Find more of my work at my blog:

www.theauthorstack.com

Find all my work at my website:

www.russellnohelty.com

Bookbub:

https://www.bookbub.com/profile/russell-nohelty

PUBLISHING IS BROKEN, BUT IT DOESN'T HAVE TO BREAK US

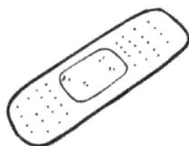

By:

Russell Nohelty

Edited by:

Lily Luchesi

Proofread by:

Katrina Roets

INTRODUCTION

This marks my 19th non-fiction book. When I got started, I thought I would write one non-fiction book, ever. Oh, how time makes fools of us all.

SOLO

- *How to Build Your Creative Career*
- *How to Become a Successful Writer*
- *Advanced Growth Tactics for Authors*
- *How to Thrive as a Writer in a Capitalist Dystopia*
- *How to Cultivate a Thriving Author Ecosystem*
- *Direct Sales Strategy for Authors*
- *How to Launch a Book on Kickstarter*
- *Write Irresistible Books that Readers Devour*

CO-WRITTEN

- *$8333: 12 concepts for a six-figure year*
- *The Author Ecosystems*
- *Direct Sales Mastery for Authors volume 1*
- *Direct Sales Mastery for Authors volume 2*
- *Get Your Book Selling on Kickstarter*
- *Get Your Book Selling on Facebook*
- *Get Your Book Selling in Print*

- *Get Your Book Selling with Cross Promotion*
- *Get Your Book Selling at Events and Book Signings*
- *How to Build a World Class Substack*

This is my 76rd book overall. In total, I've been part of 100+ books in my life. So, I have pretty good standing to say publishing is broken in fundamental ways.

Not to put a dour gloom before we even get started, but you know what book you picked up. You didn't pick up "The Publishing Company is Sunshine and Rainbows."

I also don't think that's some insightful revelation, either. By all accounts, the publishing industry is broken and has been broken since Gutenberg slid his first Bible off the press.

I contend, though, like a kintsugi bowl mended with gold, there is beauty there as well. My goal in this book is to help you smash every piece of the publishing industry to bits, pull out the parts that work for you, and then rebuild something that won't make you miserable.

This is not an easy task, because writers are prone to misery. I believe, though, that the reason stems from the fact that the publishing industry does a very good job masking its biggest flaws until you are inside it. Then, gaslighting you to believe the things you see aren't flaws but functions.

It also tends to bring people into its fold young before they truly know how the world works, or that you aren't supposed to work 100 hours a week for $30k a year and thank the publisher for the privilege. You aren't supposed to work for a year on a book, get paid a pittance, then have your book discarded without any publicity.

That's not how it's supposed to work, but that *is* how it works. So, the goal of this book is to show you how to take back agency in a world that wants to strip it away from you.

Yes, the underlying problem has a lot to do with capitalism, but there are some real doozies that are special to publishing, too.

By the time you're done, you will hopefully have found a nice little pocket of skills, tools, and mindsets that work for you…

…either that or you will run away from this industry and burn the bridge so nobody can follow you. I, personally, can't do anything else. I know, because I tried, and it doesn't work for me. Even with all its flaws, I love publishing books.

So, I have no choice but to find ways to make this industry work for me. I should note that I am an independent author and small-press publisher who mainly works direct-to-customer. I'm not an editor, or a cover designer, and while I've signed 50+ publishing deals in my life the focus of this book will be on what I know, which are those worlds.

I won't lie. While this is a solo adventure, you will get more from it if you read it in concert with *How to Thrive as a Writer in a Capitalist Dystopia* as this builds on a lot of its concepts.

Now, let's enter the suck, and figure out how to build success from it.

TECH COMPANIES LIED TO US, AND IT CREATED A CREATIVE CRISIS

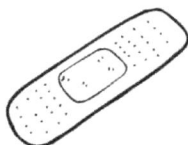

One of the great failings of tech over the decades has been the idea that the democratization of the internet meant that anyone can be successful in anything for any reason. All you have to do is make a thing and everyone will love you.

The truth is a bit more like the end of Anton Ego's famous line from *Ratatouille*: "Not everyone can become a great artist; but a great artist can come from anywhere."

Tech companies have, for the last 30+ years, focused on Auguste Gusteau's idea that "anyone can cook," without including any of Ego's subtle nuance.

And why would they?

It's easier to give people hope that they can do any old thing and be successful. That's how you get people to adopt technology.

Unfortunately, when people who believe that smack full force into reality, you get a bunch of frustrated creators who think they aren't good enough because the "magic" didn't touch them.

But it's not magic, it's strategy. There is an order of operations creators should probably take in order to be successful, and you probably won't get there if you skip a bunch of steps or do them in the wrong order. For most creators, their biggest problem is sequencing. They do step 10, then step 8, then step 15, and wonder why their business looks like a Picasso painting nobody wants.

Yes, some writers blow up overnight without following any sequence or order, their words catching fire in ways that defy explanation, and these are the people that get all the attention to "prove" the system works. Unfortunately, whatever loophole they exploited only worked for them. Once they figured it out, the universe spackled over that loophole so it will likely never work again.

That doesn't mean you have to do it this way. Sometimes chaos agents make the best entrepreneurs because they short circuit systems in weird and beautiful ways. Unfortunately, those ways tend to only work for them. That doesn't mean there aren't still loopholes. There are billions of them, enough for every human to find their own. If you have a knack for blowing things up to figure out what works, you can surely find one, too. Most of us, though, don't have the energy to blow things up for fun.

So, unless you are interested in blowing things up for laughs to find the flaws, this is probably the order you should think about things.

- **Start with the words.** This seems obvious, but in an age of platform-building and personal branding, it's easy to forget that content is still king. Write something that makes people feel seen, understood, or less alone. Write the piece that you desperately needed to read three years ago. Write what keeps you up at night, what makes you laugh, what makes you angry. The technical term for this is "resonant content," but really, it's just truth-telling that connects. The deeper your words resonate, the easier the rest of this will be, and honestly you probably shouldn't even move onto the next bit until at least a few people are ravenous for your word.

- **Finding your platform comes next.** This is where many writers stumble. They try to be everywhere at once, spreading themselves thin across every social media channel and blog platform available. ***Don't.*** Pick one place where the writing feels natural, and the readers feel right. Maybe it's Substack for your long-form analysis, or Twitter for your sharp observations, or Medium for your personal essays. The important part here is that you find somewhere that not only makes sense but also values your work enough to share it organically without you doing much promotion.

- **Build a brand identity.** "But I'm a writer," you protest, "not a brand." Wrong. Every writer is a brand, whether they like it or not. Stephen King is a brand. Joan Didion is a brand. The question isn't whether to have a brand, but whether to shape it intentionally or let it shape itself. Your brand is simply the promise you make to readers about what they'll find in your work. Make it honest. Make it clear. Make it something that the right readers recognize immediately as home. ***Why did we wait so long to build it?*** Because you don't know your brand promise until people start showing up and revealing themselves. Once you have an audience, your brand should become obvious.

- **Only after you've built this foundation should you think about monetization.** Yes, this means you might write for free for a while. Welcome to the club. We have jackets (but you'll have to buy your own). If you wait until you have an audience, they will literally tell you what they want from you in annoying and painstaking detail. Then, all you have to do is give it to them. If it's harder than that, you probably shouldn't be doing monetization yet. When you do start charging, you should probably begin with services. Editing, coaching, consulting, and things that leverage your expertise directly. They're easier to sell than products because they require less infrastructure and fewer up-front costs. Listen to what your readers ask for help with. Build that. Either that or develop a product, like a book, which is easy for readers to conceptualize since they already read your work. If you're going the product route, focus on one-off products first. Memberships are the hardest game in town. They probably shouldn't be your first sale.

- **When growth slows (it will) or enthusiasm wanes (it does), look for new channels that align with your voice.** Maybe your personal essays could become a podcast. Maybe your X threads could become a book. The medium may change, but the message remains consistent. Try to only do things you can use in multiple ways, so your time is leveraged. That social media post can become a blog post, which can become a book, which can become a podcast episode, which can become…well, you get the idea.
- **Every year, you should aim to find one strategy that works consistently for you and add it to your repertoire.** Most successful businesses are little more than a collection of platforms and skills that work consistently to grow their audience and build their

business. A successful business only needs one, but great ones have 5-10.

There's no magic bullet, despite what the latest platform, tool, or guru might promise. Success in digital writing isn't about finding the perfect channel or mastering the latest algorithm. It's about consistent, intentional growth built on a foundation of good work.

Your path won't look exactly like anyone else's. You might spend years finding your voice while someone else discovers theirs in a month. You might build a massive following on a platform that others barely understand. That's fine. The steps matter less than the progression.

Additionally, many writers had a meteoric rise and then stalled in ways that don't seem to make sense. If this sounds like you, then ask if you "skipped" one of these steps. Usually by going back and getting really clear on the ones you moved through quickly will help you get on track. You probably had success despite having a wonky structure. By going back and building those bits, you can often unlock exponential growth again.

The internet didn't lie about opportunity. It just oversimplified the process. Yes, anyone can publish. Yes, greatness can come from anywhere. But sustainable success usually follows a pattern. Understand it, adapt it, make it your own. Then get back to writing. That's still the heart of it all.

The magic isn't in the bullet. It's in the persistence, the craft, and the connection. Everything else is just details.

THE PUBLISHING INDUSTRY IS BROKEN, BUT IT DOESN'T HAVE TO BREAK US

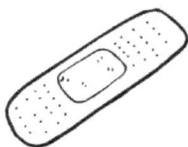

Yes, some authors can just write the next book and release a new book every month for months, or sometimes even years...

...but they almost always burn out.

My friend says you have to push hard for three years to break through, and I think that's about the limit somebody can push their body to write that much before it rebels on them.

I think most people start burning out at six months at this pace and they keep it up for two years, maybe three if they are really stubborn.

If they don't burn out, then they either transition to co-writing, transition to running a publishing company, or transition to building their brand in other mediums.

There are so many well-intentioned and helpful humans in this industry. You can basically walk up to any author, and they will spill every secret they have to you at any time.

The industry is in the best shape it's ever been...

...and everyone is still broke.

On top of that, everyone is burned out from writing and writing and writing and writing without ever getting anywhere they feel "safe" taking their foot off the gas.

"Write the next book" is still being pushed as the dominant narrative to find success in publishing, and we don't think it's doing authors any favors.

Yes, it's obviously important to have a critical mass of writing to break through and build a successful career. ***What does a critical mass mean, though?*** Is it three books? Five? Ten? Twenty? Fifty?

At what point does it become a burden instead of a blessing? Following that advice is causing people to write dozens of books for years and years while still riding the struggle bus the whole time.

If that's really the best practice to find success, then show me the receipts.

- If that's true, then why isn't it working for so many people?
- If that's true, then why is everyone at their wit's end?
- If that's true, then why do I get texts from my successful friends damn near weekly at this point telling me they don't think they're gonna make it the end of the year?

Of course, writing books is how we make money. I'm not saying you don't have to write books as an author. That would be like telling a baker to stop baking bread.

You can't have success as an author without books, but I'm not convinced writing the next book is the best marketing action for all authors at all time, just like I don't think baking bread is the best marketing action for somebody who can't drive foot traffic into their bakery storefront.

Sir Terry Pratchett wrote over 50 books in his career and has sold 100 million books in the process. Stephen King has published 65 novels in his career. Anne Rice published 37 novels. Jane Austen wrote 6 novels. Melissa Albert has also written 6 books.

Meanwhile, I've written over 40 novels and have seen almost none of the success of these people. I have a pretty decent career going, but there has to be something beyond "write the next book" that's driving these people forward. I can tell you I'm nowhere near 100 million copies sold, and I'm working just as hard as Sir Terry.

SYSTEMIC ISSUES FACING AUTHORS

- So, what's happening here? Unfortunately, it's not as easy as pointing a finger. There are systemic issues that no single author can fix by themselves, or even collectively, without a lot of help. They include, but are not limited to:
- **Capitalism, but not in the way you think:** I have plenty of vitriol to throw at capitalism, but the biggest problem for authors is capitalism works consistently, but not intuitively. People think 1+1=2, but really 1+potato=cheese sandwich. It's nonsense, but it is consistent nonsense. Once you understand how to connect the right nonsense to the right outcome, you can build predictable money.
- **Price elasticity:** Books have a very narrow band in which they can operate. They can basically be $0-$10

as an ebook or $10-$30 in print. This is what Monica called The Novelist's Dilemma. This is why we need a bunch of books before we can hope to break even on books, because we have to price low. On top of that, readers have been trained to devalue the price of a book. The hardest thing to do in business is sell on volume, and the whole industry does that, because books are so cheap there's no other choice.

- **The Power Law curve:** When you chart an industry like tech, there are companies worth trillions of dollars, which means there are a bunch of companies that are worth hundreds of billions, even more worth billions, and tons worth millions. Meanwhile, an indie author might push 8 figures, which means when you chart that power law curve back, there are fewer people at every stage, and the majority are making a pittance.
- **Trying to shoehorn everyone into a very few business models:** In the past few posts I've made, it's proven out that people still think if you do the right thing for the right length of time in the right genre then you'll still probably not make it and I just...don't agree with that. Being exposed to many other types of business this year it's clear there are hundreds of business models that might work for an author, but they are only ever exposed to but a very few.
- **The whole industry mainly knows how to do one thing:** That thing is change the price of their book. They don't use any other psychological trigger except "put book out, raise price, and lower price."
- **Only going after the 1/5:** Amazon teaches us to focus on the cheap, quick wins. If somebody isn't ready to buy now now now, then they have always been seen as being worthless to authors. However, being a sales manager I know that if you show something to 5 people 1 will say no, 1 will say yes, and the other 3 will be on the fence. What separates a decent salesperson from a

great one is the ability to convert 2-4 out of 5, instead of just that 1. You can literally double your sales if you just convert 1 out of 5 people without doing any other work.

- **Authors think about collaborations all wrong, or at least not expansively enough:** They are very good about finding collaborations with people who are the exact same as them, but they are terrible at the thing that really moves the needle once you get more success, which is finding people *dimilar* (different but complementary) than the medium you currently use. Have you ever approached a local business who does something different than you do, but has a complementary audience, to see if they wanted to offer your books in a bundle with their stuff? I hear a few authors doing it here or there, but nobody ever talks or thinks about how to make this happen outside of book bundles.
- **We are still taught that we are annoying our readers when we sell to them:** I can't believe people still say this to me consistently, but if somebody joins your list to hear about your books, you aren't annoying them by sharing your books with them. That is such a wild thing to say, and yet 95% of the authors I know still think this. They "don't want to bother their readers" and everyone just kind of agrees with that advice.
- **We have to compete against every product that has ever been made:** In very few industries are the business owners up against a 400-year-old dead person for somebody's money and attention. Maybe a winery has to compete against the past sometimes, but then at least that older wine is way more expensive which prices people out of the market for it. Even film and radio only go back a hundred years, but books have been published for thousands of years, and you can read them all for a pittance. No musical artist will ever have

to go up against Mozart, only a cheap facsimile of Mozart as told through a modern orchestra.

- **We think "x is the answer":** It doesn't matter what x is, as long as it's something authors haven't tried yet, or haven't tried in a while. This happens all the time. Direct sales is not the answer for comic book people...they already do direct sales. Fiction apps are not the answer for genre authors because they pay shit outside of romance. Community isn't the answer to anything. Community is a nice, blobby, nebulous word that is so squishy that it can mean anything. There is really a suite of answers that could help, but we have to get better at trying stuff that hasn't been done before.
- **The publishing industry is elitist:** Yeah, we are inclusive on some level, but we are super cliquey, and we don't believe everyone can or should be an author. We definitely don't believe everyone can succeed as an author. This is an industry started by elites and run by elites. For eons the only way you could prove you were really an "author" was by not needing the money, but what that really proved was you were an aristocrat, which is what they really wanted to do. Why have we carried this through to 2024?
- **Authors don't want to run businesses:** Not only don't they want to do it, they will actively sabotage themselves and the industry at every turn to "make art." Meanwhile, they wrote a book with their name on it and think they don't want attention. Why did you write the book then? Just admit you want to run a business, make money, and that it's okay to want to be seen. It is impossible to teach authors because they are gleefully ignorant of the things that they need to do, and they complain about it.
- **We actively suppress information on new things that don't fit our mental model of what "right" is:** It literally happened to me for 10+ years, and I see it

happen all the time. For something to break through, it has to be so few degrees from what is already done that it's almost unhelpful just by its proximity.

HOW DO WE FIX THESE ISSUES?

Well, there are some general things we can do to fix this at a systemic level…but honestly most of these will probably only help around the margins without traditional publishing houses on board, and it doesn't make sense for them to blow up an industry that benefits them.

- **We need more authors to make way more money, like a stupid amount more money, and then drag people up to show other people doing it.** Yes, this is also happening, slowly. Some of the price stuff is being helped by special edition campaigns pricing books at $80+.
- **We have gotta stop being scared to reach out to our fans with things they can buy.**
- **We have to be better at testing things that could work, then jettisoning things that don't, to streamline our business.**
- **We have to find ways to up the prices on books at a systemic level.** Luckily, most book publishers are pricing their trades at $18.99, which allows us to up our own prices, but still…woof.
- **We gotta start building different types of business that have never been built before in our industry.** Everyone is way too timid to do anything until they see 100 other people exactly like them do it, and by that time…it probably doesn't work anymore, or at least not as well.
- **We have to start believing everyone can succeed, but not in the way that other people succeed.** It's so

exhausting to hear the people who did succeed say that *everyone* can't succeed. It's elitist as fuck and it's gotta stop. Not everyone can succeed like you, but everyone can chart a path, even if it's never been done before.

WHAT CAN YOU CHANGE?

This has not been the most hopeful message as of yet, so let's flip this and talk about what you can do as a single human to overcome what seems like overwhelming odds stacked against them.

I have studied and thought about this a lot as Monica and I worked to figure out a way to help writers through this morass, and it really comes down to three words.

Build leveraged assets.

Yes, I know the words "building leveraged assets" is peak business speak, and your eyes are glazing over, but bear with me because those three words can change your life, reduce your overwhelm, and help you recover from (or prevent) burnout.

What is a leveraged asset? It's something that becomes more valuable with every new bit that goes into it without it making you do more work or expend significantly more effort.

- **An email list (should) be a leveraged asset.** You should make more (or at least the same amount of) money with every person that enters your list.
- *A community can be a leveraged asset if you do it right*. The main way to tell if your community works is whether your effort increases or stays the same with every person that enters. You can build a leveraged

asset if you find ways to connect people with each other instead of having to be in there every day. If it becomes harder to control, you are doing it wrong.

- *A subscription should be a leveraged asset.* If it gets harder to manage with each person, then it isn't a leveraged asset. However, if you charge enough to hire people who can manage it for you, then yes, it is a leveraged asset. It should build higher with each person who enters it.
- *Translations can be a great leveraged asset.* I mean for most of us it's not, but Lee Savino often says that she only hit seven figures once her books went into translation, and it doesn't take a lot of her energy to do. That is the ideal leveraged asset.
- *A series should be a leveraged asset, but it usually isn't right now.* If you aren't making more with each installment of a series, then it isn't a leveraged asset. We have been taught to write in a way that negates the value of a book about the minute it is released.
- *Advertising can be a leveraged asset.* If you get your ads humming, they can generate a ton of money without taking a lot of work. They usually aren't leveraged because something is broken, but they can be leveraged.

There are all sorts of leveraged assets that exist all around us. The more leveraged assets you have in your business, the better your business works.

There are hundreds of ways to build leveraged assets, and we are taught how to build exactly 1, maybe 2 of them.

Do you know why you probably hate your community, your books, your publication, and/or your email list?

Because they are not leveraged assets...yet.

If every time you wrote a post or sent an email you made more and more money without costing you more time, then you would love your email list, and love sending and posting in your community.

It's obviously possible to build an email list of the wrong humans that don't care about you, but it's equally, or maybe even more, possible to build a list of the right people who perform the wrong actions.

For instance, people often try to equate list size with list health, but that is false equivalence.

It doesn't matter if you have 100 or 10,000 people on your list if they don't actually perform the action you want them to take.

Of course, that can mean a lot of things. Do you want them to engage, to click, to buy, to join something, or what? If you're selling your own products, you probably want them to buy, but if you are trying to sell advertising, you probably want them to click and/or engage on the ads.

Those are two different metrics. My email list has a very healthy open rate and sales conversion rate for my own products, but it has a terrible ad click-through rate, which is killing us with advertisers right now.

Leveraged assets are not about more. They are about less.

We're looking for less time investment to get greater returns.

Unfortunately, up until now the whole industry has exclusively taught the "pump method" of building a business, which is when you exert some amount of force and a predictable outcome happens every time forever.

These kinds of actions are easy to start doing, so authors latch onto them.

Release a book, slam through some ads, take the win, move on to write the next book, and repeat until dead is not a sustainable business strategy for 90% of authors.

The problem with a pump is that it takes the same effort on the first pump and the thousandth pump. Yeah, it's easy to get excited to write that first book, but it takes equal energy to write the 10th book and the 40th book. Eventually, it wears on you.

Thus, burnout, especially if your money situation isn't improving with each book.

Instead, we should be thinking about the "flywheel method" wherein things are almost impossible at first, then get progressively easier and easier over time.

The first push of a flywheel is so, so hard it seems like nothing is happening for a long time, so people abandon it before it starts working.

I don't blame them, either. If they don't know what they're building, how could they possibly know to stick with something? A flywheel doesn't get easier until you've done a couple rotations, and it's difficult to get there. So, of course everyone stops before they find success with it.

That said, over time a flywheel gets much, much easier. The main reason I can keep doing this work, even with several chronic illnesses that zap my energy, is that it's easier to keep going than to stop because I've built so much momentum.

I am the king of leveraged actions. It's so natural to me at this point that, until recently, I thought this was common knowledge, but what I've learned recently is nobody is doing this...or even knows it exists.

The first thing I think about when taking on a project is how I can use it again in multiple places and formats. This post will eventually be used in an article, and probably wind up in a book, or maybe even a course or at least a training in our community.

WHAT DOES THIS LOOK LIKE IN PRACTICE?

We now have language to help us fight against the headwinds pushing against us, but how can we actually put this into practice?

It starts by prioritizing one asset first and building it to sustainability. Then, once it's humming along, we build a second one and a third once the first two are stable. Basically, we build systematically and with intention. As we build new assets, the ones we already built are getting easier and easier to manage and integrating with each other to make you more powerful every day.

- **We don't try to build 10 assets at once,** which is what everyone is doing right now.
- **We don't abandon things after a week,** which is what a lot of people are doing right now.
- **We don't keep doing things for years that never work,** which is what the rest of the people are doing right now.

Instead, we prioritize *one* thing at a time and give it *at least* three months to catch. If it does, then we keep working on it. If it doesn't, we jettison it.

Then, regardless of what we choose to focus on, we follow the best practices to succeed doing it. We don't lone wolf it.

Instead, we follow best practices from people who know what they are doing and have built the exact thing we're trying to build so we can tell if the most likely success path works for us.

Why?

Because our goal is to isolate and control, to the greatest extent possible, whether something works for us or not, in as short a timeframe as possible.

If you go out on your own, and you fail, it's impossible to know whether your process failed or the methodology failed. If you find a good teacher and follow their advice, and it still doesn't work, it's probably not right for you.

Additionally, if you follow the methodology, have success, but hate it, you can at least find somebody to outsource the work to, and they have a guide to the process already.

Or you can abandon it.

In fact, you should abandon anything that either doesn't work at all or makes you feel bad doing it.

So, at the start of every quarter, either pick something new or double down on the thing you prioritized to make it work better.

If after three months your new process does work to help you create leverage and growth, then we double down on it. If it doesn't, abandon it for something else.

How long do you keep prioritizing that one action? Until it operates on its own with very little effort or it breaks down. Then, either you keep working on it or you hand it off to somebody.

(Ines Johnson is the queen of this, BTW. She sat me down once and taught me how she uses Vanessa Vale's Box Method to systematize her publishing life and it's brilliant.)

Most importantly, we pick one thing at a time. What we don't do is drag along a hundred things that can't or won't be leveraged.

In fact, we don't drag along anything. Everything we carry forward should help us build leverage in our business.

It's too much to expect a new process to build leverage at the beginning, but if after six months it's dragging you down, cut it loose.

(If you need help learning how to prioritize things, Sarra Cannon is the best human in the world to help you with that.)

Seriously, if y'all just abandoned the stuff that wasn't working in your business, you would be so much happier and more successful, but instead you hold out hope that maybe it's gonna be the secret weapon.

There is no secret weapon.

There are only leveraged and unleveraged assets.

WHERE DO YOU START?

I've made some really, really broad statements so far about a concept you probably have never heard about before, or best-case scenario seen and run away from, so let's bring this back to a more granular level and talk about how to pick your priority.

I have never had a problem picking a priority because the thing that would move my business forward the most, take the least time to implement, and integrate easiest into my existing workflow was always glaringly obvious.

It's probably obvious to you, too. You just need some space to figure it out. Here are some exercises I recommend.

First, I recommend taking an hour and doing this exercise to help you visualize your money situation.

To do this exercise, *we start by figuring out how much money you can realistically make this year and block it out in a calendar.* So, if you want to make $100,000, but when you fill in all your launches you can't realistically make $25,000, that's a problem. If you want to make $100,000 and you can make $100k per launch...then you might be thinking too small. Literally get a calendar and put every launch into it with how much you think you will make. Don't worry about the total money yet, just plot out your next year of launches. Once they are plugged in, add in any recurring revenue or other ways you make money (consulting, ghostwriting, freelance writing, etc.). Then, add it all up and see how close you are...How can you get where you want to be? That's a good start to figuring out your priority.

Once you have that overview, n**ow *it's time to do this exercise based on a modified version of an Eisenhower Matrix*.** The Eisenhower Matrix is a powerful time management tool that helps you prioritize tasks by dividing them into four distinct quadrants: urgent and important, important but not urgent, urgent but not important, and neither urgent nor important. Building one for yourself allows you to focus your energy on what truly matters, ensuring that essential tasks are addressed promptly while avoiding the trap of busywork that often feels pressing but yields little value. My process isn't exactly an Eisenhower Matrix, but it's very, very close. Basically, you make a grid and break it into four quadrants: Don't love but need, Love and need, Don't love and don't need, & Love but don't need. Then, put everything you do in your business into one of those four boxes. Now, you assess. What is in the top right quadrant? Those should be your core products and offerings. You might even find some new services you could offer that more align with your passions. What is in the bottom right quadrant? How can you make those more important to your business? What is in the top left quadrant? How can you outsource those, or change them so you love them? What ended up in the bottom left quadrant? Cut those things ASAP.

After you finish those two exercises, the strengths and weaknesses of your business should become pretty apparent. If you're still not sure, though, I recommend taking a few of your possible choices and running a SWOT analysis on their strengths, weaknesses, opportunities, and threats.

Of course, this is just one piece of prioritizing and strategizing that's tailored toward looking at your next 90 days, but it's been super helpful for me in staying focused on both a) what's actually moving the needle, and b) what do I really want from life?

Once you finish those three exercises, the one you should focus on will almost definitely become apparent. If you're still having trouble, then what we're looking for is the one thing that will propel your business forward the most, giving you the most leverage.

This idea was popularized by The One Thing by Gary Keller and Jay Papasan. The central idea is that by identifying and prioritizing the single most important task, the "One Thing," you can make significant progress in your personal and professional life.

The book's central concept revolves around "The Domino Theory." Since a domino can knock down another domino that is up to 1.5 times its size, a rather small domino can create a chain reaction wherein it eventually knocks down a massive domino that changes everything in your business.

However, you must choose your dominos intentionally, and knock them down in the right order, if you want to cause this kind of reaction. Most people knock down dominoes at random, causing chaos and getting no results.

If, instead, you use the exercises above to find your big domino, then you can work backwards to find the actions you need to complete, and in what order, to knock over progressively larger and larger dominos, until you finally knock that big one over.

Most people don't have an execution problem. They have a prioritization problem.

They are trying to knock down a domino ten steps ahead of the action they should be working on and not getting the results they need because it's simply too big for them to push over.

Usually, what I chose to focus on was the thing that consumed my mind the most for the previous couple of months, and something I hypothesized would clear the main block that impeded my business from moving forward.

A PERSONAL EXAMPLE

Here's how this looks in my business. I've been consumed with building a membership for years. Moreso, I've been looking for a way to build sustainable revenue and growth into my business.

So, most of my prioritization decisions have revolved around bringing more recurring revenue into my business, focused mainly on recurring revenue. This has been my focus since 2020, and I still haven't fully cracked it, but I'm way closer than I have ever been before.

Since I started doing this exercise after meeting Sarra at RAM 2024 and being introduced to her HB90 method, my quarters have been:

- **Q1 2023 - Circle.** Finding a way to build a community off Facebook was the #1 thing I thought could move my business forward. It bombed, and it was very easy to see it was incongruent. However, it led me to realize I was a better part of a community rather than a leader of it.
- **Q2 2023 - Substack.** This one easily exceeded my expectations because I was getting bonkers organic growth and enjoying it. I started doing it because Monica was doing it and said it was better than Circle.

It also allowed me to become a part of a community without leading it, which was one of my big revelations the previous quarter.

- **Q3 2023 - I doubled down on Substack because it was working.** I really want you to do it for 6 months if it's working even a little bit. Substack was working well, but I also comped everyone on my list three months access so I kind of had to double down on it through at least August. I'm glad I did because revenue started to pick up after then and into September.
- **Q4 2023 - Again, I kept going on Substack.** We started making some decent money on Substack. However, I found the ROI was decreasing drastically from where I needed it to be and where it was the previous two quarters, so I had to figure out some way to supercharge growth.
- **Q1 2024 -Ads.** Ads were the easy next step after Substack growth slowed since I found several ways to test them without a lot of expense. I tested a ton of platforms and hired a growth team to help me.
- **Q2 2024 - Ads still.** I probably would have ended this earlier and picked a different priority for Q2, but I had an ad team that was contracted through May, so I kept this quarter focused on ads. It was a bloodbath, but I learned enough doing them that I thought the next step would be a daily newsletter. Again, it was clearly the next place to test because I needed a way to sustain ad growth, and I decided to try it through an ad supported daily.
- **Q3 2024 - Daily newsletter**. This is where we are now, and it's a struggle, honestly. I am having a lot of problems with ads, and it's just not doing what I need it to do to keep running ads, which is why I did them daily. That said, I'll probably keep going with it through Q4 because I have nothing else.

As you can see, almost all of them revolved either tangentially or intrinsically around this idea of subscription/membership revenue and sustainability. Additionally, they each dovetailed into the next based on what I learned during my tests.

If you're still having problems figuring it out, ask yourself these questions:

- What is the thing consuming your business and holding it back?
- What is either something you are already doing but not enough or that you aren't doing but can augment your business that you think you want to test in the near future?
- What hypothesis can you measure in the next three months that could bear fruit?

In my experience, there's always been one standout thing that I thought would move my business forward the most and the quickest.

Like with Circle, we were already doing it with Writer MBA, and I've been searching for a community thing with Wannabe Press, so it made sense to try it.

Then, when that failed, it was pretty obvious the best next step was Substack since Monica was already there and we wanted to give more value to people in the Writer MBA community. Plus, I could try another subscription platform.

Throughout this process, it was pretty obvious the things that failed were failing and the things that succeeded were succeeding. If the thing you are testing is either holding you back or barely worth it, then you should probably try something else.

Russell Nohelty

We are looking for sails, not anchors.

It's only something like this daily newsletter that's limping along where I would have any question as to whether to continue it or not, and really I would probably say if it's working even a little bit give it three more months.

From everything I've read and everything I know, these things really need six months to prove out or not.

Still, I'm getting such great responses from people who read the daily, and people coming out of the woodwork with such nice things to say that it's not like nobody is reading and it's not working at all.

It's doing everything I want it to do except book sponsors to fund continued growth. Aside from that, there's been nothing but positive growth.

If I wasn't having people reach out so often to talk about it, I probably wouldn't keep going with it after next month, but having those other metrics allows me to see there might be value from doubling down on it.

I would say if you're enjoying it but it's limping along, maybe give it another shot and try some different things. However, if you're not enjoying it, it's probably best not to reup for another three months of torture.

I really enjoy doing this daily. It might be the most enjoyable single thing I've ever done, and I do over-index for enjoyment. It's probably not a bad idea for you to do the same.

Finally, I want you to remember this bit. You wrote something with your name on it, or at least your words in it.

It's okay to want people to read it. It's okay to want money for it. It's okay that you want fans to obsess over it.

Money flows with your energy and is blocked by your blocks.

You are not bad for wanting attention. You are not bad for wanting money. You are not bad for seeking notoriety.

If you have a negative view of money, then it won't flow toward you. If you are hostile toward attention, then it won't come to you. If you can't accept having fans, then they won't accept you.

The biggest thing you can do is clear those blocks before they hold you back for one second longer.

CHARTING YOUR PATH FROM STYLE TO SCALE

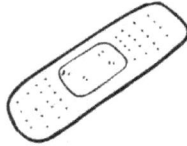

Creators often ask me what they should be doing to grow their publication, and that is a really, really tricky question to answer, because it kind of relies on how much work you've done before this point. Growth isn't a one-size-fits-all solution; it's a journey, and your starting point is unique to your experience.

Before I even started my first blog, I had written 10+ screenplays and directed a movie. Before I started my Substack, I had close to 15 years' experience blogging and podcasting.

Some people will come to this work with an MFA in creative writing and others haven't done much more than write Facebook posts. So, I've outlined the stages I think people need to go through in order to grow sustainably and consistently.

Not all of you will start in the same place, and just because you've been doing things for a while, doesn't mean you've been doing it with intention. You might have been writing every day for months, but without varying your styles, you aren't going to get far.

Additionally, I've added how long each of these bits might take, but it could take way longer or a little bit shorter depending on how much time you have allocated to doing it. Each stage is broken up into three-month chunks. This is because I believe you should choose one singular area of focus every quarter. Additionally, I believe that if something is working, you should focus on it for two quarters, or six months.

Most things can't be neatly wrapped up in three months, but it should be possible to see growth after three months, and whether you're ready to move on after six months.

STAGE 1: NAIL YOUR STYLE - 3 TO 12 MONTHS

When you first get started, all you need to do is write, and write, and write. Write every type of story in every format you can to find out what resonates with you. I am an excellent writer, but I'm an excellent writer because I'm constantly trying to reach just outside my grasp. Not only have I written in tons of formats from movies to comics to novels to non-fiction, but in just about every style I could find to see if there was anything to make my own writing stronger.

COMMON MISTAKE

Rushing through style development — one of the biggest mistakes is trying to settle on a style too quickly. Many creators lock into one format or tone too early, limiting their growth. Instead, take the time to experiment widely. Try different genres, perspectives, and even platforms before deciding what feels right for you.

EXERCISE

Write one short story or article each week in a completely different style or format than the previous week. At the end of each week, reflect on what came naturally, what felt challenging, and whether you enjoyed the process. Track these reflections in a journal to help identify patterns.

STAGE 2: NAIL YOUR VOICE - 3 TO 6 MONTHS

Voice might feel like style, but it's very different. When you're trying to nail your style, you should be trying to write the "perfect" encapsulation of that kind of writing. You're doing a whole lot of mimicking and, frankly, writing a lot of things you don't really care about in the end. Nailing your voice is about finding what you want to say and how you want to say it. Your voice comes through beyond the style, and you're often using different styles to amplify your voice.

COMMON MISTAKE

Ignoring voice in favor of mimicry — while learning from others is important, many creators get stuck mimicking successful voices instead of developing their own. If you notice you're constantly writing in someone else's style or tone, step back and ask what *you* want to say and how *you* want to say it.

EXERCISE

Choose a topic you're passionate about and write about it in three different styles (e.g., formal, humorous, conversational). Compare how each style affects your voice. Which one feels the most authentic? Use this as a foundation to develop your unique voice further.

STAGE 3: NAIL YOUR PLATFORM - 3 TO 6 MONTHS

Once you've got your style and voice, it's time to figure out what platform(s) work the best to amplify it. The most important part of a platform is that it multiplies the efforts you already do and enjoy. Just because TikTok can get lots of people to look at your work, if you hate video then you probably shouldn't be there. Now that you have a style and a voice, you can plug it into a lot of different platforms and find which one works for you. I'm not so ideal as to think you haven't been doing this already, so really, what you want to do is find the platforms that feel the best and have the best engagement for your work. It might be something like Instagram, but it could be something like Kickstarter or Quora, too. Every website that aggregates an audience is a platform, and now we need to figure out what works for you.

COMMON MISTAKE

Overcommitting to the wrong platforms — some creators feel pressured to be everywhere all at once, on Instagram, TikTok, YouTube, Substack, etc. This leads to burnout. Focus on the platforms that genuinely amplify your voice and feel sustainable to manage. Quality engagement on one or two platforms is far more valuable than being spread too thin.

EXERCISE

Post one piece of content across 3-5 different platforms over the course of a month (e.g., Instagram, Substack, Quora, Medium). Track the engagement you get on each platform and reflect on which platform felt most comfortable for you to use, as well as which led to the most meaningful interactions.

STAGE 4: NAIL YOUR AUDIENCE - 3 TO 6 MONTHS

Notice, up until this point, I haven't talked about readers, and that is intentional. We're so obsessed with building an audience, but until you have a style, a voice, and a platform, it doesn't really matter who reads your work, or at least it shouldn't be a focus. Don't get me wrong, during those first three steps you'll definitely pick up some people who love your voice and your style, and this is the point where you need to look back and say, "Who actually does love my work, and why?" We're looking for both demographic (age, sex, location, etc.) and psychographic (attitude, tastes, vibes, etc.) data here to develop an amalgamation of who resonates the most with your work and evangelizes for it the most. I recommend reaching out to the people who engage the most with the stuff you write; try to interview them to figure out what makes them tick and why they love your stuff.

COMMON MISTAKE

Chasing readers before you're ready — *i*t's tempting to focus on building an audience as soon as you start creating, but this can backfire. If you're constantly promoting work before you've honed your style and voice, you risk alienating potential readers with content that doesn't yet reflect your best self. Take time to refine your craft before worrying too much about audience-building.

EXERCISE

Create a survey for your existing audience with questions that focus on why they connect with your work. Include questions that help you understand both demographic information (age, gender, location) and psychographic details (interests, values, emotions your work evokes). Use this feedback to adjust your messaging or topics.

STAGE 5: NAIL YOUR BRANDING - 3 TO 6 MONTHS

Now that you've gotten this far, it's time to really look at your brand and make sure it speaks to the people who are most likely to love your work and that it feels good to you. Your brand is the intersection of what you and your audience love so that your readers can create a nice little home for you in their heart and know the exact vibes you're going to put in there. The more cohesive you can make your brand, and the louder it speaks to what you do, the easier it will be for people to know they are in the right (or wrong) place and get them to buy into your writing quicker. Lots of people won't even give your writing a chance if they don't think they are in the right place, so this is about giving as many people as possible the chance to give your writing a try.

COMMON MISTAKE

Inconsistent branding — your brand should be a natural extension of your voice and your audience's expectations. If your branding is all over the place—one week professional, the next casual, with no clear throughline—it can confuse your readers. A cohesive brand builds trust, so don't overlook this stage.

EXERCISE

Create a mood board or a brand style guide that visually represents your work's tone, values, and aesthetics. This can include colors, fonts, imagery, and words that represent your brand. Share this with a few trusted readers or peers and get feedback on whether it aligns with how they perceive your work.

STAGE 6: NAIL YOUR OFFER - 3 TO 6 MONTHS

Now that you know what you're writing, why you're writing, how you're writing, where you're writing, and who will read it, only now does it make sense to start selling something. However, nailing your offer isn't just about having something to sell; it's about finding the right product that aligns with both your audience's needs and your personal strengths.

In earlier stages, you've likely experimented with a few products or services. Maybe you tried selling an ebook, offering a course, or launching a membership. Now it's time to take a step back and evaluate which of those felt most authentic to you and resonated best with your audience. Here's how to approach this stage in more detail:

- **Evaluate Early Data**: Look at any experiments you've run in the past. What products sold the most? Which ones led to the highest engagement or satisfaction? Just because something didn't make a lot of money doesn't mean it wasn't valuable—pay attention to feedback and how much joy you got from delivering the offer.

- **Refine Based on Audience Feedback**: At this stage, your audience should be fairly established. Use their feedback to shape your offer. Did they express interest in certain types of content or products you haven't fully explored yet? Consider running a quick survey or hosting a Q&A to get direct input on what they want to see from you next.

- **Test Smaller Offers**: Before locking into a larger, long-term product, start with smaller, limited-time offers. For instance, if you're thinking about launching a full course, try offering a one-time webinar first. If you're considering a paid subscription, start with a low-commitment product like a digital download or mini-course to gauge interest.

- **Align with Your Brand**: Make sure that what you're selling fits seamlessly into your brand and voice. If your writing or content has been about helping creators find their voice, your offer should logically extend from that—whether it's a coaching package, a workshop, or a resource guide. The best offers feel like a natural progression of your core message.

- **Create a Value Ladder**: Instead of thinking about one product, think about how you can offer a range of products at different price points. For example, a value ladder might start with a free ebook, move up to a paid course, and then lead to a more personalized, premium service like one-on-one coaching. This way, you can attract readers at different stages of their journey with you.

COMMON MISTAKE

Launching too soon without a clear offer — some creators rush to monetize without fully understanding what their audience wants or what they're best suited to offer. This can lead to frustration and missed opportunities. Don't be afraid to test and tweak your offers before committing to a large-scale launch.

EXERCISE

Develop two to three different offers that reflect what you enjoy creating and what your audience has shown interest in. Test these offers with limited-time sales or pre-orders, and evaluate which brings in the most engagement, satisfaction, and revenue. This will help you home in on your core product that can form the foundation of your business.

By the time you've nailed your offer, you'll have a clear sense of what works for you and your audience. From here, scaling becomes much easier because you're no longer guessing, you have data and feedback to guide you.

STAGE 7: NAIL YOUR SCALE - 6 TO 120 MONTHS

Now, you should have a killer offer, an amazing audience, and great products that make you money, and a cohesive brand. You should be growing pretty well organically. At this point, when you already have a little fire, it's time to throw gasoline on it. You've probably done some PR in the past, or guest blogging, or even ads, but now it's time to put growth strategies into overdrive…because now it will pay off. So many people do this work in the wrong order, and it fails because they don't have the other bits in place first. Growth tools are great assets for people who are ready to scale, but they don't have great ROI until you have a fire going. If you don't know you've built fire, then you probably need to go back and make the other bits work better.

COMMON MISTAKE

Scaling without a solid foundation — one of the biggest mistakes creators make is trying to scale before they have a strong foundation. Scaling efforts, like paid advertising or PR, can backfire if your offer, brand, or audience isn't fully developed. Another mistake is scaling too quickly without the systems to handle the increased demand, which can lead to burnout or customer dissatisfaction. Make sure you've fine-tuned the earlier stages and built the right infrastructure before trying to grow exponentially.

EXERCISE

Develop a growth plan that includes one paid strategy (e.g., Facebook ads or sponsored posts) and one organic strategy (e.g., guest posts, collaborations). Implement these over a three-month period and track their ROI carefully. Be prepared to scale or adjust based on what works best.

Building a sustainable and thriving publication takes time, intention, and a willingness to embrace the process. Each stage of growth is a step toward not just becoming a better creator but also refining your message, your brand, and the connection you build with your audience. Remember, these stages aren't linear, and it's normal to revisit earlier steps as you evolve.

The key to long-term success is patience and persistence. Growth doesn't happen overnight, and the creators who find the most fulfillment are the ones who continue to experiment, learn, and adapt. By focusing on developing your style, voice, platform, audience, brand, offer, and scaling with intention, you'll be well on your way to building something meaningful.

As you move through these stages, keep in mind that the journey is uniquely yours. Don't compare your timeline to anyone else's and allow yourself the grace to grow at your own pace. Ultimately, the most important thing is that you create work you're proud of and that resonates with the audience who values it.

THE ART OF SUSTAINABLE PRODUCTIVITY

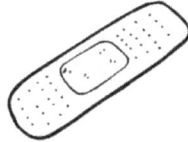

For years, I've heard the same advice repeated in the writing community: write more, publish more, market more. The modern writing world seems obsessed with churning out content at an ever-increasing pace. But after spending over two decades in this industry, I've come to realize we've been thinking about productivity all wrong.

When I talk about productivity, I'm not interested in cramming 200 hours of work into a 20-hour week. I'm focused on something far more valuable: leverage. What I mean by productivity is doing an hour's worth of work in 10 minutes. I don't want to fill up the rest of those 50 minutes. I just want to do the work efficiently so I can move on with my day and have more time for myself.

This perspective shift is crucial. True productivity isn't about doing more, it's about getting more value from what you do. Consider an email list: whether you have 100 subscribers or 1,000, you're still writing one email. The leverage comes from having your same effort reach more people, create more impact, and generate more results.

Before we dive into productivity strategies, I need to address something vital: you don't need to be productive to be a writer. This isn't just feel-good advice. It's an important truth I've seen proven time and again throughout my career. You can write less than one book a year. You can write articles instead of books. You can focus on short stories. You can write one book and share it with friends. Your legitimacy as a writer isn't tied to your output.

I understand the many valid reasons why someone might not be able to maintain high productivity. Maybe it's your day job, your health, or caregiving responsibilities. Perhaps it's financial constraints or social obligations. Or maybe you simply choose to work at a different pace. Each of these is completely valid.

THE FOUR PHASES OF A WRITING CAREER

When I started my writing journey, nobody explained that careers develop in distinct phases. Understanding these phases has transformed how I approach productivity and success. Let me walk you through them.

THE LEARNING PHASE

Most writers want to start with their dream project; that epic fantasy series they've been imagining since childhood or the great American novel they know will change literature forever. I understand the impulse, but it's usually a mistake. Here's why.

Starting with your dream project often leads to spending years churning on the same idea without making real progress. Instead, I recommend beginning with more structured projects. Mystery, romance, or other genres with clear frameworks give you something concrete to learn from. You can judge your progress because there are established patterns to follow.

I spent my first decade writing and getting nowhere, but each finished project taught me something valuable. Even my documentary that didn't work out, my failed movie scripts, and my early attempts at different genres - they all contributed to building my skill set. The key was finishing things, even when they weren't perfect.

THE DISCOVERY PHASE

Once you understand the basics, you enter a phase of finding your voice and what you really want to say. This is when you should experiment with different genres and styles. I wrote comics, then novels. I tried romance, YA, and various other forms. Each attempt added new tools to my creative toolkit.

It wasn't until 2018, after writing *Anna in the Dark Place,* that I felt I truly understood how to write romance, how to pace a story, how to write monsters, how to handle contemporary settings, and how to write *anything.* I was 20+ books in at that point, after starting serious writing around 2001. The discovery phase takes time, but it's essential for developing your unique voice.

THE MONETIZATION PHASE

Here's something crucial: you can't scale your business until you know how to put in a dollar and reliably get at least a dollar and one penny back. Preferably closer to two dollars, but let's start with that penny of profit.

Many writers, myself included, have made the mistake of trying to scale before establishing this basic profitability. You need to understand what works consistently before you can grow it effectively. This might mean writing in a specific genre, building a particular type of audience, or focusing on a specific marketing channel.

THE SCALING PHASE

Only after you've mastered the previous phases can you effectively scale your writing business. This is when you can take what's working and amplify it. Your writing speed naturally increases, your quality improves, and you can handle multiple projects without losing effectiveness.

Even at this phase, you're still learning and adapting. These days I write fewer books than I used to, but they're better books. I'm more selective about my projects, only taking on things that truly excite me and fit my long-term goals.

Yes, you can make money before reaching the scaling phase. Plenty of writers do well writing formulaic works in popular genres. But if you want to develop a sustainable, fulfilling career that plays to your strengths, understanding and respecting these phases is crucial. Don't rush through them. Each phase builds the foundation for the next, and trying to skip ahead usually leads to frustration and burnout.

The goal isn't to race through these phases but to use them as a framework for understanding where you are and what you need to focus on next. Whether you're just starting out or well into your career, knowing which phase you're in can help you make better decisions about where to spend your energy and how to measure your progress.

UNDERSTANDING RESISTANCE

Your body doesn't want you to succeed. I know this sounds weird, but evolutionarily speaking, your body cannot tell the difference between physical harm and mental danger.

Most productivity advice skips over the most fundamental challenge. Your body is actively working against you. This isn't metaphorical. It's biological. Your body cannot tell the difference between physical danger and mental danger. When you try to push past your comfort zone as a writer, your body interprets that like it would interpret being chased by a lion.

When you're going into mentally dangerous territory, like a place outside your comfort zone, your body wants you to stop. It wants you to stay in the safe space because if you stay in the safe space you know, you won't die. We haven't evolved past this primitive response, even though the "dangers" we face as writers are more about ego than survival.

What makes it harder is that everyone around you also wants to stay in their safe space. They have all evolutionarily been brought up to be in that place too. So, you have to break through a lot to do this work. The best writers have broken through hundreds of these blocks to be able to speak authentically and vulnerably.

I've spent years observing this in myself and other writers. When we try to level up our craft, push into new territories, or put our work out into the world, our bodies start throwing up warning signals. Your brain is screaming "DANGER! RETREAT TO SAFETY!"

And it's not just your body. Everyone around you is hardwired the same way. When you try to do something risky or different, you're not just fighting your own evolutionary responses. You're fighting against a whole society of people whose bodies are telling them to stay safe, stay small, stay in the known territory.

This is why it's so hard to build a writing career. Every time you sit down to write something new, every time you try a different genre, every time you publish a book, you're going against millions of years of evolutionary programming telling you to stick with what's safe. Your body wants you to stay in your comfort zone because, historically, that's what kept our species alive.

Successful writers aren't just good at writing. They're good at pushing through this biological resistance. The best writers have broken through hundreds of these internal blocks to be able to speak authentically and vulnerably. Each time they pushed past their comfort zone, they expanded what their body considered "safe territory."

This is why positive self-talk is so crucial. Your body is already telling you negative stories about danger and safety. You need to actively counter those stories. You need to remind yourself that stretching beyond your comfort zone is how you grow, that the discomfort you're feeling is the sensation of progress.

And this never fully goes away. Even after writing dozens of books, even after building successful businesses, I still feel this resistance. The difference is that now I recognize it as a signal that I'm pushing into new territory, that I'm growing, that I'm doing something worthwhile.

Understanding this biological resistance has transformed how I think about productivity. It's not just about time management or writing techniques or business strategies. It's about learning to work with, or despite, your body's primitive survival instincts. Every time you sit down to write, you're not just crafting words - you're engaging in an ancient battle between your creative aspirations and your survival programming.

The resistance you feel is natural. It's biological. It's human. But it's also outdated. Your body thinks it's protecting you, but it's actually holding you back from the very things that will help you grow and thrive in the modern world. Understanding this is the first step to building a sustainable writing career.

THE COST OF CONTEXT SWITCHING

Research shows that every time you switch between ideas or tasks, you lose about 40% of your productivity. That's not a small number. Lost productivity due to context switching costs the global economy an estimated $450 billion annually.

This is why finishing projects is crucial. If you just complete the thing you're working on, you'll be 40% more productive than if you keep jumping between projects. That doesn't even include all the time you've already sunk into the current project.

Even if you don't love what you're working on, figure out a way to finish it. You learn so much from just finishing something. The last 10% is often where a piece becomes exceptional.

The middle isn't sexy. After the initial rush dies down, when no one's cheering you on, staying with a project is hard. But that's exactly why finishing is so valuable. Each completion teaches you something new and builds your creative resilience.

Remember: the hard thing about hard things is that they're hard. That's their defining characteristic. You cannot write books, build businesses, or have success if it's not hard. And if it's going to be hard, we have to accept that it's hard and push through anyway. Because that's what professionals do.

THE ONE THING PRINCIPLE

Let me tell you about my favorite concept in all of productivity. It comes from a book called *The ONE Thing* by Gary Keller and Jay Papasan, and it's about unlocking the one thing that will take your career to the next level.

So often, we're scattered through 100 different things. But if we just take that same energy and line it up the right way, we can use it to create a domino effect. There's one task that, if you finish it every day, you will knock down the big domino. It's about finding these little dominoes that lead to the next domino.

A domino can knock over another domino 1.5 times bigger than it. Stack them right, and after 10 dominoes, you're knocking over something enormous. That's what we're talking about here — little, continuous tasks that compound into something huge.

For me, at different times, it's been writing 5,000 words a day, editing 25,000 words a day, getting people on my mailing list, or running ads. Whatever your goal is, if you work backwards and say, "I'm going to expend all of my energy on this one task instead of across 50 tasks," you'll see exponential results.

Instead of starting 10 social media accounts, start one on a platform you love. Once that's up and running, do the next one and the next one. Take all of the energy you have and condense it. You'll not only save that 40% of productivity lost to context switching, you'll also be able to push progressively bigger and bigger dominoes over with very little effort.

Think about what you're trying to achieve. What's the one thing that would make everything else easier or unnecessary? That's where you need to focus. Not on doing everything, but on doing the right thing consistently.

Every time you perform an action, it should get more and more powerful. That's how you build true momentum. That's how you create lasting change. That's how you transform your career - one focused action at a time.

The beautiful thing about this principle is it simplifies everything. You don't have to worry about a hundred different tactics or strategies. You just need to identify and execute your ONE thing. Everything else becomes secondary.

I know it sounds too simple. That's why most people ignore it. But in my experience, the simpler the strategy, the more likely you are to actually do it. And doing it, consistently, day after day, is what really matters.

TIME BLOCKING YOUR WAY TO SUCCESS

If you're trying to avoid context switching, then the best method I have found is called time blocking. It's something I learned in my old school sales days, and I still use it today.

First, I block out every day as a specific type of day. Writing days, editing days, promotion days, launch days. Then I define what green time means for that day.

Green time is sacred. These are the things that will directly lead to me making money. That might include writing words for a book, doing sales calls, running ads, taking meetings, doing coaching calls. The key is that doing coaching calls on a writing day isn't green time because it's taking away from the main focus. Green time is immovable. Nothing else goes where green time goes.

Then there's yellow time, which is the ancillary stuff that relates to your job but doesn't directly make money. Answering emails, doing promotion on podcasts, writing blog posts, PR activities, etc. are all yellow time activities. These activities might lead to money eventually, but they're not direct revenue generators.

Finally, there's red time. These are the things that have nothing to do with making money. Picking kids up from school, having lunch, doctor's appointments. You're not going to make money picking your kids up from school. I'm sorry to tell you.

Time isn't inherently good or bad. It's about how you use it. Sometimes taking a nap is more valuable than a sales call. Sometimes eating lunch with your child is the most important thing you can do that day.

I love my green time activities because they're focused and productive, but I love my red time activities, too. The yellow time activities? Some I like, like writing blog posts. But there's a lot of administrative stuff that at this point I probably should offload.

The goal isn't to eliminate red time or even yellow time. It's to be intentional about how you use each type of time. When I'm in my green time block, I'm fully focused on that revenue-generating activity. When I'm in red time, I'm present with my family or taking care of myself.

This system works because it acknowledges reality. You can't be in revenue-generating mode all day. You need breaks, you need administration time, you need life time. The trick is to stop pretending all time is equal and start being strategic about how you use each type of time.

Remember, some days I don't have any energy, and taking a nap is more valuable than anything else I could do. If I don't do something with my hands during yellow time, I'll start thinking too much, and my brain will start associating or dissociating things I don't necessarily love.

Additionally, not everyone has the same amount of time, despite what cheap gurus and trite aphorisms tell us. A single mother with two kids working three jobs does not have the same amount of time in a day as somebody who is a full-time writer with a supportive wife who makes enough money to support the household.

Even if we did all have the same amount of time, that time would be disbursed differently. That mother would have considerably more red time than somebody in good health who has no kids because they are juggling three schedules instead of one.

The power of this system isn't in maximizing every minute. It's in being honest about how time really works and using that understanding to create a sustainable schedule. Because at the end of the day, productivity isn't about doing more. It's about doing the right things at the right time.

BUILDING SUSTAINABLE SYSTEMS

When I was younger, I thought productivity was all about speed. How fast could I write? How many projects could I juggle? Now I understand it's about building systems that grow stronger over time.

I think about my body like a computer with a specific amount of RAM. When you're a novice at something, it takes up 80-90% of your bandwidth. You're learning the basics, figuring out what works, making all the rookie mistakes. You can barely think about anything else when you're working on it.

But over time, as you become a pro, that same task might only take 1-10% of your bandwidth. Keep going, become an expert, and it drops to a tenth of 1%. I've been doing this so long that giving presentations takes very little of my bandwidth. It still takes energy, but I can do it while managing other tasks because I've mastered it.

The trick is understanding that you can't do more than one novice thing at a time. You can't do more than three things you're a pro at in one day. You have to respect your bandwidth limitations. So many of us try to open five novice programs at once and wonder why our system crashes.

Some tasks take a long time even when you're an expert. If I can write 2,000 words a day and I'm writing a 100,000-word book, that's still 50 days. That's still almost a sixth of my year writing that book. Then I have to edit it.

The key is accepting that mastery takes time, but it does come. When I write a nonfiction book now, I almost don't know what it's going to say until I finish editing it and take all the stuff out. Then I'm like, "Hey, that is what I think about this topic."

When you're learning something new, try not to learn other things simultaneously unless you're already an expert at them. Focus on turning as many novice skills into pro skills, and pro skills into expert skills, as you can. That's when you start doing these things on autopilot.

If something is exhausting you right now, you're probably not far enough along on it. You need to at least get to a pro level at it or figure out a way to offload it or delegate it before you can move on to the next thing.

This is why it's so important to give yourself space. Your speed of creating things will increase with each stage, along with the number of projects you can produce. But you have to respect the process. You have to understand that your capacity grows naturally over time, and you can't force it.

Even expert-level tasks can take significant time and energy. When I do an expert-level task like giving a presentation, it takes all my focus and energy because I have to be present. The difference is that I know how to manage that energy now, how to prepare for it, and how to recover from it.

This is the reality of sustainable growth. It's not about suddenly becoming superhuman. It's about gradually building your capacity, understanding your limitations, and creating systems that work with your natural rhythms rather than against them.

THE MINDSET FOR SUCCESS

It's okay to want attention. It's okay to be successful. It's okay to want fandom. It's okay to want your book to sell a million copies. It's okay. I genuinely like the books I write. I don't understand people who don't like their own books. Why are they writing those books?

If you don't believe that, lie to yourself until you do.

Sometimes you have to trick yourself into liking yourself before you actually like yourself. I know that sounds strange, but it's true. Here's what nobody tells you about building a creative career. If you tell yourself you're bad, you will start to believe you are bad.

But it works the other way too. If you tell yourself you are good, and the things you are doing are good, and you surround yourself with positivity and people that push you forward, then your whole mindset will change.

This isn't about living in a bubble. It's about refusing to let yourself talk to yourself negatively. If you wouldn't let someone talk to your friend that way, you can't let yourself talk about you that way. If you say something negative to yourself, I want you to say, "Don't talk that way about my friend."

One of the big problems with success is that whether you're going to fail or succeed looks exactly the same in the middle. If they drop you in the middle of an ocean in the dark of night and you start swimming, it's 50-50 whether you're swimming to shore or doing worse for yourself. You don't know in the moment. You just have to keep swimming.

Because if you don't believe, then you're going to stop swimming. Then you definitely won't make it to shore.

This might be the most important thing I say in this entire book: you are good. You are valuable. You deserve to be here. Even if you don't believe that yet, you have to at least say it. You have to say it to yourself all day, every day. Every time something negative comes up, put something positive in its place.

The beautiful thing is that when you stop letting yourself talk negatively to yourself, you'll stop letting other people talk to you negatively too. Your standards for how you should be treated, both by yourself and others, will rise.

This isn't just feel-good advice. Every successful writer I know has had to learn this. Because the path is too hard, the journey too long, to survive without building this foundation of self-belief.

The path of a writer is challenging enough without being your own worst enemy. Build yourself up. Protect your creative spirit. Trust in your journey. The rest will follow.

Everything I've shared here comes from twenty years of writing, failing, succeeding, and figuring it out along the way. Some days I still struggle. Some days I still doubt. But I've learned that productivity isn't about doing more. It's about doing better.

The hard thing about hard things is that they're hard. That's their defining characteristic. You can't write books, build businesses, or have success if it's not hard. But we can do hard things as long as we know they're not supposed to be easy.

Start by understanding where you are in your journey. Learn the fundamentals. Discover your voice. Build your foundation. Then scale what works. Don't try to rush the process; each phase teaches you something essential.

Most importantly, be kind to yourself along the way. Your body might fight you. Your mind might doubt you. But you have the power to push through, to build systems that work for you, to create success on your own terms.

TURNING YOUR NATURAL WRITING PATTERNS INTO AUDIENCE GROWTH

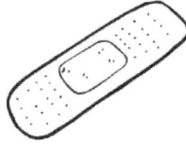

I spend a lot of time on consulting calls talking people through about how to get more people reading their work. Often, this is about turning subscribers into paid members, but just as often it's about getting people to subscribe to their publication in the first place.

After talking around the issue for a little while, it almost always comes down to not knowing what their publication is about or even who it's trying to reach in the first place.

Sometimes, people have done the work of finding a generic ICA (ideal customer avatar) and might even have "content pillars" or something similar that defines the types of things they write.

100% of the time, these two things which drive their publication are conceptualized wrong, or are too broad to work well as a guiding light for their work. I spend a lot of time breaking down these to their base level and building them back up with clients.

This work generally comes down to three questions.

1. WHAT ARE YOU ALREADY WRITING ABOUT?

People often come with me asking for my opinion on what they should write or how they should change their publication, and I generally have one answer to this question: "It doesn't matter what I think. It matters what you're already writing."

Writing is something we are almost always doing for free, and if you're doing something for free, you should enjoy the thing you're doing.

We can create a methodology to make any kind of writing work with people, but we can only build on writing we actually, well, write.

Now, you might think that you're a unique snowflake that never writes the same thing twice, but I guarantee there are patterns to your writing. If there aren't, you need to keep writing until you see the patterns, because they are there.

You're looking for things that keep popping up over time, either thematically or topically.

I call this "being back on my bullshit." It's the stuff I talk about all the time, and I keep coming back to over the years. It's so much easier to go back on your bullshit than to force yourself to write something that doesn't resonate with you. Additionally, it's so much easier to make the stuff you're writing resonate deeper with people than to change your writing to fit something that doesn't resonate with you.

2. WHAT IS YOUR IDEAL READER'S "WIN STATE"?

I've spoken at length about your win condition, but this isn't about you. It's about conceptualizing how your ideal reader walks through the world after they have "won the game." Assuming they follow everything you say, eliminate all the flaws in their process, and build all your best strategies into their life, how do they walk through the world? What job do they have? What have they accomplished?

This is critical information because it drives the fear you are trying to flush out of their system.

If you want to make the most money from your work, it behooves you to serve people in transition, and specifically at a transition point that brings them a lot of uncertainty.

So, the win state is imagining a person who is no longer filled with that uncertainty. Then, working backwards to find the transition point and transformation that matters most to them. Finally, you define who the person is before they encounter your work.

If you can define these three items, you can create every piece of content around them and how to get somebody from one to the other. Ideally, you would attract both the person who's already reached their win state as well as people still in flux, because then the people in their "win state" can help refer other people to you. Besides, people in their win state will do almost anything to stay in it.

If you're struggling to pinpoint this, try writing a day-in-the-life narrative for your ideal reader, imagining them having achieved all their goals. What does their life look like? What challenges have they overcome? Who do they become? Writing this out can clarify the transformation your content should be guiding them through.

3. WHAT 3-5 THINGS DOES YOUR IDEAL READER HAVE TO LEARN IN ORDER TO GET THERE?

Now that you have your "win state" avatar, it's time to go back and define the 3-5 things that a person in flux needs to master in order to get there.

When I started, my first book was called *How to Build Your Creative Career*, and it was built around five pillars: Making Great Content, the Fundamentals of Selling, Building and Audience from Scratch, Selling at Live Events, and Launching Products Successfully.

It's almost ten years later, and these are still the five pillars that I believe it takes to build a creative career. All my work revolves around one (or more) of these five pillars. They drive everything about my content…but they are not what most people think of as content pillars.

People think content pillars are "Ultimate Guides" or "Cornerstone content," but it has nothing to do with what types of content you publish. It's all about the pillars that somebody must master to reach their ideal end state.

If you've been writing for a while, it should be easy to go back and categorize each of your posts into buckets, at least very broad buckets. It's very important here to catch trends in your own thinking and find ways to create categories for them, because it's stuff you'll probably be talking about for a long time, especially since you have already talked about it for a long time.

Ideally, you would create an acronym of these pillars so that it's easy to follow and remember. I don't have a nice, easy acronym though, and it's still worked for me. If you can find one, it makes the message go down easier.

Once you have these three elements ironed out, you should be able to more easily conceptualize your messaging around them to bring the right people into your writing. It should also help you stay focused on your audience's needs while creating content that is consistent, relevant, and easier to write because it aligns with what you're naturally drawn to in the first place.

THE MODERN PRODUCTIVITY PARADOX

The challenge I see many writers face isn't that they're not productive enough. It's that they're trying to be productive in unsustainable ways. They burn themselves out trying to match someone else's pace, or they scatter their energy across too many projects, diluting their effectiveness.

Sustainable productivity looks different. It's about creating systems that grow more powerful over time. It's about focusing energy where it matters most and building momentum through consistent, manageable effort. It's about understanding and working with your personal limitations and making your work compound in value.

Think of it like compound interest for your creative career. Just as a smart investment grows over time without additional effort, well-designed creative systems should deliver increasing returns without requiring proportionally more work.

This is the foundation of sustainable productivity. It's not doing more but doing better. It's about building systems that grow more valuable over time, creating work that compounds in impact, and maintaining a pace you can sustain for the long haul. In the following sections, I'll show you exactly how to build these systems and create this kind of leveraged productivity. But remember: the goal isn't to exhaust yourself doing more. It's to create more impact with the energy you have, while maintaining the space and freedom to live your life.

ENGINEERING WINNING DAYS

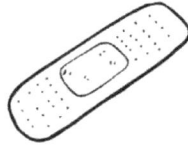

How many days a year do you really need to "win" to be successful? Is it 100? 50? Maybe 20?

What if I told you it's just 1–2?

And by "win," I don't mean having a good day or crossing tasks off your list. I mean those days; the ones where everything aligns. The book launch that shoots into the stratosphere. The post that spreads like wildfire. The moment when your hard work finally gets the spotlight, and it feels like the world is cheering for you.

We think we should be having those days all the time because we constantly see other people having them. It feels like everyone is always winning, doesn't it? One person's big launch, another's viral post, a third's glowing feature; it all adds up to an overwhelming sense that success is constant for others and elusive for us.

But that's just not the truth. What we're witnessing is a collection of different people winning on different days. It's not a steady stream of success but a patchwork of moments spread out over months and years.

We've been conditioned to believe that winning should be a daily occurrence, especially in an era where social media bombards us with highlight reels of other people's lives.

But most of those highlights are the result of long, deliberate efforts. Nobody wins every day. They don't even win every week or month. Success is about what happens in between those days; the quiet grind, the unglamorous prep work, and the steady laying of foundations.

If we accept that winning is rare, we can shift our focus. Instead of chasing daily wins, what if we concentrated on creating the conditions for a massive win every 6–12 months? What if we embraced the idea that most of our time is better spent behind the scenes, moving pieces into place for those rare but significant moments when everything comes together?

WHAT IT TAKES TO ENGINEER A WINNING DAY

Success isn't usually random; it's almost always engineered. It begins with knowing what a winning day looks like for you. Is it a book launch that hits bestseller status? A viral article that brings in thousands of new readers? A surge in email subscribers after a carefully crafted campaign? *Clarity is the first step.*

The biggest problem creators face is that they don't define the win condition. They flail and flit, trying things, but never knowing if they work to reach their goal because they don't know their goal. The biggest shift any creator can make is to clearly define the singular goal they're working toward, and they align all their resources toward getting it.

Once you've defined success, *the next phase is preparation.* Winning days are built on strong infrastructure: a polished product, an engaged audience, and systems that amplify your reach when the moment arrives. This might mean months of building an email list, crafting irresistible content, or refining your product until it's undeniably excellent.

The final step is execution. When your moment arrives, you need to be ready to seize it. That means having clear messaging, a distribution plan, and the confidence to step into the spotlight.

The people who "win" aren't just lucky. They've set themselves up to capitalize on opportunities when they come.

If winning isn't about luck but about preparation, how do you prepare?

1. **Define what winning looks like:** Before you can engineer a winning day, you need to know what it looks like. Is it a book launch that sells 10,000 copies? A viral article? A surge of new subscribers? Be specific about what success means for you.
2. **Build the infrastructure:** Winning days require a foundation. This might mean setting up a strong email list, creating content that resonates with your audience, building a network of supporters, or refining your product until it's irresistible.
3. **Create your opportunities:** Successful launches and viral moments don't happen out of thin air. They're often the result of deliberate planning, timing, messaging, and amplification. Schedule your efforts around strategic windows when you're most likely to make an impact.
4. **Stay focused on the long game:** Most of your time will be spent in preparation, not celebration. This is the unglamorous reality of success: months of quiet work leads to those rare moments of visibility. Embrace the grind, knowing it's a necessary part of the process.

5. **Execute with precision:** When your moment arrives, make it count. Be ready with everything you've planned, including clear messaging, polished deliverables, and a distribution strategy that maximizes your reach.

One thing I want to make sure to mention is that launching doesn't necessarily mean a winning day. In fact, most of my launch days don't win the day. Often, I launch a book just to my list or launch it without even sending an email. People often assume that when you launch you have to go big and win huge, but I think in reality you only get to win 1-2 launches a year, and the rest of them have to be more modest hits, which is why I'm so adamant about choosing different launch lengths for each project. Yes, your winning launches probably need to be 30-60 days to capitalize on the hype and buzz, but sometimes a launch might only warrant a 5-day launch if you don't think there's a very big audience for it. I often have one day launches now, which don't get any fanfare and bring in very modest bumps in revenue.

When you're setting up your launch schedule, pick your winning launches, and then slot in the other launches around it. One of the most dangerous things creators do is assume every launch will win, when only a very few launches will win every year.

THE "BORING WORK" THAT NEEDS DOING

Winning days don't happen in a vacuum. They're the result of months, sometimes years, of unglamorous preparation. It's the kind of work that rarely makes headlines but lays the foundation for success. This is the "boring work" framework: a disciplined approach to building systems, relationships, and momentum during the quiet times, so when your moment arrives, you're ready to seize it.

The problem is, many of us resist the boring work. We crave the instant gratification of visible progress, the thrill of daily wins. But the reality is, those quiet, under-the-radar efforts are where real growth happens. Let's break down what this behind-the-scenes work looks like and why it's so essential.

- **Building your community:** At its core, success is about connection. Whether you're an author, entrepreneur, or creative, your audience is your lifeline. But building a community isn't just about broadcasting your message—it's about fostering relationships. Think about your emails, social media posts, or even in-person events. Are they inviting dialogue, encouraging loyalty, and making your audience feel seen? These interactions may not result in immediate sales or viral moments, but they cultivate trust. Over time, that trust transforms casual followers into superfans, the people who will rally behind you when your big moment comes. The work here can feel slow and unglamorous. It's answering comments, crafting thoughtful newsletters, and showing up consistently even when it feels like no one is paying attention. But each touchpoint builds a thread of connection, and over time, those threads form an unbreakable web of support.
- **Refining your product:** It's easy to romanticize the idea of launching something perfect on the first try, but the truth is, most success stories are built on relentless refinement. Your book, product, or service isn't just a one-time effort. It's a living, breathing thing that evolves with time and feedback. Refinement means taking the time to polish every detail. *It's rewriting that book draft until it sings.* It's tweaking your course

curriculum to ensure it solves your audience's problems. It's iterating on your service offerings until they're irresistible. This stage isn't flashy. It often involves long hours, trial and error, and learning from what didn't work. But when you focus on making your product the best it can be, you're setting the stage for a winning day where your audience can't help but notice.

- **Strengthening backend systems:** While the spotlight shines on launches, viral posts, and public-facing success, the real work happens in the backend systems that support those moments. These systems are the invisible gears that keep your operation running smoothly, allowing you to focus on the creative or strategic parts of your work. This might mean setting up automated email funnels that nurture your audience while you sleep, creating content schedules that keep you consistent, or diving into analytics to understand what's resonating with your audience. These tools ensure that when your winning day arrives, you're not scrambling to keep up with the momentum. Think of it like building a house. The visible structure gets all the attention, but it's the foundation and plumbing that make it livable. Backend systems are that foundation. They may not be glamorous, but they're absolutely essential.

- **Networking with intention:** No one succeeds alone. Behind every big moment is a network of people who amplified the message, shared the vision, or opened doors. Networking isn't just about attending events or collecting business cards. It's about building genuine relationships that are mutually beneficial. Think about the peers, influencers, and collaborators who can help you amplify your reach. How can you add value to their work? Can you share their projects, offer your expertise, or collaborate on something meaningful? These relationships don't blossom overnight, but by consistently showing up and supporting others, you create a network that's ready to back you when your winning day comes. Networking is also about reciprocity. It's not just about what others can do for you but about creating a sense of community where success feels shared. When you lift others, they're more likely to lift you in return.

The boring work isn't glamorous, but it's what separates fleeting success from sustainable growth. Each email you send, product detail you refine, system you build, and connection you nurture adds another brick to the foundation of your future success.

When you embrace this work, you stop chasing the illusion of constant wins and start building something far more valuable: the infrastructure for consistent, meaningful progress. Winning days may be rare, but the effort you put into the quiet moments makes them not just possible, but inevitable.

So the next time you feel like your work isn't visible or exciting enough, remember: this is the work that matters. This is the foundation that will hold up when the spotlight finally finds you.

THE REALITY OF FAILURE

Of course, not every attempt will succeed. Some launches will flop. Some campaigns will underperform. But these moments aren't failures in the traditional sense—they're data points. Each misstep teaches you something valuable about what doesn't work, allowing you to refine your approach.

Think of the setbacks as stepping stones. They're not barriers to success but part of the path leading to your next win. For instance, an underwhelming email campaign might reveal weak points in your messaging, giving you the insight you need to craft a stronger one next time.

This is the work of the in-between days. The time between winning days can feel uneventful, even frustrating. It's the long stretch of preparation where you're building the systems, connections, and content that support your success. This is where the real work happens; quietly refining your craft, engaging with your audience, and strengthening the foundation that will hold up when the spotlight finally finds you.

Winning days don't just happen. They're the result of countless hours spent creating a product worth talking about, a network willing to share it, and a strategy to ensure it lands with maximum impact.

When a winning day does arrive, the work isn't over. In fact, it's just beginning. That viral post or successful launch opens a window of opportunity, but it's up to you to keep the momentum going.

Engaging with your new audience is critical. Follow up with thoughtful emails, offer additional value, or simply thank them for their support. Analyze what worked and why, so you can replicate and improve on it next time. Wins aren't endpoints—they're springboards for what comes next.

THE MENTAL SHIFT WE ALL NEED

Entrepreneurs often fall into the trap of believing they're failing if they're not winning all the time. But understanding that success is rare by design can be liberating. When you realize you're not supposed to win every day, you free yourself from the exhausting chase of constant validation.

Instead, you can focus on progress, the slow, steady effort that leads to big moments. Celebrate the milestones along the way: completing a draft, growing your audience, or refining a strategy. These are wins in their own right, even if they don't come with fanfare.

Entrepreneurs often struggle with mental health because they feel like they're failing if they're not winning constantly. This mindset shift can help:

1. Recognize that "winning" is rare by design. It's supposed to be special.
2. Track progress in smaller increments, like the number of audience touchpoints or content created.
3. Celebrate preparation milestones, such as completing a book draft or launching a new website.

The path to success isn't paved with daily wins. It's marked by quiet, deliberate preparation punctuated by rare but extraordinary moments. Those moments aren't accidents. They're the result of your effort, strategy, and patience.

So, stop chasing the illusion of constant success. Embrace the work behind the scenes. Build the kind of infrastructure that allows you to rise when your moment comes. Because when it does, it'll be worth every ounce of effort you invested. Winning may be rare, but it's always worth it.

WHY SEQUELS FAIL

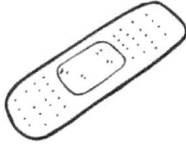

I run into writers all the time who say some version of "I'm giving people what they say they want," or "I'm writing more about my most popular topics, but I can't replicate my success." Basically, even when they follow the data and give people what people "want," they still can't make anything new pop with their audience.

Combating this is one of the toughest bits about building a thriving creative career. Customers will confidently tell you what they think they want…except that what they say and what they will actually buy are two very different things.

It turns out that while people know how they want to feel when they interact with your product or service, they struggle to articulate exactly how to get there again. They'll ask for more features, more options, or more of what they've already experienced, but what they're really asking for is a way to recapture an emotional high. To truly succeed, we need to decode these requests and focus on delivering the emotional experience that keeps people coming back.

It's the reason sequels fail (or succeed). Failed sequels come from creators listening when the audience says, "more more more," but failing to hear the "…of this feeling please" between the chanting. Successful sequels deliver on giving audiences the same feelings as the original, instead of just the same structure and characters.

Like children (and most adults, honestly), customers rarely articulate their emotional needs directly. Often, they don't even understand their emotional needs enough to articulate them.

They focus on tangible requests like "I want more sex" or "Give me more of this relationship" but that's not really what they want. Readers don't have the language to express what they really want, so they instead fall back on the language they do have, even if it is imperfect at best and wildly incorrect at worst.

What they're really expressing is a desire to feel something specific. Maybe it's the thrill of discovery, the satisfaction of efficiency, or the comfort of feeling understood.

The key is to listen beyond the words. Instead of taking requests at face value, dig into the emotions behind them. What made the customer satisfied in the first place? What are they trying to replicate?

A customer might ask for more articles on a specific topic, but the deeper emotional need could be a desire to feel that same emotional catharsis again. Simply adding more articles likely won't fulfill that desire within them unless you can replicate the same feeling again.

It's important to ask what emotional outcome your customers are chasing. Once you understand that, you can design solutions that meet the deeper need, even if they don't look exactly like what was requested.

This is the counterintuitive part about listening to your audience, because hearing them is really about translating what they are saying into what they really want, which might not seem like listening to them at all in the moment.

When customers give feedback, it's important not to stop at their first answer. Instead, dig deeper to uncover the emotional motivation behind their request. The first thing they mention is usually a surface-level solution, not the root of the problem.

Getting to the heart of what people really want requires not only asking the right questions, but also the right follow-up questions. Instead of asking, "What characters would you like to see?" ask "What relationship resonated most deeply with you?" or "How did you feel when you finished reading?"

Asking deeper questions helps you move away from simply delivering what's been requested to designing an experience that taps into what people actually care about.

A really great game to play is the five whys, which involves asking somebody "why is that important?" or some variation five times about the same topic to draw out their true feelings.

- Why do you feel that way?
- Why is that important?
- Why did you like that?
- Why does that matter to you?
- Why do you think that is?

Even better, if you know your audience well and understand their problems on a deep level, then you can predict which problem you're solving with anything you launch, and how to deliver something that will resonate with them.

Remember, you are the expert delivering what your customer needs, even if it is buried under a mountain of false beliefs of what they say they want. It's your job to uncover what they want, both through their words and their actions.

Customers say one thing, but their actions often tell a different story. By observing how people engage with your work, you can get a clearer picture of what they really value. Behavior is often a more reliable indicator of needs than verbal feedback.

If you see people reading a particular type of article from you or spending more time in one part of your catalog, that's a signal to dig deeper. Look for patterns in behavior that reveal what's resonating emotionally. What do they keep coming back to? What sparks engagement?

Don't rely too much on using engagement as a metric unless that was the point of your article. Everything you write should have a clear objective, from writing a comment to subscribing to becoming a paid member of your community. Yes, everything you write will lead to a bevy of different outcomes depending on the reader, but it's important to know what your intention is before you decide if it aligns with your reader's actions.

If you write a sales post that doesn't get any sales, but gets tons of engagement, that's probably pretty terrible alignment. It's also going to severely affect your bottom line. Engagement don't pay the soup man, as they say.

By observing how customers behave, you can align your future offerings to enhance the emotional aspects they're most drawn to, even if it's not something they've explicitly requested.

That said, when you enter another community, people there might behave a lot differently towards you than in your own community. This is often because this new audience:

- Doesn't know who you are, so they don't trust you yet.
- Don't have the language to talk about or even understand what you're talking about.

Integrating into a community usually involves both building trust and disseminating the language needed to understand, explore, and be transformed by what you're trying to talk about with them.

As a Kickstarter expert, I'm often called to talk about crowdfunding with other communities. When I do, I focus mainly on explaining the opportunity Kickstarter provides and giving the new community the language to translate what they know into how this new platform works.

I'm not going too deep into the nitty-gritty of Kickstarter because I don't want to overwhelm them. Meanwhile, my own audience is very well-versed in Kickstarter, so we can talk about crowdfunding on a much deeper and more nuanced level.

That doesn't mean there aren't new things to introduce to my audience, though. I've spent a decade laying the groundwork with my most ardent readers about how to thrive in capitalism, mainly by showing them how to use platforms and get in the right mindset to thrive.

Crowdfunding is one factor in that equation, but it's far from the only one. So, we expanded the message into direct sales, retailers, and mindset and allowed all of that to permeate through our community until they understood the full scopes of the problem. Only then, after disseminating the aspect of the conversation for years, did I feel confident my audience was ready for the next part of the conversation and the transformation that comes with it, which was when I introduced my book How to Thrive as a Writer in a Capitalist Dystopia.

Once you understand the emotional drivers behind your customers' needs, your next step is to innovate around that emotional experience. This doesn't mean simply adding more features or rerunning the same playbook. It means designing experiences that evoke the right feelings. The goal is to enhance the emotional payoff while surprising your customers with new ways to achieve it.

Instead of writing about a particular topic just because people ask for it, think about how you can amplify the feeling that's driving their request. People don't buy books. They buy the feelings that come with them. When communicating the value of your work, focus on the emotional impact it creates rather than just listing topics or technical details.

Customers care about how your product makes their life easier, better, or more enjoyable, so lead with that bit first.

Instead of focusing solely on what your writing does, emphasize how it makes readers feel. Are you giving them peace of mind? Empowering them to do something they couldn't before? Streamlining a process that causes frustration?

When you position your writing around emotional benefits, you're speaking directly to the deeper needs of your audience. This helps you connect with them on a more personal level, making it easier for them to see how your offering fits into their life. Apple's marketing doesn't just list features. They focus on how their products make people feel creative, inspired, and in control. You should do the same by highlighting the emotional outcomes your product delivers.

Here are some practical ways to apply these insights and start delivering on your customers' true emotional needs:

- **Focus on the emotion behind the request**: Don't just give them what they ask for directly. Instead, figure out the emotional experience they're trying to achieve, and offer a solution that delivers that feeling.
- **Ask "why" multiple times**: Keep asking "why?" until you uncover the emotional driver behind a request. The first answer will rarely get you to the core of the problem. That said, it's important to note that whenever your audience tells you something is wrong, they are right, but if they tell you how to fix it, they are almost always wrong. It's your job to translate what they say into what they mean and implement it.
- **Test emotional outcomes, not just features**: When launching new products or features, test how they make your customers *feel*. If the emotional payoff isn't there, no amount of functionality will save it.
- **Create an emotional journey**: Design your product experience to guide customers through an emotional arc—from solving a pain point to delivering satisfaction or excitement.
- **Triangulate your audience**: I like to "plunge the depths" of what my audience wants by offering a lot of different articles with different hooks and use the successes to guide the fence around which I operate. If you haven't been doing this for a while, then it takes a while to know the bounds by which your audience will engage with your work, and it's different for everyone. Once you can triangulate your signal around several different points, you'll have a stronger relationship with your audience, and what they want.

That said, you could do all this and fail. That's just part of it and why you need to take a bunch of angles with any launch. Even if you do everything right from design to execution, some things just won't resonate. These are all just strategies to help you separate the chaff from the wheat, so you fail less over time.

At the core of every piece of writing is an emotional experience. Readers might ask for more of what they've already had, but what they truly want is to feel the way they did when they first connected with your product. By understanding these emotional drivers and innovating around them, you can deliver more than what people say they want. You can give them what they actually need.

Focus on the feeling, and you'll build deeper, more lasting connections with your customers.

BOOK CATALOG AS INVESTMENT PORTFOLIO?

I've spent years watching the publishing industry obsess over book launches. We pour endless energy into those first few weeks, treating them as the ultimate measure of success. But after managing over 60 books throughout my career, I've learned something crucial: we're thinking about this all wrong.

That's not to say launches aren't important. They bring in revenue, boost the exposure of a book, and keep our cash flow positive, but especially in this day and age where everything is in print forever, the book launch is less important than ever.

Once you break even on a book's costs, both your time and money, that book becomes an asset forever. Forever. Even if it only makes $10 a year in profit, year after year, it's still an asset in your portfolio.

Large publishers know the power of the "backlist," which is books that have passed their launch window. Publishers can make more than half their income from backlist books in their catalog. However, these books are not evenly distributed. Even with a thousand book backlist, only a small percentage will be making significant money at any one time.

Similarly, when you think about an investment portfolio, you'll have individual stocks that rise and fall, but it's the overall growth that matters most. In fact, having a varied portfolio full of large cap, small cap, technology, healthcare, and other types of stocks helps smooth out the dips in any one sector. If you over index on one industry in the good times, you'll be uniquely exposed to losing money on the bad days.

In my catalog, I have over 60 books that can make money for the rest of my life. Most of them look pretty pathetic at any one time, pulling in maybe $10-$50/yr on retailers.

But these same books still generate revenue behind publication paywalls and in various bundles. More importantly, even if they never earned another dollar, they've already broken even on my time and effort. That's my key.

If a book can merely break even at launch, then they become an asset forever, instead of a liability.

Think about having 50 books in your catalog, each bringing in modest annual profits. Maybe it's only $500 total per year. That might not sound impressive but remember that these are permanent assets. That money adds up over time, especially if you're smart about reinvesting it into index funds or other growth vehicles, including future books.

I've talked before about how to build a body of work as a way to fight imposter syndrome, but once you've got that body of work built, and you're not in the red on them, you suddenly have a powerful investment vehicle you can lean on forever.

I've learned to live primarily on my frontlist books when they launch, combined with contract work, and make anything I earn from retailers be bonus money, but that won't always be my plan. My goal is that in the next few years all my books will be launched, and I can start to make real money on my backlist…

…which is incredible, because you can always try to get your old books to sell. I would recommend not trying to go full-bore on it until you have at least 4 books in one series that get good reviews, but my friend Kevin McLaughlin talks often about his goal of having 4 series of 12 books that each make $10k in profit a month.

You don't get there in one day, you can always get there, and you can always redesign everything once a book breaks even, forever and ever. Even your heirs can get your book to sell, generation after generation, once you've built those assets.

Here's the strategy that's served me well: I focus intensely on breaking even at launch. If you need $5,000 to break even on a book, that's actually quite achievable with a well-planned Kickstarter campaign. If you follow our strategies, you should be able to sell 100-200 copies from a modest launch, break even, and then never have to worry about it again.

Now I write much faster, but for the first decade of my career I was basically a one book a year author. From 2011-2017, I would put out an average of less than two projects a year.

That's not much production compared to where I'm at now, and I couldn't retire on those launches, but by 2017 I had 12 books out, and since I broke even on all of them using a combination of Kickstarter and conventions, within three months of launch those books broke even and have been earning a little bit every year since then.

When my career took off, people went back to those old books, too, making them even more valuable as time went on and more people cared about my work.

Even if you can only put out one book a year, by the end of a decade you'll have ten books, which can be an incredible asset. If you can earn some money by releasing episodes of your book on Substack, Patreon, or some other platform, you can get several bites of the apple. Publishing is a war of attrition, where every dollar counts, so every dollar counts.

Since I started my career, I've rarely failed to break even on a book either at or soon after launch and have never had an unprofitable book. This might not sound very impressive, but most publishers lose money on up to 90% of their books, but I am always profitable, if only barely, on every launch, and have been since 2016, well before I even built a name. The books I've tried to launch on retailers first are the only ones that have ever failed in my whole career.

I'll be the first to admit very few of these books have exploded into massive bestsellers or made me rich overnight. That's not the point. I deliberately over index on breaking even at launch because I want to move each book from the liability column to the asset column as quickly as possible.

When you start thinking this way, something remarkable happens. The pressure of needing every launch to be spectacular begins to lift. You realize you're not just publishing for today - you're building something for your future self. Whether that's your 40s, 50s, or beyond, you're creating a foundation that will continue generating value long after the initial release excitement fades.

The real power of this approach becomes clear when you look at multiple revenue streams. Traditional retail sales are just one piece of the puzzle. Your books can earn through:

- Digital platform subscriptions
- Bundle deals with other authors
- Special editions and repackaging
- Publication paywalls
- Direct sales through your own platforms
- Library lending programs
- Educational licensing

Each of these streams might generate modest income individually, but together they create a resilient income portfolio that isn't dependent on any single channel.

Once you have a story that works, it tends to keep working far into the future. The key is to make sure that story is rock solid. Then, even if it doesn't sell today, you set yourself up to earn on it for a long time.

Looking ahead, I'd love to see our industry shift away from its launch obsession. Instead of pouring all our resources into those first few weeks, what if we spent more time thinking about creating lasting assets that we loved? What if we approached each book as another piece in our long-term investment strategy?

Because if we do that, then we can stop focusing on writing to market, writing cookie-cutter books, and writing what's hot and can start making books that resonate deeply with readers. Trends change, readers move on from cheap stories, but those books that resonate will always connect with readers, no matter what they are about today.

The financial reality of publishing often gets obscured by stories of breakthrough bestsellers and seven-figure advances. But for most authors and publishers, success comes from building a sustainable catalog of assets that generate steady returns over time. It's not glamorous, but it's effective.

I've found immense freedom in this approach. When you know each book you create has already covered its costs and moved into the asset column, it changes how you view your entire career. You're no longer just as good as your last launch. Instead, you're building a foundation of intellectual property that works for you continuously.

A book's value isn't determined in its first month of sales. Sometimes the real returns come years later, through channels you never anticipated when you first published. By building with this long view in mind, you're not just publishing books - you're creating assets that can support you for decades to come.

It's about being kind to your future self. Each book that breaks even represents one more brick in the foundation of your long-term security. That's a weight lifted off your shoulders, an investment in your creative and financial freedom. And in my experience, that's worth far more than any single bestseller could ever provide.

HOW TO MARKET YOURSELF WITHOUT FEELING GROSS ABOUT IT?

I hear this question all the time and it's kind of the whole game, right? If you can figure out how to market yourself without feeling scuzzy about it, then you'll probably have success. If you can't, then you'll probably be doomed to obscurity.

Yes, there are instances where you could skyrocket to success despite yourself or market yourself with no success for years, but in general there's a strong correlation between marketing success and overall success. I know personally it was a game-changer for me.

Once you have an audience and you can make cool things, then it's all about building better and better product-market fit that resonates deeper and deeper with your audience with every project.

It's hard before you have an audience because you're just guessing what people will like, but once you have even a small audience, it gets increasingly easier to build something that sits at the intersection of their interests and your interests.

My best advice toward this end is not particularly fun, but it is effective.

To get you into the right mindset to succeed, first we have to break down a lot of the beliefs creatives have about their work. This is meant to break you down to the core so we can rebuild you back stronger.

- **Almost nobody sees the thing you do.** This doesn't even include the suppression platforms force upon you (wherein barely 1-2% of your followers see what you post on most platforms). Even if you could reach every one of your followers, you still are being followed by effectively nobody in the world even if you have an audience of millions.
- **Even fewer people click on the things you are doing to buy it.** Unless you can explain something succinctly in a way that resonates with people, they aren't going to take action. A good result from a sales campaign is 1-2% of your audience buying from you, which means at any time, 98%+ of your audience isn't funding your work. Even then, you usually have to make a dozen or more different pitches using slightly different angles to convince somebody to buy.
- **Even when they want to buy, they don't have money.** Over 66% of Americans live paycheck to paycheck. Roughly 1 billion people in the world make less than $1/day. Lots of people might want to support you, but they don't have the money to spare.
- **Life is chaos, and even when people want to follow up, they won't**. I feel like this is self-explanatory, right? Nobody has their stuff together, right? This means you have to keep popping up to remind people, because they wait until the last minute to make a decision. They have other stuff occupying their time, just like you.

I fully accept all these things, and that's difficult even for me to read. The most important bit to pull out is that people not paying attention to you or buying your stuff has nothing to do with you. It has everything to do with what they have going on in their lives.

I talk with a lot of long-term customers during my launches who just lost their job, or got a cancer diagnosis, or ended up in the hospital, or had their only car break down, or just lost somebody close to them, or just moved, or…well, they just have stuff going on. Often, they apologize for not being able to support me, which is very kind, but I never expect anyone to buy my work, especially if they just don't have it in them to make it a joyous experience.

Those are just ones that connected with me, too. How many of my fans face the same adversity, but just never tell me about it? Probably a lot. Once, somebody messaged me after a campaign asking for a refund because they were in the hospital. Not only did I process that refund, but I also sent them the book because man, that is a tough row to hoe and a free book makes it a little better.

Everyone in the world has their own stuff going on that's more important to them than anything you are doing (unless it's directly related to helping them deal with their own stuff).

Creatives think that people hate their work when they don't buy. The truth is that most people never think about you at all.

I've been doing this for a long time and millions of people have been exposed to my work. Meanwhile, I've collected about 200,000 email addresses in my career. Of those, 45,000 of them are currently active on my email lists, and I make about 2,500 sales a year, with hundreds of people paying at least $1 for my publication.

That math sucks, but it's better than my friend's client, who collected 4 million emails to get 100,000 engaged subscribers to find 1,000 customers.

It also gets better at scale. If I had collected 2,000 emails, had 450 people on my list, made 25 sales a year, and had 8 people paying for my publication, that would not be great, even though the ratios are the same.

One thing I learned studying hundreds of companies of all sizes is that most businesses only work at scale. Their metrics suck when you look under the hood. Yes, there are also great businesses that work with just a few great clients, but they aren't the ones that make the news.

Another thing I learned is that even the biggest companies in the world can't get everyone to use their products, even for free. For instance, there are 8 billion people in the world and Facebook had 3.05 billion monthly active users in July 2023, which is a ton, but it's less than half the world's population. Open AI has been an internet darling the last few years and had 1.7 billion monthly users in July 2023. TikTok has over 1 billion monthly users, which is a ton, but still not the majority of the world.

None of these super successful companies can get everyone to use their product for free, let alone pay for it. So, you should probably cut yourself some slack if everyone you talk to doesn't buy from you. Facebook hires the best salespeople in the world, and they can't figure it out, either. Heck, only half of active internet users search on Google, and they have as much market share as it's probably possible to have for a company.

I've been doing creative work for 20 years and maybe, just maybe if I stretch, I've been exposed to 8 million people. That's a ton, but in a world of 8 billion people, that's only

.1% of the population that have even had a chance to make a decision about my work.

There are still literally billions upon billions of people who have never been exposed to my work at all.

At the end of the day, you should feel good if 10% of people you talk to care about your work (with 1-2% of your engaged audience loving it enough to buy it), and 10% will hate it, but that means 80% have no opinion. They saw what you want to put out into the world and gave a collective shrug of "meh."

So, if you want to make $50,000 on your $50 product, you need to make 1,000 sales, which means you need to have access to 100,000 people in your audience, which means you probably need to expose yourself to somewhere between 1 and 10 million people to find that audience. We've certainly had $50,000 launches with just a couple thousand on our list, but those were very, very motivated buyers who were ready to buy from us immediately.

If you're failing at this, it's probably because you're simply not balancing the math equation properly. It's not you, or people hating you. Like with most things, math is both the problem and the solution.

The whole of this work is swimming through the rejection to find that 10% who love what you have to say. They will be different to everyone, but if you want to make sales, you have to swim through lots of people who hate you, tons of people who don't care about you, and a bunch of people who love your work but don't, won't, or can't buy it to find that 1 in 100 person who will buy from you.

BUILDING YOU BACK UP

By now, you should be pretty well broken down to the core. Once you are lying in a heap on the floor, then we can build yourself up again because there are several truths that work in your favor.

- **You effectively have been exposed to 0% of the world's population, which means you have nothing but upside.** There's almost no chance you have spoken with as many people as me, and even I haven't spoken to 99.9% of the world. So, you have at least that many people. Even if 99% of them don't like your work, that's still millions of fans waiting out there to meet you.
- **It is statistically impossible that in a world of eight billion people that a bunch of people don't have the same interests as you**. Even if 1% of the adult population of the USA's 258.3 million people share your interests, that's 2.58 million people. If you expand that to a global scale, that's 6.6 billion total adults, and 66 million who, probably, on some level, share your interests.
- **It's financially impossible in a capitalist system that if you show those people something that interests them that some percentage of them will pay for it.** You can do a really, really bad job and still make a lot of money if enough people know about it. If even 1% of 1% of the adult US population will pay for your work, that's 25.8k people. If you expand that to a global scale, that's 660k people who might be willing to pay for what you're doing. There is nothing but opportunity out there. You just have to find them.
- **If you gather enough people who care about the same things you do and make something that tickles**

that interest, then you will be successful. It's literally impossible for you not to be successful if you dump enough money into finding enough people who have enough money to support your work.

Hopefully that gets you fired up. It always fires me up to know even with as much work as I've done, there is tons of opportunity out there to succeed if I just do the work.

Now, it's mainly a numbers game. The more people you talk to, the more people will hear and make a decision about your work. The more people who make a decision about your work, the more they will decide they like what they hear, and the more people who will decide to buy.

Our goal then becomes finding enough people who care about your work without going broke in the process, which means you need enough runway to succeed.

Runway basically means "money in the bank". If you have enough money in the bank, or can find ways to keep refilling your coffers, for long enough to find an audience that wants to buy your stuff, you will make money. Almost all businesses go bust because they run out of runway and crash spectacularly.

Even if the concept of a runway is an easy one to define, it's much harder to define what it means to you. Do you need to find 4 people to pay you $10,000 or 10,000 to give you $10? Do you have a 10% profit margin or a 90% one? How much overhead do you carry for hiring help? How much competition do you have for your work?

Books are hard because they are almost exclusively small margin, low cost, high competition products, and those are the hardest to sell. In general, you should endeavor to create a service-based business first, as you build up your product line and audience because it's exponentially easier to find 1 person to give you $2,000 than 2,000 people to give you $1.

It is almost impossible to get somebody to part with that first $1. Once they see the value in your work, getting them to go from $1 to $2,000 is much easier.

Regardless of your situation right now, success is still largely a numbers game. If you gather enough people, you will almost assuredly uncover at least 1 willing to buy from you. It might be 5, 50, 500, 5,000, or 50,000 people, but there is a ratio where your business will start to bring in money.

Profitably? Well, that's another thing.

Which is why we need to be strategic about where we share our stuff and show what we make, because both money and energy are finite resources that need to be replenished.

However, there are really two main issues you are facing right now if you're not having the success you want.

- **If nobody engages with you, it either means you haven't done a very good job finding people who care, or you aren't making them feel seen**. People engage with you when they feel seen. If your plight mirrors their plight or if you speak to their experience, then they will engage. Otherwise, they won't. It's not personal. We're all selfish creatures, including you and me. Even if you don't get traditional engagement, if they are reading your work then they are engaging through the work, which is the most important type of engagement for most writers.
- **If nobody buys from you, it means either you haven't made something enough people care about,**

you have gathered the wrong people, you haven't gathered enough of them, or you suck at explaining what you made. Every single one of these are fixable issues. You can start working through them one by one and shore up your business in the near future.

All of these problems suck, but even if you've spent years building an unresponsive audience, you literally have 99.9%+ of the world left to find a new one.

If you aren't where you want to be, you might need to:

- Find more people *(outbound marketing)*
- Make your publication better aligned with your perfect customer *(branding)*
- Make people understand the value of what you have *(sales)*
- Get people who love your work to buy again *(customer satisfaction)*
- Make things more aligned with your audience's needs *(R&D)*

If you get those things cranking, you'll at least be on the right track. I suggest trying to get your branding and marketing message right first before you start to find new people. The easiest and cheapest fix in your business is always going to be getting the branding right so it calls out to the right people.

There are only two things you have to be great at to have a successful business; the thing you do and marketing.

Nobody likes marketing, at least at the beginning. We all want to do nothing but write all day, but so do doctors and plumbers. No matter the business, everyone is mostly stuck doing the administrative tasks that allow them to practice their craft. Nobody wants to fill our quarterly profits or keep their books accurate, except maybe bookkeepers. You should expect to spend 80% of your time doing tasks you don't like, even if you have a business you love.

That's why we hire people, but at the beginning we're not making enough money to do so and break even, so we are usually stuck doing everything ourselves. However, if we can make marketing work, we can generate enough money to offload a lot of this stuff so we can focus more and more on the work we love.

GETTING YOUR MARKETING RIGHT SO MONEY FLOWS

There are four major marketing channels you can use to stabilize your revenue. You should work toward being excellent at a minimum of one if you want to build a successful business. It doesn't matter which one, but it is much better to be a master at one than pretty good at all four.

- **Owned Media Channels:** Owned media refers to the platforms and content that you have complete control over. These are the channels that you directly manage and where you can consistently communicate your message without relying on external parties. Owned media is essential for establishing your brand, building a loyal audience, and creating a hub where people can regularly engage with your work.
- **Paid Media Channels:** Paid media involves any form of advertising or promotional content that you pay for to reach a broader audience. This includes ads on social media, search engines, display ads, paid influencers, sponsored posts, and more. Paid media is an effective way to quickly increase visibility, drive traffic, and

boost engagement, especially when you're looking to reach specific demographics or expand beyond your existing audience.

- **Earned Media Channels:** Earned media refers to the exposure you gain through organic, unpaid methods—essentially, it's the recognition you "earn" rather than pay for. This includes any media coverage, word-of-mouth, social media mentions, shares, reviews, and any other form of promotion that comes from outside your direct control. It's often seen as one of the most credible forms of media because it's driven by others talking about your work rather than by your own marketing efforts.
- **Borrowed Media Channels:** Borrowed media, sometimes referred to as "shared media," involves leveraging someone else's platform to reach their audience. This type of media includes guest appearances, collaborations, or content that is published on platforms or channels not owned by you but where you have permission to share your message. The key here is that you're using someone else's established audience to amplify your voice, often through partnerships or mutual agreements.

Inside each channel there are dozens of strategies that might work for you. The Author Stack literally has dozens of articles on these strategies.

Personally, my business is built upon owned media, with a significant amount of borrowed media, a little earned media, and paid media sprinkled in to keep growth steady.

If somebody says "you gotta do this," no you don't. You can just do one of the other things listed above and still succeed. I know great businesses that do each of these well, while doing almost none of the other three, and still excel.

You can build a great business mastering any of these, and, if you are already great at one, consider partnering with somebody great at one of the other channels to grow faster and amplify your effort.

If you are going to hire, find somebody either better at you at the same channel (if you want to offload your own work) or a master at a different channel than you (if you want to scale faster).

HOW DOES ANY OF THIS MAKE MARKETING FEEL LESS GROSS?

This is the million-dollar question, right? We've now gone over 3,000 words on building an audience, but how does this make you feel any better about actually doing it?

Because you'll actually be talking to people who want to hear from you.

If you feel gross about marketing, it's probably because one day you flipped a switch and started selling to people in your audience, even if they never for one second knew you were a writer or chose to enter your audience in the first place.

If you start promoting on your personal Facebook page, then you've probably got people who became friends with you in high school. If you only started writing 10 years after graduation, then they never gave permission for you to market to them about your work. Neither did your cousin or your old co-worker.

That doesn't feel great.

When we grow our audience with intention, we are actively talking to people who chose to join our audience. They definitionally want to hear about what we do because they made the conscious choice to enter our audience in the first place.

Seth Godin calls this *permission marketing.* The more times somebody actively asserts they want to remain in your audience, the more congruent you should feel marketing to them.

This is why I believe in culling your email list at least once a year. If somebody isn't opening, they might no longer be interested in what you have to say. Before I delete them, though, I send them a series of emails to make sure they really don't want to be on my list anymore. Often, somebody really does want to be there and either they aren't registering or life happened and they got busy.

As long as somebody wants to be in my audience, I want them to be there, even if they aren't buying, or opening. Many people over the years have told me that they don't open my emails but they like that I show up in their inbox because it shows I still exist.

All of that is permission.

Another thing I offer in my newsletter is the chance to unsubscribe from any section without unsubscribing from anything else. So, if I'm doing a launch, people can opt-out of getting those emails. I also allow people to choose how often they want to hear from me. If they only want to hear from me weekly, monthly, or at launches, they can make that choice.

All of these permissions are set up so that I send emails to people who want to hear from me at the cadence they want to hear from me about what they want to hear from me. As long as people are properly informed, I can feel good about sending anything I want to them, within reason.

Making things is an act of service for an audience that wants or needs it. Even those supermarket ads that feel so gross to some people have lots of people waiting to gobble it up.

Once you align your work with people who want to hear it, then it's no longer marketing. It's service. When people are excited for your new things, it's no longer scammy to sell them because they already want them.

It's impossible to feel good selling something to a person who doesn't want it. Best case scenario, it feels like you're tricking them.

However, when you sell something to people who either already want it or don't know if they want it yet, then all those other problems fade away. No, you won't always hit a home run, and you will have stuff that flops, but it will always be in service to an audience, which makes you feel good about marketing.

Then, it's barely marketing at all.

THIS IS NOT ABOUT YOU

If you want to have success, then you have to become comfortable with one more thing. Success is all about what you can do for the person buying from you.

It. Has. Nothing. At. All. To. Do. With. You.

The better you are at making people **feel seen** and showing them the value they will find in your work, the more you will succeed. Even your personal memoir written in your own blood will only sell if you can get somebody to see themselves in those pages.

This might sound horrible, but it's actually quite liberating because none of this is about you at all. It's all about the reader. They are the protagonist of their own story, and sometimes they might use you as a conduit to explore and make sense of the world.

Even Stephen King can only rely on 1-2 million sales per book, and he's the most exposed author in the world. Yet, still less than .005% of the world's populace choose to buy his work.

You should not take it personally because it is not personal, even if what you have written is very personal. It is all about what the reader has going on and whether it hits for them. Very little of it has anything to do with you.

There are a finite number of functions that people will pay money for consistently:

1. **Curation of information/saving somebody time** - If you are curating good information and people can trust you, then people will pay for it. Similarly, if you make a better sponge, then you're saving time and people like that. They'll probably keep buying your stuff until something better comes along or you break that trust. Either that or they just don't have space for it anymore in their lives. Every act of curation is really about saving somebody time and energy.
2. **Making somebody money** - This is why finance blogs do so well, because you can tangibly bring this back to money. The same is true with couponing content. If you

can save somebody $20, people will probably give you a few bucks for it. It's easy math. I pay money to my financial advisor every quarter, but they make more than they cost so it's fine.

3. **Bringing something new/interesting/entertaining into somebody's life** - This is generally categorized as "helping people forget their lives and letting them dream about some other (better) existence." Lots and lots of fiction falls into this category, but so does much of this series.

Every successful product is designed toward one of these ends and will attract different types of readers. Some might overlap, but others will only want one experience.

The Author Stack articles are about bringing a new perspective into your life and making somebody feel seen runs under that function. Every successful writer is really an expert at making people feel seen at scale. Giving people the shared language to communicate with each other is a huge skill and very valuable, especially now with such a loneliness epidemic facing humanity right now.

If you are a good writer but your stuff doesn't resonate with people, it is probably because you need to double or triple down on making people feel seen by your work. It is what separates world class writers from very good ones.

The more you can fit into one (or more) of those buckets and build a world-class product that stands above the rest, or is remarkable as Tara McMullin says, the better chance you have of reducing your cost per acquisition and increasing your lifetime customer value, the two most important metrics in making this stuff work.

The final thing I will say about this, and something that I'm still learning, is that the biggest market, when people are most likely to spend money, is when they are in transition.

Whether that is having a baby, or changing jobs, or starting a business, retiring, going to college, raising children, starting a new hobby, or any number of other things, if you want to make this stuff stick quickly, find a transition and drill down deep into it. That's where you're going to find a deep vein of gold.

This is true in both fiction and non-fiction. If you want to make a career, focus your work on a specific group of people in a chaotic moment of transition.

I have stumbled on this by mistake multiple times in my life, but I was only given the context to understand it recently. If you're not having success, one of the first questions you should ask yourself is what transition you are servicing with your work.

HOW TO AVOID SMASHING INTO BRICK WALLS

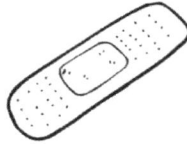

At the beginning of your writing journey, growth is easy and everything moves quickly. You're seeing progress, hitting milestones, and the road ahead seems wide open. Then, you smash into a brick wall, and it feels like nothing you do can break through it.

Maybe it takes a couple months or a couple years, but we all hit that same brick wall, and it's right about the time we start to question whether we're any good or should just give up.

The answer's a little more complicated than just yes or no, but the truth is that your early success lied to you. This stuff is haaaard.

Most of the people you flew past aren't really playing the same game. Some have one foot in, others gave up a long time ago, and a lot of accounts are just inactive.

So yeah, at first, you're making great strides, but you're mainly leaping over folks who aren't all that committed. Even though there's a ton of people flooding the market every day, it would be a mistake to assume most of them are trying.

This gives people a false sense of confidence and makes the crash even worse when they eventually reach resistance.

They don't hit resistance because their work is "bad", or they are awful. It's because the people making real money are actually trying. They've been doing it for longer than you, and they want to keep doing it.

Remember, Stephen King, Elizabeth Gilbert, and frigging Shakespeare are crammed up at the top of the publishing pantheon, and the fact that you're good enough to be mentioned in the same breath as them is incredible. Sure, you've maybe leapt past 85% of the people, but those people haven't really done much, and those that once did have all but given up.

Yes, you've probably leapt over some fancy names, but when was the last time they did anything? How often do people talk about them? How much space do they really consume in the conversation?

Probably not much, and it probably didn't take much effort to zoom past them. The people dominating the conversation right now are a different matter, though, and it takes more effort to join that conversation than ever before. Yes, Shakespeare is an old, dead playwright, but people still perform his plays and talk about his work regularly.

Do you have millions of people talking about your work every day? Probably not, which is why you hit the wall. It's not because you're doing something wrong. It's just part of the journey. The further you get, the more you'll realize that the people ahead of you are working just as hard, if not harder. They've been doing this for years, they're skilled, and they've figured out systems that work for them. You're not just coasting past people anymore; you're up against serious creators.

When you reach this stage, frustration can creep in as all your tricks and strategies stop working. The same tactics that worked before aren't as effective, and it might feel like your progress has stalled. But this isn't failure. It's a sign you're moving into the next level of your craft. The question is whether you push through or let the resistance get the best of you?

The creators who are doing well aren't just talented. They know what they're doing. They have a plan, they've built systems, and they've refined them over time. These people aren't winging it; they've figured out how to engage their audience, how to keep their content fresh, and how to keep improving. Breaking into this space isn't just about working harder. It's about working smarter.

You're going to need more than raw talent to stand out. You need a deep understanding of who your audience is, what your strengths are, and how you can consistently deliver value. This is where intentionality comes in—you can't just throw content out there and hope it sticks. You have to be deliberate, constantly learning, and evolving along the way.

Honestly, have you done any of this work or are you just winging it and assuming it's going to work?

Even if you're building systems and going about it strategically, you only get 1-2 shots a year to uplevel yourself. I spend almost my entire year finding ways to maneuver myself to take advantage of opportunity, and I still fail about half the time.

If you're hitting a wall and you're just smashing against it without any rhyme or reason, you almost certainly won't get past it.

That's bad news, but the worse news is that even once you do smash down that wall, there's going to be another one blocking you in new and horrible ways before long, and it will take a whole different set of skills to break down.

On top of that, the higher you go, the more effort each small step requires. Think of it like this: getting from the 1st percentile to the 10th? That's relatively easy.

But from the 10th to the 20th? You're going to need to work twice as hard.

By the time you're aiming for the 90th percentile, the effort required to make each small jump feels overwhelming. Basically, it's the same energy as moving from 1 to 89 combined, and every subsequent percentile gets progressively harder in the same way.

This is the point where a lot of people drop off because it's exhausting.

Those who stick with it don't just work harder; they work smarter. They start to refine their processes, focus on what truly matters, and cut out the fluff. It's all about putting your effort into the right places. No more busy work—just smart, calculated steps forward.

One of the biggest problems with publishing is that you can't just stop at the 80% percentile because most of the money, fame, and recognition goes to a tiny fraction of writers.

- **The top 5%?** They're the ones reaping the rewards.
- **Everyone else?** Well, they're fighting for whatever's left. It's the harsh reality of a power law market, where the best of the best get the most, and the rest are scrambling for visibility. Being "good" isn't enough. If

you want to succeed in publishing, you've got to be exceptional—and smart about how you position yourself.

Hitting a plateau can be a real emotional rollercoaster, but it's also a financial one. Your position in the industry directly relates to how much money you make, which intertwines your sense of self with your bank account.

When you've been riding high on progress and suddenly everything slows down, it's easy to start doubting yourself. You might feel frustrated, burned out, or even question whether you're cut out for this. It's normal to hit these moments, but what matters is how you respond. Do you let it derail you, or do you dig deeper and push through?

When you're feeling stuck, it's important to remember that plateaus are just part of the process. Everyone hits them. What separates those who succeed from those who don't is how they handle that resistance. Take it as a signal that you're growing, and you'll come out stronger on the other side.

To survive long-term, you need to be adaptable. The landscape is always shifting—whether it's audience tastes, new technologies, or changes in how content is consumed. The most successful creators aren't the ones who stick to a single formula forever—they're the ones who can pivot and evolve when needed. Flexibility isn't just a nice-to-have; it's essential. You have to be willing to try new things, learn from mistakes, and change direction if your current approach isn't working.

The good news? Being adaptable means you're always growing. Embracing change can open new doors and lead to opportunities you might not have expected. Staying curious and open-minded will help you stay ahead of the curve and keep your creative spark alive.

Writing is a journey filled with highs, lows, and plenty of in-betweens. Early success can feel exhilarating, but it's not the whole story. The real test comes when you hit resistance, when progress slows, and when the effort required starts to outweigh the results. The publishing world is ruthless, with only a small slice of creators truly breaking through. But the ones who make it? They've adapted, refined, and pushed through every challenge.

Keep refining your craft, stay flexible, and remember that success isn't just, or mostly, about talent. It's about persistence, learning, and never losing sight of why you started this journey in the first place.

Why does it feel so hard? That's easy. Because it's really hard.

You are basically trying to convince somebody who already has a list of things they love to not only consume your work, but enjoy it enough to add it to their TBR pile, read it, fall in love with it, obsess about it enough to buy it, and tell everyone they know how they should read it, too.

Yes, that's really hard, and it's way harder than flippantly saying "It only takes 1,000 true fans".

That's what we say when the unfathomable unknown of doing the thing seems impossible.

And guess what? It is frigging impossible. That is the little secret nobody tells you. *It feels impossible because it is impossible.*

All these strategies we teach are meant to tilt the universe in your favor a little bit and make the impossible a little bit more possible.

Make no mistake, though. Everyone who's done it has done the impossible, which is simply proof that it is possible…

…and therein lies the logical fallacy inside it all. It is possible to do the impossible only if you believe it is possible, but believing it is possible only becomes possible with strategy and time.

HOW AUTHORS CAN STAND OUT BY DEFYING LOGIC

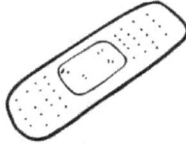

The publishing industry, like most sectors of our economy, operates on careful calculations of profit and loss. Publishers need to justify every investment, agents need to secure favorable deals, and authors are expected to treat their work as a product to be protected and monetized. Capitalism's core assumption is that rational actors will always maximize their financial returns. But what if breaking these rules could actually help authors succeed?

Consider how capitalism shapes the modern author's journey. Traditional wisdom says to guard your work carefully, publish only through established channels, and never give away what you could sell. This makes perfect sense within capitalism's framework, where every resource must be monetized for maximum profit.

Publishers, who operate under shareholder expectations and market pressures, literally cannot afford to be systematically generous. They must protect their assets, maintain their profit margins, and justify every decision in financial terms.

Knowing this, one way to fight the power imbalance inherent in the system is to make financial reckless choices that would destabilize bigger companies. Sometimes, making financially ruinous decisions is strategically advantageous.

For instance, recently I released a framework I've been working on for six months to the public in a 16,000-word article for free. That was probably 200+ hours' worth at least five figures or more. Surely, it would have been better to at least put it behind the paywall, right?

Or what about when Monica and I released over 50,000 words of our Author Ecosystems methodology for free? Companies charge thousands to access their proprietary framework, and we gave it away for free.

These are bad ideas, right? Except that while hundreds of people might have been exposed to our book if we started by charging for it, we've been able to access thousands of authors at all stages of their career.

The framework I developed is what I go through with clients at the beginning of our time together. So, if I want to find more clients, it helps to introduce them to the system I put out for free.

Even without those things being true, one marketing concept that has stuck with me over the years is that the person who can spend the most on marketing wins. By giving these away for free, it is investing in our relationship, and helping it reach as many people as possible.

By making these financial reckless decisions, we actually help create more value for something like a movement or a methodology, because those types of things are more valuable at scale, and benefit most from the network effect. Thus, making them easily accessible to the majority is a winning strategy.

The power of this approach scales directly with the perceived value of what you're giving away, though. The more powerful the transformation you offer, the more people value when you give it away.

When E.L. James first shared what would become Fifty Shades of Grey as free Twilight fan fiction on FanFiction.net, she was essentially giving away a complete novel for free. The story, originally titled Master of the Universe, grew to over a thousand pages and attracted millions of readers. This "financially reckless" decision to share such substantial work for free helped build a massive, dedicated following that eventually translated into unprecedented commercial success when the work was later adapted into an original novel, a movie series, and a brand worth millions.

Similarly, Andy Weir initially released The Martian chapter by chapter on his blog for free. When readers requested an easier-to-download version, he created a Kindle edition for the minimum price Amazon would allow. This apparent disregard for maximizing immediate profit helped build the groundswell of support that ultimately led to a traditional publishing deal and a Hollywood film adaptation. The more valuable the free content, the more remarkable the act of sharing it becomes.

Consider also the case of Hugh Howey, who gave away the first story in his Wool series for free and priced subsequent entries extremely low. This strategy seemed financially unsound at the time, but it created such strong word-of-mouth momentum that it eventually led to a print-only deal with Simon & Schuster while Howey retained his valuable digital rights.

The impact of generous sharing increases with the perceived value of what's being shared. When Margaret

Atwood shares detailed writing advice on platforms like Masterclass, she's giving away insights gained from decades of experience that could easily be packaged into expensive courses or consulting. When Amanda Palmer responds to fan questions on Tumblr with detailed advice, she's sharing expertise that many would pay significant amounts to access. These acts of generosity become more remarkable precisely because of the high perceived value of the knowledge being shared.

This approach works because it exploits a fundamental limitation of capitalist systems. As we talked about above, large publishers and established authors operate within strict financial constraints. They must show returns on investment, maintain certain profit margins, and justify their decisions to stakeholders. They cannot systematically undercharge or give away valuable content, even if doing so might build audience loyalty in the long term. Their fiduciary responsibilities and market pressures make this impossible.

The main exceptions to this rule are when they are releasing a new book in the same series or when a book is not popular enough to sell on its own. These two exceptions should clearly be in our toolbox, but that's just scratching the surface. People expect those kinds of deals and often wait for them. The more unexpected you can make your generosity, the more off-balance people will be when it comes, and the more remarkable you become.

The strategy becomes particularly powerful when authors share not just their work, but their process. Brandon Sanderson's extensive writing lectures from his BYU course, freely available on YouTube, represent hundreds of hours of valuable teaching that could have been monetized. This level of generosity with high-value content creates a strong connection with audiences precisely because it seems to defy market logic.

As a Tundra who thinks in launch cycles, I tend to think the best strategy is to give something big and flashy out a couple times a year for a very short time. Whether that is dropping the price of your publication or offering something packed with value, or putting together a bundle that expires after a week, these are the things I look for to draw attention to the event and allow it to disseminate naturally through the community as more and more people talk about it.

Whatever the strategy, the key is to give away things that are valuable enough so people question your judgment. When potential readers ask themselves, "Why would they give this away?" you've achieved something powerful. You've made them stop and think about your motivations, and in doing so, you've become memorable. Your apparent financial recklessness becomes part of your story.

This strategy builds trust through demonstrated sacrifice. When you give away valuable work for free, you're showing that you prioritize reader engagement over immediate profit. This signals authenticity in a landscape where most content is behind paywalls or tied to purchasing decisions. The trust and goodwill generated often lead to stronger long-term relationships with readers.

THE PSYCHOLOGY OF UNEXPECTED GENEROSITY

Our brains are wired to notice exceptions. When every author and publisher follows expected market behaviors - protecting their work, maximizing profits, carefully controlling access - the ones who break this pattern become instantly memorable. This isn't just about standing out; it taps into deep psychological principles of reciprocity and trust. When we receive unexpected generosity, we feel a natural urge to reciprocate and form a lasting connection with the giver.

Consider how E.L. James first shared what would become Fifty Shades of Grey as free Twilight fan fiction. The story grew to over a thousand pages, attracting millions of readers. This wasn't just sharing; it was sharing something of obvious value, something that represented thousands of hours of work. The sheer scale of the generosity made it remarkable. Similarly, when Andy Weir released The Martian chapter by chapter on his blog, he wasn't just giving away content - he was sharing a meticulously researched, carefully crafted novel that represented years of effort.

The impact of generous sharing increases exponentially with the perceived value of what's being shared. When Brandon Sanderson uploads hundreds of hours of detailed writing lectures for free, the gesture becomes remarkable precisely because everyone understands the high value of this knowledge. The more valuable something appears, the more attention-getting and loyalty-building its free release becomes.

This principle extends beyond just the monetary value. When Margaret Atwood shares intimate details about her writing process, she's giving away something arguably more valuable than a free book. The perceived value makes the generosity more remarkable, which in turn makes it more effective at building audience connection.

THE PLATFORM REALITY

Modern technology platforms both enable and constrain this strategy. Substack allows writers to mix free and paid content strategically. Amazon's Kindle Direct Publishing permits limited free promotions but requires specific approaches. Social media platforms enable direct sharing but often limit reach unless you pay for promotion. Understanding these platform dynamics is crucial for implementing a generosity strategy effectively.

Hugh Howey navigated these constraints masterfully with his Wool series, using Amazon's systems to price the first entry free while charging incrementally more for subsequent entries. This created a natural progression that readers understood and accepted, demonstrating how platform constraints can be turned into advantages.

When authors share valuable work freely, they often trigger a powerful community-building effect. Readers who receive unexpected value feel motivated to share their discovery with others. This word-of-mouth marketing carries special weight because it comes from genuine enthusiasm rather than promotional effort. The community that forms around this shared appreciation becomes a powerful force for building an author's platform.

But this raises an important challenge: how to maintain the value of your work while being generous with it. There's a real risk of becoming known as "the author who gives everything away," which can create expectations that make it difficult to monetize future work. The solution lies in strategic framing and clear communication about value.

HANDLING INDUSTRY PUSHBACK

This strategy comes with important challenges that need careful navigation. The most significant risk is becoming known primarily as "the author who gives everything away." This reputation can create expectations that make it difficult to monetize future work and can potentially devalue your creative output in readers' eyes. Some authors who started by giving away their work have found themselves trapped in a cycle where readers resist paying for subsequent books, expecting everything to be free.

The solution lies in being strategic about what you give away and how you frame it. Think of it like a premium restaurant offering an extraordinary happy hour. The generous happy hour prices draw people in precisely because they contrast with the regular menu prices. The restaurant isn't known as "the place with cheap food" but rather "the excellent restaurant that has an amazing happy hour deal." The high quality of the regular menu actually makes the happy hour more remarkable, while the happy hour makes the regular menu feel more accessible.

If you give away crap, then you'll be seen as shitty. The remarkability of the give is tied to the perceived value of it.

Any author can apply this same principle. Instead of giving everything away, create clear distinctions between your free offerings and your premium work. You might release a complete novel for free while making it clear this is a special launch strategy, not your standard practice. Or you might share extensive behind-the-scenes content and writing advice while maintaining normal pricing for your books. The key is to position your generosity as a special opportunity rather than a permanent business model.

Consider how Andy Weir navigated this transition with The Martian. While he initially shared the story for free, he later began charging a minimal amount on Amazon in response to reader requests. This created a natural progression that his audience understood and accepted. When the book was later traditionally published at full price, readers didn't balk because the earlier free version was clearly positioned as a special early-access opportunity, not a permanent pricing strategy.

The timing of generosity also matters. Early career generosity often builds goodwill that supports later monetization. Brandon Sanderson's free writing lectures helped build his reputation as an authority on crafting fantasy novels, which in turn supported his book sales rather than undermining them. The lectures were complementary content that enhanced the value of his books rather than replacing them.

This approach requires clear communication with your audience about the value of your work. When you do give something away, explain why it's valuable and why you're choosing to share it freely at this particular moment. This helps readers understand that you're not devaluing your work but rather making a conscious choice to share something valuable as part of a larger strategy.

Some authors successfully maintain this balance by creating different tiers of access. They might share drafts or works-in-progress freely while selling polished final versions or offer free serialized content while selling collected editions. This strategy allows them to maintain the benefits of generous sharing while establishing clear value for their paid work.

The goal is to make your generosity remarkable without making it expected.

Each act of generosity should feel special and intentional rather than routine. This way, you can maintain the attention-getting power of financially reckless generosity while building a sustainable creative career.

BUILDING THE STRUCTURE FOR YOUR NEXT LAUNCH

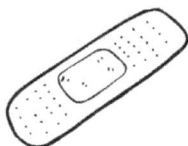

When people come to me after a poor launch, often even after gathering a big audience, I always ask this question:

How many people were around during your last launch?

If you've followed my work for any length of time, you have probably heard me talk about the power of the email list and building a fandom. Following that, you've probably gathered a lot of people from your last launch who have never seen you launch before to get excited about it.

And yet, when you hit that launch button…all you get is crickets. Then, you start feeling ways about things and me, specifically a combination of rage and shame that you can't figure this out.

Don't worry. You're not bad and you're not dumb. You just fell victim to one of the biggest misunderstandings in the game.

The people on your list between launches will see your current launch and usually get excited for your next launch.

You aren't building your audience to monetize them today. You're building them so you can monetize them 6-12 months from now. I know this is a gut punch, and there are certainly things you can do to move them along their customer journey, but the best thing you can do to convert your subscribers into sales is letting them get to know you, which just takes time.

Most of the new people you convert from this current launch have probably been with you for at least 2 launches.

I treat every launch (aside from a way to make money) as a chance to show people how much fun it would be to get behind the paywall so that next time they are ready for it.

The people who can launch effortlessly have spent years building and supporting their audience. If you're just starting your journey, you literally can't rely on that because you haven't built up that cache with the people on your list. They just don't know you enough to buy from you on autopilot yet.

I heard from Tyler James once that many people are on his list for 1-2 years before he can rely on them to buy consistently. Alex Hormozi said the same thing a few months later. Then, I looked back on my launches and as much as I hate it, YUUUP, most of my best customers have been on my list for 1-2 years before they start to buy frequently from me.

The word frequently is doing a lot of work there. What I mean is that, even though people often buy something from me during their second launch, that is just a tryout.

After they get their new book, they usually sit on it for months and use the third or fourth launch as an incentive to read the thing they bought from me and decide whether they are in for the long haul.

The buying cycle often looks like this once a subscriber joins my list.

- **Launch 1:** *Build excitement.* Somebody probably isn't going to join you the first time. They are just trying to get the vibes of your launch, whether you're cool, if they want to hang out with you, and if you've got something they want to read.
- **Launch 2:** *Try the goods.* By now they've known you 3-6 months and know your style. They've probably read some of your posts, maybe a sample of your books, and are ready to get excited for what you have to sell. If it's something they are into then it's a good bet they'll at least put it on their to-read list for later.
- **Launch 3:** *Reminder they need to read.* Once you deliver the book, it goes to the bottom of the pile, so the next launch is a great way to get your book bumped up higher in the queue. Honestly, every touch point is a little reminder. When I did shows full-time people would come up and apologize that they hadn't read my book yet...even a year after buying it. Getting people to read my work and form an opinion *after buying it* is easily the hardest part of the game for me.
- **Launch 4:** *Read the thing, finally.* By this point, you are probably near the top of their to-read pile, and the fact you are launching again will probably guilt them into reading the book. However, *it can take a whole year or more* for somebody to read one of my books after they get it. Once they do, they'll make an opinion to either become a big fan, follow a series, or put you on the scrap heap. However, I've known people for 5+ years who still haven't read a book they bought from me a dozen launches ago.

If you launch every three months, like I do, then the best case scenario is that a subscriber is literally one year from getting on your list to buying everything.

In my opinion, you should launch things more often so you can audition yourself to potential readers more often and win them quicker. You don't have to launch a book. You could launch your membership, or a set of pins, or a map, or a calendar. It just has to be something where people can get a sense of your vibes.

Even with that it could take a year or more, and that's somebody who's on the ball. It could take even longer, which is why you have to take a longitudinal view of your career.

This is also why you need a good content marketing strategy that warms people up for your launch, and why you need to be constantly building your fandom

You're always 1-2 years behind monetizing your audience.

If you want money now, you should have built the structures 1-2 years ago, but if you want to avoid that mistake in the future, you need to make audience-building a part of your practice all the time.

In my sales management days, we used to say that what you do today is predictive of your sales in six weeks, but you are really working on a much longer time horizon if you want to have any stability in your career. It wasn't until I was doing sales for over a year and had repeat buyers that I started to feel stable in my job.

The biggest habit I had to break in my salespeople was their constantly working on a boom/bust cycle.

Somebody on my team would have a bad month and have to scramble to close deals so they could hit their numbers. In doing so, they would scrape by that month, but they would have performed a ton of actions that paid off six weeks later.

All that effort while they were struggling brought them a windfall the next month, which would cause them to take their foot off the gas. Since they were still living off all the work they did, they would equate laziness with success and struggle with work. even though it's exactly the opposite. If they could just keep their foot on the gas all the time, they would be unstoppable, but it's a very hard habit to break.

Even the best salespeople dealt with this all the time. I'm not the best salesperson, but I can just show up longer than anyone else without taking my foot off the gas.

The single best predictor of success was whether a salesperson could break that cycle in and of themselves, and the same is true for creators.

If you use your launch wisely, you can use your current launch to build the structure you need to succeed better next time, whether that means hiring people, building our partnerships, creating new material, building your mailing list, or something else that will help the lift become easier each time.

I spent 5 years funneling all my money back into projects so that I could prove to people I was serious and wasn't going anywhere. These are the two biggest fears people have when they assess a creator, and there's very little you can do about that except let time happen and keep showing up.

If you're not using your current launch to build some buffer for your next launch, then it will be a lot harder to build once that launch is over and everything crashes to the ground.

LSS: The people you bring onto your list today probably won't pay off for 6 months and won't become consistent buyers for 1-2 years.

That's even true with Substack.

My last pay-what-you-can-afford pledge drive was 2.5x better than my last one, and wouldn't you know it, most of the people who bought got on my list around September last year.

Yes, some people became paid members before then, but not many. That said, it was still only a small fraction of my list who chose to buy, and I still have fewer than 2% of my list converting to paid membership, but it keeps growing over time. Two percent of 40,000 is a lot bigger than 10% of 4,000.

So, honest and true, do you have a strategy to get you 1-2 years down the road? Or are you just planning for people to buy quickly? Are you launching enough to audition for your readers? Do you have a 1 to 2-year launch strategy to pull people through your funnel?

YES, WRITING A GREAT BOOK PEOPLE READ IS MARKETING, TOO

Lots of people tell me they hate all marketing and "only want to write the next book" which is wild because, and I know this is gonna get your dander up if you're new to this, but writing the next book *is* marketing.

In fact, for over a decade writing the next book was basically the only strategy that "gurus" said was valuable. The idea was simple: the more books you have, the more opportunities there are for readers to discover your work. A larger backlist increases your visibility on digital platforms, making it more likely for readers to find your books through recommendations, algorithms, or simply browsing.

Then, you either put your books in KU (Amazon exclusive) and live on page reads or you put your first book in series free to give people a taste on all platforms (Amazon, Barnes & Noble, Kobo, Google Play, etc). Every time you launch, you slam through ads and/or book a bunch of book promo sites to get you in front of readers, rinse, and repeat.

That's literally the indie stack everyone ran for years and years and years. Writing a better book than the last time is still probably the best marketing (to a point).

The reason I say to a point is that if you only have a couple books, and not a body of work, you probably should work on writing the next book and getting your books hookier.

Once you have a body of work, though, Monica is absolutely right. The bottom line is that writing a book your readers love so much that they share it is a major function of marketing.

I can't imagine you being a writer if you didn't want to connect with more readers on a deeper level so they fall further in love with your work, and that is the core of marketing.

Everything else is just throwing gas on a fire, but if there is no fire, then you're just making a stinky pile of wood.

This first bit might have offended your delicate sensibilities because your writing is art and art is only great if it's completely devoid of marketing, but the truth is that every decision you make in a book either increases or decreases the audience for it, and every word you write gets readers to fall deeper in love with your work.

So, whether you call that marketing or not, you're certainly making decisions during your writing process that determine the marketability of your work.

WRITING VS. "WRITING AS MARKETING"

Let's say we all have the same "full-time" writing time and we split it down the middle, 20 writing hours and 20 marketing hours. I understand not many people have full-time hours to devote to their work, but if you have both writing and marketing time, then this might be a good frame for you.

Yes, those 20 writing hours are spent writing books, but what do we do with the marketing hours?

Most people default to one of the following as their main form of marketing:

- **Dissemination of information** - Another group spends those 20 hours blogging, tweaking SEO, getting on podcasts, guest blogging, and basically borrowing other people's audiences to expand their reach. They aren't writing more books in that time, but they are preparing a lot of other material to build interest in their work.
- **Building toward and executing a launch** - This group is doing a lot of audience building activities and then flushing them out with a launch. Yes, everyone launches, but these people put outmoded attention to a launch. For almost a decade I lived on a cycle of building an audience, monetizing them with a launch, letting my audience recover before the next launch.
- **Nurturing their community** - This group is deep in their community, doing live videos, picking people up, making people feel seen, and growing their community and making it stronger. This creates a group of devotees who talk about the community and bring in new people, hopefully growing it organically.
- **Securing partnerships** - This group is trying to expand their network through aligning themselves with other people to bring their work into other formats or create new experiences. Partnerships are about working together to bring something new into the world.
- **Write more books** - These people spend those additional 20 hours writing more and not doing much else. They fall back on the old "the best marketing is the next release," so they likely create 2x the output of any other author, but they aren't doing much more

marketing than just writing the book. That's where the extra 20 hours go.

We consider the first four things marketing for sure, but there is a large group of people who are basically exchanging marketing time for more writing time like I talk about in the last bullet point. Because it looks like writing time, it's easy to say, "I hate marketing", but, in reality, spending more time writing the next book is its own type of marketing.

Making a book so amazing people can't help but talk about it is part of a marketing strategy called "ambassador marketing" and revolves around the act of turning fans into evangelists of your work who go out and proselytize about it.

The #1 way to excel at ambassador marketing is to write the best books ever.

If you write a book your fans talk about, they will bring in new fans. If you write a book that fans can't stop talking about, they will naturally bring in new readers, creating a powerful, organic marketing engine for your work. To achieve this, focus on writing a story that deeply resonates with your ideal reader—something that speaks directly to their interests, emotions, and needs.

Craft compelling, relatable characters, and include memorable moments that evoke strong reactions, whether through laughter, tears, or surprise. When readers feel emotionally connected to your book, they're more likely to recommend it to others who share their tastes, spreading the word in a way that no amount of paid advertising can replicate.

Once you start seeing more humans organically coming into your ecosystem and reading your books with more fervor, it means you're writing the kind of books that are shared with people, and that those people are able to easily talk about your book.

Doing this intentionally is the crux of our Storyurge course, where you're baking these elements intentionally into your book. One of the best ways to bake this into your book is through creating a shared language that allows your fans to communicate together on a deep level without you needing to be in the mix at all.

Shared language is a set of phrases, terms, or ideas that become a common reference point for a community. In the context of books, shared language helps readers connect with your work on a deeper level and makes it easier for them to discuss it with others. This might include catchy phrases, memorable quotes, or unique terms specific to your book's world or themes. It also means dropping in easter eggs from pop culture that people can bond over.

Shared language creates a sense of belonging among readers and makes your book more memorable and easier to talk about, effectively turning your fans into ambassadors who naturally promote your work.

To create shared language, start by identifying the key themes, emotions, or concepts in your book that resonate most with your ideal reader. Develop distinctive phrases or terms around these elements that readers can latch onto. Examples of shared language in books include George Orwell's 1984 with terms like "Big Brother" and "Orwellian," J.R.R. Tolkien's The Lord of the Rings with "Hobbits" and "Middle-earth," and Stephenie Meyer's Twilight with phrases like "Team Edward" and "Team Jacob." These terms not only define the world of the books but also create a common vocabulary that fans use to connect and discuss the stories.

Incorporate these terms consistently throughout your writing and marketing. Encourage their use by including them in your book's blurb, on social media, and in any promotional materials. The goal is to make your language not just a part of the reading experience, but also part of the reader's everyday vocabulary when they talk about your book.

CONCEPTUALIZING WRITING AS MARKETING

So, if you "just want to write the next book," awesome. Here are some things to think about as you're designing your series to make it more marketable without you doing more marketing.

- **How are you helping your readers talk about your work?** To help your readers talk about your work, you need to give them the tools and language they need to easily describe your book to others. This can include a compelling tagline, a memorable quote, or a clear description of the themes or problems your book addresses. Create shareable content, like graphics or short excerpts, that readers can easily post on social media. Encourage your readers to share their thoughts through book clubs, social media challenges, or even through incentivized reviews. Remember, word of mouth is powerful, but it only works if readers have the right words.
- **How are you making your book packaging so killer that people have no choice but to one-click buy it?** Your book's packaging is the first impression it makes—it's your silent salesperson. Invest in a professional cover design that speaks directly to your

target audience and genre conventions. Your title and subtitle should be clear, compelling, and keyword-rich to catch the attention of both readers and algorithms. The blurb needs to be concise, intriguing, and promise a clear benefit or resolution that the reader craves. Incorporate testimonials or review snippets that create social proof. Your goal is to eliminate any hesitation in the buyer's mind and make the book look so good that it's an instant 'add to cart.'

- **How are you signaling to the right people to buy your book?** Signaling to the right audience is about aligning your book's presentation with their expectations. This starts with understanding your ideal reader: What do they value? What do they want? Use targeted language in your marketing materials, and make sure your cover design, blurb, and even your author bio speak directly to them. Use keywords in your book's metadata that your ideal readers are likely to search for. Run ads that are narrowly targeted to demographics that match your readers. Your goal is to speak so clearly to your intended audience that they recognize the book as something made for them.

- **How are you using your book to build your audience and your list?** Your book isn't just a product; it's a lead magnet for building a deeper connection with your audience. Include a call to action in your book to join your mailing list in exchange for something valuable, like a free bonus chapter, a workbook, or early access to new content. Use the end of your book to link to your social media or website, inviting readers to engage with you beyond the last page. The goal is to turn one-time readers into lifelong fans who eagerly anticipate your next release.

- **How are you taking advantage of trends so that your books have virality?** Staying current with trends can help your book tap into the broader cultural conversation. Monitor what's popular in your genre, on social media, and in the wider entertainment landscape. Leverage these trends by tying them into your marketing efforts, whether that's through timely social media posts, themed content releases, or even adjusting your advertising language. However, be genuine—only align with trends that naturally fit your book and brand. The goal is to make your book feel relevant and timely, increasing its chances of catching the wave of virality.

None of this is about "writing to market," either, at least not in the traditional way we tend to mean that phrase.

Yes, anything you write is written to *a* market, even if it's a market of one, but "writing to market" is the specific process of creating books that cater specifically to current market demands and reader preferences of the broad publishing landscape, despite how you might feel about them.

It doesn't mean researching popular genres, trends, and broad reader expectations to align a book's content, style, and themes with what is selling well.

It does mean writing a book with the intention to resonate deeply with people, and that there are enough people to share your work to build a fandom.

Then, it means packaging your book in a way that people who will resonate deeply will immediately know they are in the right place with your book, with a great, on-brand cover, blurb, and look inside for people to discover and fall in love with easily.

On top of that, it means designing your entire online experience (website, blog, social media, etc) so that those same people can understand what they are going to get in your work.

"Writing as marketing" means thinking about the "ambassador journey" and making it easy for people to talk about your work to people who would like it.

To make it easy for readers to talk about your work, provide them with the tools and language they need to share it effortlessly. A catchy tagline or hook that encapsulates your book's core appeal can also serve as a quick, memorable way for readers to pitch your book to others. Additionally, including discussion guides or book club questions at the end of your book can spark deeper conversations and make it easier for readers to articulate what they loved about your work.

Encourage readers to leave reviews and recommendations by offering simple calls-to-action in your book, emphasizing that even brief comments can have a big impact. By removing barriers and making it simple for readers to promote your book, you can turn their enthusiasm into effective word-of-mouth marketing, amplifying your reach through genuine, organic advocacy.

Additionally, if you do a good job with your shared language, then you empower your readers to talk with each other, and you don't have to do much aside from nudging them together. It also gives them a clear "entry point" for your writing that people can easily send others to where they can discover, understand, and engage with your book, even if they've never encountered your writing before.

This starts by crafting a compelling hook—a strong first chapter, an intriguing blurb, or a striking cover design— that immediately grabs attention and sets the tone for what's to come. Your entry point should clearly communicate the core appeal of your book, whether it's the unique storyline, relatable characters, or the emotional journey it promises. A well-crafted blurb that highlights the main conflict or question your book addresses can serve as an effective entry point, drawing readers in with a clear sense of what they'll gain from diving into your story.

Additionally, it's important to make your book easy to find and accessible across multiple platforms—whether it's available in print, ebook, or audiobook formats. Ensure your website or author platform clearly directs new visitors to a dedicated landing page that introduces your work and offers a free sample, like the first chapter or a short story, to entice them further. Consider creating a series starter or a prequel that serves as a low-risk entry point, offering potential readers a taste of your writing style and story world without the commitment of a full-length book. The key is to eliminate any confusion.

PRODUCT-LED GROWTH

I know you're ready to tune out hearing a business term like Product-led growth (PLG), but I swear it's relevant to you as an author, so stick with me for like five more paragraphs.

Product-led growth is a business strategy where the product itself drives customer acquisition, conversion, and retention. Instead of relying primarily on traditional sales and marketing tactics, companies using PLG focus on creating a product so compelling and easy to adopt that it attracts users organically. Examples include:

- **Slack**, which grew by offering a freemium model that lets teams start using its collaboration tools for free, making it easy to scale within organizations as its value becomes apparent.

- **Dropbox** also utilized a freemium approach, allowing users to store files for free with the option to upgrade for more space, driving growth through user referrals incentivized by additional free storage.
- **Zoom** is another prime example; it provided free access to its video conferencing service with limited features, which became a standard tool for remote work and virtual meetings due to its simplicity and user-friendly experience.
- **Canva** grew rapidly by offering a free, easy-to-use graphic design platform with powerful features that cater to non-designers, encouraging users to explore premium options as they become more invested in the product.

I know thinking about business terms can make writers zone out, but does any of that sound familiar to you? Freemium to hook people, focusing on the product to sell itself, organic growth through attracting new buyers and having them evangelize for the product?

Doesn't that kind of sound like books to you? It definitely does to me. Books can be seen as product-led growth in several ways:

- **The book itself as the product:** The core of PLG is letting the product demonstrate its value, and in the case of books, the content is the product. A well-written, engaging book that resonates with readers can naturally lead to word-of-mouth recommendations, reviews, and social media shares, driving organic growth without direct marketing.
- **Free samples and excerpts:** Similar to freemium models, offering free chapters, excerpts, or sample

audiobooks allows potential readers to engage with the content before purchasing. This strategy helps hook the reader by giving them a taste of the book's value, which can lead to increased sales and reader loyalty.

- **Reader experience and retention:** Books that provide a memorable and impactful experience encourage readers to return for more, follow the author, or explore other works by the same publisher. This is akin to the retention aspect of PLG, where the product keeps users engaged and drives repeat interactions.
- **Building a community of advocates:** Books can foster a community of dedicated fans who actively promote the content, akin to turning users into advocates in PLG. This happens through book clubs, fan pages, or even social media discussions, where readers share their enthusiasm and encourage others to read.
- **Low barrier to entry:** E-books, affordable pricing, and availability on platforms like Kindle Unlimited or other subscription services reduce the barrier to entry, making it easier for readers to discover and commit to new books, similar to how PLG reduces friction in the adoption process.

In essence, books embody product-led growth by leveraging the quality and appeal of the content to attract and retain readers, fostering organic growth through reader satisfaction and advocacy.

Books, publications, and anything where you are trying to get people to read your work as the main vehicle for growth is a PLG company. Free first in series, a trial membership, free book giveaways, etc, are all ways to hook people through a product. PLG companies are wildly successful, with some of the highest profit margins in all of tech.

Using a PLG strategy with books means taking the friction of sales away and making it easy to consume your work before they know they love it. Thus, either putting it into KU, where they can read for free, or offering at least one book free so that people can try it.

The biggest cause of friction is money, and removing it is the best way to convince people to give your book a go.

While it's not the *only* method to market your books, "writing the next book" is traditionally the one book marketing experts talk about the most. So, if all you want to do is write the book, how are you making that book shareable? How are you writing a beloved book that people can't help but tell others about?

Are you joining group promos, anthologies, and deeply discounting your books during sales events to find new people to read them? Do you have a Bookfunnel or Storyorigin account? If not, then why not?

It's so easy to book a promotion with Written Word Media and drop your pricing. It's so easy to join a Booksweeps or even just put your book free.

So many of my friends use that as their only strategy, and guess what? That's marketing, too. If you love writing great books that people love, then congratulations. You love marketing.

THE ONLY GOOD MARKETING IS THE MARKETING YOU DO

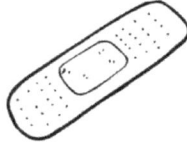

The best way to make money as an author is to not grin and bear something you don't like. It's to find something you already innately understand and obsess about learning how to use it more effectively.

If you get jazzed about virality, then you should spend all your time trying to figure out how to hit the algorithm right. If you don't obsess over that stuff, you should stop worrying about it now. If you love crowdfunding, then you should run a bunch of campaigns. If not, then there are better uses for your time. If you love community, then you should learn everything about having a successful one. If you don't love it enough to obsess about it, then you don't need to do it.

There are no magic bullets...or, more accurately, there are millions of magic bullets, but they are all piled in a heap in the middle of the floor with no rhyme or reason.

You have to find the strategies that work for you.

We live in a world run by obsessives. The most successful authors and entrepreneurs today aren't dabbling in a bit of everything—they are fully immersed in the strategies that they innately understand and are driven to master. They don't just participate; they dominate their chosen platforms by learning every angle, every trick, and every subtlety that others overlook.

- I spent a long time doing conferences because I innately understood how to sell in person. I got really good at it because I did over 200 shows in a short time. I made a full time living from shows for years.

- I love Kickstarter because I understand innately how to launch products to people and build a hype train. I've run dozens of campaigns in the publishing category because it worked. I've raised over $600k on my own projects.

- I love Substack because I understand how to build consistent value thanks to Monica. I love scrolling the platform and figuring out how to hack it for people. I built my publication up to 1000+ members and $30k in recurring revenue.

- Before I write a new series I obsess over reading everything in that genre, and I only really write in genres I already obsess over anyway. I've written 40+ novels that way and made over $1 million from my creative endeavors in the past decade.

You excel at things you obsess over. When you obsess over something, you naturally invest more time, energy, and attention into it than others who merely dabble. This deep, sustained engagement leads to a level of expertise and proficiency that sets you apart. It is how you win.

The great thing about this is that you already have things you obsess over! You don't even have to dig deep to find them. Are you on Instagram for hours on end? Do you make TikToks all day? Are you backing dozens of Kickstarter campaigns?

Using something significantly more than other people is a great start to an obsession. Spending 30 minutes daily can lead to initial proficiency within 2-4 months (about 30-60 hours), intermediate mastery in 1-2 years (around 200-300 hours), and advanced expertise after several years (1,000 hours or more). While advanced mastery takes time, you can become proficient in something with far less effort. Regular practice of 30 minutes a day, focused and deliberate, builds your skillset steadily and keeps you adaptable in evolving fields.

If you put in the effort, you'll be surprised how little it takes to become an expert in something. The key is consistency, as even small daily actions compound into substantial results, allowing you to progress towards expertise without overwhelming your daily routine.

Obsession creates an environment where learning and improvement are constant. It's not just about putting in the hours. It's about immersing yourself in the process, experimenting, failing, and iterating until you find what works. This relentless pursuit of mastery means that you not only learn the basics but also uncover the nuances and shortcuts that give you an edge. In a world where many are content to just get by, your obsession can be the differentiator that propels you to the top.

Stop forcing yourself to obsess over things you hate, kicking and screaming the whole way. It's not doing you any favors and could seriously be hampering your success.

Forcing yourself to obsess over things you dislike is a surefire path to burnout and frustration. It's not just about disinterest. It's about the immense mental and emotional energy required to stay engaged with something that doesn't resonate with you. This approach is unsustainable because it cuts against your innate natural tendencies, draining you rather than fueling you.

Instead, build on the strategies and platforms that already make sense to you. Look for platforms that already work in the way you need them to work.

Look for strategies you already gravitate toward without needing to be prodded. Do things you already do naturally. Ask yourself what aspects of marketing and sales you naturally enjoy or find easy to maintain. If you're a data-driven individual who thrives on analytics, you might find platforms that offer robust ad targeting or SEO optimization particularly rewarding. Alternatively, if you love storytelling and content creation, blogging or serialized fiction platforms could be where you truly shine.

We live in a world where you can make money on almost anything if you obsess about it enough. After finding that obsession, you will likely be able to manufacture asymmetric, exponential growth using it. Then, you can use that growth to build a stable, steady stream of income from it.

Once you have that one stream humming along, then use the excess revenue you made to hire other people to run those parts of your business you don't like or spend time learning another bit that fascinates you.

I'm not saying those things you hate doing aren't important, but you aren't going to do things you don't like, and the only good marketing is the marketing you do.

I'm gonna say that again.

The. Only. Good. Marketing. Is. The. Marketing. You. Do.

The only marketing that works is the marketing
you do. You only make money on things you do, and you
only do things that work. The emphasis should be
on doing—taking consistent, actionable steps that keep
your name and your work in front of readers.

Whether it's a weekly newsletter, regular social media
updates, or a new book launch, the key is to keep moving
forward. You learn what works by doing, and you refine
your approach through action, not theory.

The most successful authors aren't necessarily the ones
with the most polished strategies. They're the ones who are
out there, trying things, iterating, and consistently showing
up. You are wasting precious resources half-assing a dozen
things instead of full-assing one thing.

Guess what, though?

There are other people out there that love the things you
hate, and they are great at making money doing those
things. You can just hire those people with the money you
make doing the thing you love. We think that just because
we hate something it means everyone does, but that's just
not true. Similarly, there are things you do with ease that
other people can't stand (and you can charge people to do
them for you, if you want).

These people know the tricks you'll never know because
you hate doing it.

For instance, if you ask me about Kickstarter or Substack, I
will tell you so many things about them you never thought
to ask or wanted to know. All of these people know things
you'll never know because you haven't done it at a high

enough level and/or you don't care enough about the topic to obsess about it.

I have spent hundreds of hours on Substack in the past year, and even more hours on Kickstarter since back in the day to learn every trick that I could find about them. You probably aren't going to do Kickstarter as well as me unless you obsess about it and/or read our book/take our courses.

It's very unlikely.

So, stop doing things you hate. Stop doing things you don't understand. Stop doing things you fight tooth and nail to avoid.

If you aren't having success with a strategy, you probably aren't obsessive enough to develop an asymmetrical advantage using it.

If this sounds like you, then it's time to go find something you already love and somebody you resonate with who already does that thing better than you. Then, learn from them how to be better than almost anyone.

Experiment until it works for you.

After it clicks, double down on your success until you stop getting exponential growth from it. Every strategy loses effectiveness over time. Once you reach the limit of your success running one strategy, find the next thing you love and try again.

Keep exploring things you love until you can't grow anymore, then use your excess cash to find things you hate and hire people to do them. If a strategy doesn't make intuitive sense to you, then you will probably suck at it, abandon it, and waste your resources on it.

So, stop doing it.

Consider this permission to burn everything that doesn't work tonight.

The #1 thing I've learned from seven figure authors is that when they want to do something, they find somebody who already knows how to do it and pay them.

Do you know why they can do that? Because they made money doing things they liked that worked. Then, they reinvested it in doing things they like less to help stabilize their business.

It's probably a pretty good model for your career, too.

SOCIAL. MEDIA.

Peter Yang from Creator Economy has been living rent free in my head for years due to his writing this about the two different types of social media companies, and how we're thinking about them all wrong.

"Social media" actually refers to two very different types of apps:

- *Social: "I want to connect with others."*
- *Media: "I want to be entertained."*

An app that pursues both at once is destined to lose.

Social media has always been a catch-all term that implies every platform works the same way, and that's why we're all failing at it.

It turns out that some platforms exist to create and deepen relationships. These are social apps. Others are built to broadcast content to as many people as possible. These are media apps. The difference between the two is massive. Social apps thrive on conversation. Media apps thrive on content.

A *social app* is about two-way interaction. It's a space where direct connection is the priority. Growth comes not from reach, but from deepening relationships. Think about Discord or WhatsApp. Success there isn't measured by how many people see a post but by how often people engage in ongoing conversations. These platforms don't reward virality because that's not the goal. They're about sustained engagement, not passive consumption.

A *media app*, on the other hand, is about pushing content to an audience at scale. Platforms like TikTok, YouTube, and Instagram aren't designed for conversation. They're designed for discovery. The goal is to capture and hold attention through compelling content. The better your content performs, the more the algorithm distributes it, whether you have one follower or a million. This is where virality happens. Media apps don't care about your personal connections, they care about what keeps people watching.

This is why so many creators struggle. They're trying to play both games at once. They're chasing virality on platforms that don't support it or expecting deep engagement from audiences that are there just to consume content.

If you're on a social app, success comes from direct participation and relationship-building. If you're on a media app, success comes from creating content that gets seen by the most people possible.

And if you don't know which one you're using, you're probably wasting time.

What type of platform do you naturally gravitate toward?

Before you decide where to focus your efforts, you need to ask yourself a critical question: Do you naturally engage as a creator the same way you engage as a consumer?

Most people assume the answer is yes, but that's not necessarily the case. As a consumer, you might love scrolling through TikTok, consuming hours of short-form video, or passively watching YouTube. As a creator, you might thrive in a conversation-driven space, where you build relationships and get direct feedback from your audience.

Or it could be the opposite. You might love lurking in communities, but when it comes to your own work, you prefer broadcasting content rather than responding to every message.

- **Social-first creators** thrive on conversation and direct interaction. They like two-way engagement, discussions, and relationships.
    - **Best Platforms:** Discord, WhatsApp, Facebook Groups, Substack Chats
    - **Challenges:** Harder to scale; requires constant engagement
- **Media-first creators** thrive on one-to-many content distribution. They like creating polished content and seeing it reach large audiences.
    - **Best Platforms:** TikTok, YouTube, Instagram Reels
    - **Challenges:** Harder to build deep engagement; success depends on algorithm performance

This disconnect is important because it shapes your instincts. If a platform feels exhausting, it's often because it doesn't match how you naturally engage with the world. The best platform for you isn't just the one where your audience is. It's the one where you can show up consistently without burning out.

If you've ever wondered why a platform feels draining instead of exciting, this might be why. You're forcing yourself into a model that doesn't match how you naturally engage. Your business might need a different platform than the one you personally enjoy.

This is where many creators get stuck. They build a strategy around the kind of engagement they enjoy, rather than what actually serves their goals.

Maybe you're drawn to social-first platforms because you love community, but your business relies on reaching as many people as possible. You could spend all day having great conversations in a Facebook group or on Discord, but if your business model depends on growing an audience for a book, a course, or a product, you need new people constantly discovering your work. And social platforms aren't built for discovery.

On the other hand, maybe you thrive in the one-to-many world of media apps, crafting polished content that gets pushed out to thousands of people. But if your business model is based on long-term relationships, like coaching, memberships, or direct sales, you'll struggle if your audience is built entirely on viral reach. People might see your content, but they won't stick around.

This is why so many creators feel stuck. They assume they need to do everything, but that's a losing game. If you try to do both at the same time, you'll end up overextended, posting into the void, and wondering why nothing is working.

The solution isn't to force yourself into a model that drains you. It's to pick one platform that aligns with your natural strengths, then build a strategy that supports the areas you struggle with. If you're social-first, you can use media platforms as a traffic source, directing people to your community space. If you're "media first," you can create a lightweight way to engage deeper, like an email list or a paid membership.

But the key is knowing which one comes naturally to you first because the platform that matches your instincts will always be the one where you can build momentum without grinding yourself into the ground.

Personally, I'm great at media apps and generally suck at social apps. I'm a pretty good member of a community, but I stink at leading one. Monica and I struggled with it for years at Writer MBA, and I still marvel at people who can get deep engagement.

Meanwhile, we are both great at the media part of the social media equation and generally excel at platforms where that is the focus.

SOCIAL APPS: RELATIONSHIPS DRIVE SUCCESS

If media apps are built for broadcasting, social apps are built for connection. These are the platforms where success isn't measured by how many people see your content but by how deeply people engage with you. Growth on a social app isn't about going viral. It's about building a space where people actually want to come back day after day.

Think about the last time you joined a truly engaging online community. Maybe it was a Discord server where conversations kept flowing without feeling forced, or a WhatsApp group where people actually responded, instead of just dropping links and ghosting. These spaces thrive because the engagement is two-way. Unlike media apps, where the goal is to get your content in front of as many people as possible, social apps reward direct participation.

This is why these platforms are powerful for businesses that rely on trust. If you're a coach, a consultant, or running a membership community, social apps create the kind of high-touch engagement that makes people stick around.

Someone might stumble upon your work on a media platform, but they stay because of the relationships they build in a social space.

Many people go wrong because they treat a social app like a media platform. They post as if engagement should just happen, but that never works. Social platforms are built around conversation, not consumption. If you want engagement, you have to start engagement. You have to reply to comments, ask follow-up questions, and create a space where people feel like their participation actually matters.

Social apps take work. They demand consistent presence, not just content. If you're not the kind of person who enjoys regular interaction, maintaining a thriving social-first platform will feel exhausting. That's why many creators love the idea of a strong community but struggle to maintain one. A social app isn't about posting and walking away. It's about being there, and that kind of consistency isn't easy.

Still, if building deeper relationships is central to your business, social apps are the best way to create the kind of loyalty that media platforms can't replicate. The trick is knowing whether you have the bandwidth and desire to show up in the way these platforms require. Because if you're expecting to succeed on a social-first app without actually being social, you're better off somewhere else.

MEDIA APPS: THE ENGINE FOR VISIBILITY

If social apps are about engagement, media apps are about attention. These platforms aren't designed to deepen relationships. They're designed to get content in front of as many people as possible. The goal isn't conversation. It's consumption.

Think about TikTok. The entire platform is built around the For You page, not your follower list. The algorithm doesn't care about who you are or how long you've been on the platform. It cares whether your content stops the scroll. If it does, it will push that content to more people. If it doesn't, it will disappear into the void.

YouTube works the same way. While subscribers still matter, most people find new creators through algorithmic recommendations. A video doesn't usually succeed because of who posted it. It succeeds because it's what people want to watch.

Media-first platforms are built with the best discovery engines available. You don't need an existing audience to get traction. If you can create compelling, high-quality content, the algorithm will do the work of finding people who might be interested. That's the power of a media-first platform: you can reach thousands, or even millions, of people without any direct connection to them.

But that's also the problem.

While media apps are great for discovery, they're terrible for retention. Just because someone watched your TikTok or YouTube video doesn't mean they'll remember who you are, let alone follow you long-term. The average TikTok user watches hundreds of videos per day. Expecting them to develop a meaningful connection with you just because they saw one post is wishful thinking.

This is where so many creators get caught in the trap. They assume that visibility equals stability, that if they just keep posting, eventually the algorithm will reward them with a big enough audience to make their business work. But media-first platforms don't care about your business. They care about keeping people on the app.

That's why creators who rely only on media apps often struggle to convert their audience into actual customers. They're playing a game of constant production, always chasing the next viral hit because they know that yesterday's success doesn't guarantee anything tomorrow.

But that doesn't mean media apps aren't useful. If your business requires a steady stream of new people discovering your work, there's no better place to be. The trick is understanding their limitations and making sure you have a strategy for what happens after people find you. Because if you're only focused on going viral, you might get famous, but fame alone doesn't build a business.

TRYING TO DO BOTH IS A RECIPE FOR FAILURE

Every creator has, at some point, tried to "be everywhere." It feels like the smart thing to do. After all, why limit yourself to just one platform when you can reach people on multiple? The problem is that social apps and media apps require fundamentally different skill sets and time commitments. Trying to do both at the same time almost always leads to burnout, mediocre results, or both.

At first, it seems doable. You post on TikTok to reach new people, then invite them to join your Discord or Facebook group. Maybe you write long-form content on Substack while also trying to grow on Instagram. But then reality hits.

Social platforms demand presence. You need to interact, reply to comments, and keep conversations flowing.

Meanwhile, media platforms demand production. You need to keep making new content to stay relevant in the algorithm. If you're doing both, you're constantly shifting gears, trying to be engaging in one place while churning out content in another.

The worst part? The metrics don't sync. On media apps, success is measured by reach and views. On social apps, success is measured by depth and engagement. What works well on TikTok won't necessarily translate to a thriving community. What makes a Substack post go viral won't guarantee people will interact in your chat.

Then there's the issue of audience behavior. People who love consuming content on YouTube or TikTok don't always want to engage in a community space. And people who love deep conversations in a social app might not care about short-form content. Just because someone follows you on one platform doesn't mean they'll move with you to another.

This is where so many creators get stuck. They spend time building a presence in both places, but instead of getting the best of both worlds, they get the worst of both worlds. Their media content isn't optimized enough for virality, and their social presence isn't strong enough to build real relationships.

The answer isn't to try to master both at once. It's to pick one primary focus and structure your entire strategy around that. Then, once you have momentum, you can layer in the other in a way that actually makes sense.

If you spread yourself too thin, you'll always be busy, but you'll never be effective. The goal isn't to "be everywhere." It's to be strategic about where you spend your energy. And that starts with choosing which game you actually want to play.

THE TWO-STEP STRATEGY

If trying to do both at the same time is a guaranteed way to burn out, then what's the right approach? The answer isn't to ignore one side completely. It's to sequence your efforts in a way that aligns with your strengths and business needs. Instead of trying to master social and media apps simultaneously, start with one, build momentum, then layer in the other strategically.

Most creators and businesses fall into one of two categories: they either need visibility first, then engagement, or engagement first, then visibility. Your job is to figure out which path makes the most sense for you.

PATH 1: MEDIA FIRST, SOCIAL SECOND

If your business relies on audience size, like selling books, digital products, or advertising-driven content, then you need new people finding you constantly. That means starting with a media app like TikTok, YouTube, or Instagram Reels, where discovery is built in.

Your goal here isn't deep engagement. It's capturing attention and funneling people into a place where they can engage more deeply later. Once you've built an audience, then you can introduce a social platform like Discord,

WhatsApp, or a Substack chat to create a space where your most engaged followers can stick around.

Example:

- A nonfiction author starts by posting **short, engaging educational videos** on TikTok, building a following.
- Once they have an audience, they invite their biggest fans to join a **private newsletter or community**, where they can deepen relationships and convert attention into book sales.

The mistake most people make here is trying to force deep engagement too early. If no one knows who you are, starting with a Facebook Group or Discord server is a waste of time at the beginning

PATH 2: SOCIAL FIRST, MEDIA SECOND

If your business relies on trust and relationships, like coaching, memberships, or high-ticket offers, then you need depth first, then reach. Starting with a social app allows you to build strong connections and conversions early, even if your audience is small. Then, once you have an engaged community, you can introduce media content to bring in new people.

Example:

- A business coach starts by creating a **private WhatsApp or Discord community**, offering direct access and high-value discussions.
- Once they have a strong foundation, they expand into media apps, **posting clips from coaching calls or creating content that attracts new leads**.

The mistake in this model is relying on social platforms alone and expecting them to bring in new people. If you never introduce a media component, your growth will eventually stall,

Most creators instinctively gravitate toward one path or the other. They're either better at capturing attention (media-first) or better at deepening engagement (social-first). The trick isn't to force yourself into both at once but to sequence them in a way that feels natural and sustainable.

Start where you're strongest. Build momentum. Then, when the time is right, layer in the other piece in a way that supports your business without pulling you in two directions at once.

WHEN IS IT TIME TO ADD THE OTHER PATH?

No matter whether you start social-first or media-first, there will come a point when you hit a ceiling.

If you've gone "social first," you might notice that while you have an engaged community, growth has stalled. You've built strong relationships, but new people aren't finding you. Your revenue is stable, but it's capped because you aren't bringing in fresh leads.

If you've gone "media first," you might see your content continuing to reach thousands (or even millions), but engagement is shallow. People watch your videos, but they don't stick around. You have visibility, but conversions are low because there's no deeper connection.

These are the signs that it's time to integrate the other path—but the way you do it depends on where you're starting from.

IF YOU STARTED SOCIAL FIRST

Social-first creators reach a point where their community is thriving, but their audience isn't growing. They've built strong engagement, but they're relying on the same people over and over.

Here's how to know it's time to add a media strategy:

- You're **running out of new leads**, your growth has plateaued, and it's getting harder to attract fresh members to your community.
- Your revenue is **reliant on repeat customers**, but you're not seeing enough new buyers.
- You feel **stretched thin**, constantly engaging without bringing in passive audience growth.

The next step: Introduce scalable content.

Start creating evergreen media content that can work for you while you focus on engagement. Choose a platform that fits your strengths (e.g., if you're good on camera, try YouTube or Reels; if you prefer writing, try SEO-driven blogs or newsletters). Use your media content as a lead-generation tool, always pointing new viewers toward your social space.

Example: A business coach who built a thriving WhatsApp community realizes that growth has slowed. To attract new people, they start posting short-form educational content on Instagram and TikTok, using those platforms to drive people toward their private group.

IF YOU STARTED MEDIA FIRST

Media-first creators eventually face a different problem: people see their content, but they don't stay. They might have a large audience, but that audience isn't turning into long-term fans or buyers.

Here's how to know it's time to add a social strategy:

- Your content **keeps reaching people, but engagement is low**—you're getting views, but not enough meaningful interactions.
- Your audience feels **disconnected from you**—people recognize your name, but you don't have a core community of engaged followers.
- You're **struggling to convert followers into customers**—people consume your content but aren't taking the next step (buying, subscribing, joining your list).

The next step: Introduce a deeper engagement channel. Create a dedicated space for your biggest fans, like a private chat, membership group, or subscriber-only discussion. Start engaging in the comments and DMs. Instead of just posting content, actively build relationships. Shift some of your content toward direct audience interaction, like Q&As, live sessions, community features.

Example: A YouTuber with 100K subscribers realizes that while their videos get views, they don't have a strong connection with their audience. They start a private Substack chat for their most engaged followers where they can interact more deeply and offer exclusive insights.

The mistake most creators make is waiting too long to add the other path. They either burn out trying to maintain engagement without growth, or they keep chasing reach without ever turning that reach into something sustainable.

The best way to avoid this? Keep an eye on your numbers and your energy.

- If your audience is **growing but not converting**, it's time to add a social element.
- If your engagement is **deep but stagnant**, it's time to add media for reach.
- If you feel like you're **spinning your wheels, always "on" but not moving forward**, it's time to adjust.

When you add the other path at the right time, you don't just grow your audience. You build a system that works together, where visibility feeds engagement, and engagement fuels long-term success.

If you've ever felt like social media isn't working for you, the problem probably isn't your content. It's that you're applying the wrong strategy to the wrong platform. Social and media apps are two completely different ecosystems with different rules, different success metrics, and different expectations.

Trying to master both at once is exhausting. But picking the right one for your strengths and your business model? That's the key to making social media work for you instead of against you.

So ask yourself:

- Are you better at starting conversations or creating content?
- Does your business need deep engagement or broad reach first?

- Where do you naturally show up consistently without feeling drained?

Once you know the answers, you can stop wasting time on the wrong platforms and start building a strategy that actually fits, because success on social media doesn't come from being everywhere. It comes from being in the right place, with the right focus, at the right time.

MASTERING THE ART OF ATTENTION AS A WRITER

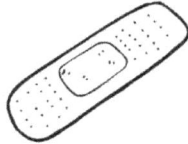

Whether you're a novelist, blogger, poet, or nonfiction writer, the ability to capture and hold an audience's attention can make or break your career. Attention not only brings visibility to your work but also opens doors to new opportunities, collaborations, and financial support. Therefore, understanding how to effectively attract and maintain attention is crucial for any writer looking to thrive in the literary industry.

Attention is about being noticed and remembered.

In a market flooded with books, articles, and stories, standing out requires more than just skill with words; it requires a strategic approach. Capturing attention means getting readers to notice, engage with, and remember your writing. This visibility can lead to increased book sales, higher engagement on social media, or invitations to speak at events. Without attention, even the most beautifully crafted stories can go unread.

The importance of attention cannot be overstated. It is the currency of the modern literary economy, determining who gets read and who remains in obscurity. Successful authors understand that attention is not just a byproduct of good writing but a crucial element that needs to be actively pursued and managed. By effectively capturing attention, you can build a loyal readership, create a lasting impact, and ensure that your writing efforts translate into tangible success.

At its core, gaining attention involves strategic thinking and a deep understanding of your audience and the platforms they use. It's about knowing where people are already focused and finding ways to become part of that conversation. It's also about creating work that is so compelling it naturally draws people in. Both approaches require different skills and strategies but mastering either one can set you on the path to success.

There are two primary ways to achieve this attention, and you must excel in at least one of these methods to thrive. While mastering both can provide a significant advantage, being adept at one can already set you on the path to success.

FINDING WHERE THE ATTENTION IS

This method involves identifying the platforms, trends, and moments where people are already focused and then inserting yourself into that spotlight. If you're adept at social media platforms like Bluesky or Instagram, you excel at this. You understand what's trending and how to weave your writing into those narratives to capture some of that existing attention.

EXAMPLES:

If you're good at social media, you know how to join trending conversations and create tweets that resonate with current events or popular topics. Take the

#WritingCommunity hashtag, for example. By participating in these discussions, you ensure your content is seen by a large audience interested in writing and literature.

On Instagram, you might leverage popular hashtags or participate in bookstagram challenges to insert yourself into ongoing conversations. For instance, when a book-related challenge is trending, and you use the relevant hashtag, your posts gain visibility among those following the event. This ability to adapt and integrate into what's already popular is key to finding where the attention is.

TURNING THE ATTENTION TO SHINE ON YOU

Conversely, this method focuses on creating something so compelling that it attracts attention to you. Platforms like Substack or Patreon are perfect for those who excel at this. It's about building a community or project that draws the spotlight toward you, even if it's not the main focus of the broader public at the moment.

EXAMPLES:

If you're successful on Kickstarter, you're skilled at crafting compelling narratives and presenting unique ideas that draw people in.

Consider a unique book project that offers exclusive content or experiences. Even if such projects aren't trending globally, your initiative can capture significant attention due to its innovative nature.

On Patreon, those who build a dedicated following are adept at creating content that continuously attracts attention. An author offering exclusive chapters, writing tips, or personalized feedback can draw a loyal audience willing to support their work financially. This ability to turn the spotlight towards your creations is crucial for sustained success.

CELEBRITY EXAMPLES

Some people are exceptional at both methods. Beyoncé, for example, is a master at turning the spotlight on herself. Regardless of current trends, when she releases new music or announces a project, the world's attention shifts to her. Her ability to command attention on her terms demonstrates mastery in creating and drawing the spotlight.

On the other hand, Kim Kardashian excels at finding where the attention is and inserting herself into it. Whether it's a social media trend, a viral topic, or a popular event, Kim consistently positions herself within these narratives, ensuring she remains a constant topic of conversation.

PRACTICAL IMPLICATIONS

If you find yourself struggling to gain traction, you might be using the wrong platform or not effectively leveraging these methods.

If you're successful on Amazon but struggling on Kickstarter, it might be because Kickstarter requires you to draw attention to your project, whereas Amazon benefits from existing traffic searching for books. The chaotic nature of Kickstarter means you must excel at drawing that spotlight.

Similarly, if you're doing well on Substack but not on Threads, it's likely because Threads requires you to insert yourself into ongoing conversations, which might not naturally align with your content. Substack, on the other hand, allows you to build a dedicated readership that seeks out your work.

IMPLEMENTATION

To improve your ability to find where the attention is, start by:

1. **Monitoring Trends:** Use tools like Google Trends and Instagram's Explore page to stay updated on what's popular. These platforms provide real-time insights into what people are talking about, allowing you to tailor your content accordingly. Regularly checking these tools helps you stay ahead of the curve and capitalize on emerging trends before they peak.
2. **Joining and Researching Communities:** Join relevant online communities, forums, and groups where trending topics are discussed. By actively participating in these spaces, you can gain a deeper understanding of what interests your target audience. Engaging with these communities also helps you build relationships and establish yourself as a credible voice within those circles.
3. **Creating Timely Content:** Produce content that aligns with current trends and topics. The quicker you can jump on a trend, the more likely you are to capture attention. This might mean adapting your content strategy to be more flexible and responsive to what's happening in real-time, ensuring your work remains relevant and engaging.

To enhance your ability to turn the spotlight on yourself, focus on:

1. **Building a Strong Brand:** Develop a unique voice and style that sets you apart. Consistency in your branding helps in creating a recognizable presence. This includes everything from your visual identity to the tone of your messaging, ensuring that your audience can easily identify your work amidst the noise.
2. **Engaging Your Audience:** Interact with your audience through comments, messages, and exclusive content. Building a loyal community can help draw attention to your work. Personalized interactions make your audience feel valued and connected to you, increasing their likelihood of sharing your content and advocating for you.
3. **Creating Resonant Content:** Invest time and effort into producing content that deeply resonates with your audience. Understand their needs, preferences, and pain points, and tailor your content to address these. When your audience feels understood and connected to your content, they are more likely to engage with and share it, naturally drawing more attention to you.

To thrive in the literary world, you need to be great at either finding where the attention is or turning the attention towards you. Mastering these skills can mean the difference between staying obscure and gaining widespread recognition.

If you find success in one method but feel capped, consider developing your skills in the other to amplify your success and reach.

Implementing these strategies can help you master both aspects, ensuring you stay relevant and continue to grow your creative endeavors.

Developing your ability to find where the attention is means staying agile and constantly scanning the landscape for new trends and opportunities. This proactive approach allows you to stay ahead of the curve and insert yourself into conversations that matter. By doing so, you can capture the attention of a broader audience and ride the wave of existing interest to amplify your reach.

On the other hand, turning the spotlight on yourself requires a deep understanding of your unique value proposition and how to communicate it effectively. It involves crafting narratives and creating content that speaks directly to your audience's interests and needs. By building a strong brand and consistently engaging with your community, you can create a loyal following that actively seeks out your work and spreads the word on your behalf.

Balancing both methods can lead to a more sustainable and impactful presence in the literary world. While finding where the attention is can provide quick wins and boost your visibility, turning the spotlight on yourself helps in building a long-term, dedicated audience. By integrating these approaches, you can create a dynamic and resilient strategy that ensures continuous growth and recognition.

7 UNCONVENTIONAL WAYS TO SUCCEED AS A WRITER

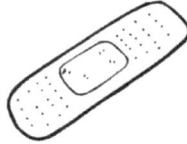

We've all come across classic writing advice like be consistent, engage your audience, find your authentic voice, and so on. It's solid guidance, but it's also what literally every other writer on the planet is doing. If you wanna break through, you often have to break the mold.

There's an old saying in Hollywood. There might be a million ways to break in, but nobody breaks in the same way twice. Once somebody uses a strategy, the powers that be pave over it so nobody can do it again.

As cool as it might be to send a shoebox to an agent with a note that says, "Trying to get my foot in the door," that's already been done and probably definitely won't work again.

Love where your head is at, though. Let's see if we can fill it with more thinking like that. The approaches below might feel a little risky or weird at first, but they can also help get you noticed for all the right reasons.

1. **Be comfortable being unliked.** If you want some people to have strong positive feelings about you, then you have to get comfortable with the idea that other people will have strong negative feelings about you. A

magnet's polarity works both ways. If nobody is ruffled, you might be playing it too safe. It's not about being a troll or intentionally offensive, but if you have a bold opinion, don't water it down just to keep everyone happy. Writers with a strong point of view attract an audience that genuinely cares, rather than one that vaguely hovers.

2. **Ignore "finding your voice" and try borrowing voices to discover your own.** Maybe for a week, try composing short stories inspired by Ernest Hemingway's sparse prose. The following week, mimic a breezy style akin to Nora Ephron. You might even merge journalistic objectivity with comedic ranting just to see what happens. Through these experiments, you'll start picking up bits and pieces that resonate with your natural inclinations. Over time, the mishmash of influences will crystallize into something original. Your voice, built through playful borrowing.

3. **Weaponize your worst moments**. On social media, it's tempting to present only the highlight reel like bestseller lists, glowing reviews, or that time you got 1,000 claps on Medium. But let's be honest. Everyone has meltdown moments, like the day you got a harsh rejection letter or the time you froze during a live reading in front of 50 people. When you open up about these moments, your readers see someone relatable, not an untouchable success story. Share the lessons you learned, the secondhand embarrassment, and the messy process of getting back on your feet. The honesty makes your triumphs feel more earned. Plus, there's an odd power in showing you're not afraid to talk about mistakes. It's a signal you care more about authenticity than polishing a perfect image.

4. **Steal like a data analyst**. Let the numbers reveal your hidden strengths. If you have a newsletter, look at open rates for various subject lines. If you post on Substack,

pay attention to which pieces receive the most highlights or reader comments. On social media, see which posts spark meaningful conversations rather than just likes. Use that data as a flashlight. Maybe you notice that whenever you talk about personal finance, people perk up and share your posts. Perhaps your comedic rants always get more engagement than your straight-laced essays. Incorporate more of those elements. This isn't about chasing trends. It's about noticing genuine reader interest so you can lean into your natural strengths.

5. **Publish in imperfect formats**. Half-formed and quick doodles can spark more inspiration than polished prose. You might publish a weekly "scribble section" or photographs of notepad pages alongside bullet points about what you're learning. They're not polished, but they attract curious readers who want to see behind the scenes. Share rough drafts, half-outlined thoughts, or even audio recordings of your brainstorming sessions. It's a refreshing contrast to a platform full of neatly packaged articles, and it fosters a sense of co-creation with your audience.

6. **Curate more than you create**. Some of the most influential people in any field got there by being excellent curators. If there's a subject you're passionate about, start curating the best work you can find. Share quotes, snippets, and links with your own unique commentary. Over time, you become a trusted source for filtering through the noise. It's as valid as creating new content and often more valuable.

7. **Don't just write, create cultural moments.** Writing can be a solitary act, but it doesn't have to stay that way. Think about hosting a virtual event or a writing challenge that sparks collective energy. For instance, you might invite readers to write a single paragraph based on a prompt you provide, then share their results

in the comments section of your blog. Or organize a short daily livestream where you spend ten minutes freewriting and encourage viewers to do the same. Moments like these turn your platform into more than just a source of reading material. They become community touchstones, shared experiences that people look forward to. When everyone can participate rather than passively read, you create real bonds.

By mixing risk-taking (like encouraging controversy or sharing failures) with deliberate experimentation (like imitating styles or analyzing data), you sidestep the trap of generic content creation. Going off the beaten path can be daunting, but it's also what helps you break away from the sea of identical advice.

There's no single secret formula for writerly success, and that's what makes the journey both maddening and magical. When you give yourself permission to step outside tidy guidelines, you allow yourself to uncover surprising strengths.

Don't be afraid to polarize, to play with different voices, or to showcase your failures. Post something that isn't polished or spend a week shining a spotlight on others' brilliant work. If you're willing to do things a little differently, you just might find an audience that respects your courage and rallies behind you all the more.

In a world filled with repetitive advice, these approaches stand out because they embrace experimentation and honesty. Try one or two ideas and see what happens. You might alienate a few readers along the way, but the ones who remain will feel more connected than ever, like they're part of a creative revolution. And for a writer, that bond is worth more than any safe, one-size-fits-all strategy.

TAKING A KNOCKOUT PUNCH WITHOUT GETTING KNOCKED DOWN

Sometimes it doesn't work. You make assumptions and it turns out you weren't just wrong, you were laughably, calamitously, epically, ruinously wrong; the kind of wrong that could actually bankrupt you or cause serious harm to yourself and/or those you love.

And right there, in that moment when you're living it, you have a choice about how to react. You can curl up in a ball and let it happen to you, learn how to make it just a little bit worse every day so maybe it doesn't hurt so many people, or pivot in a way that turns your failure around and redirects it somewhere that doesn't hurt anyone.

The longer I do this work, the more I think that these moments, and how you choose to react in them, make or break somebody's spirit.

Luckily, this isn't magic. It's strategy.

People talk a lot about getting up from the mattress once you've been knocked down, but truly, the secret is how you take the force of a blow that was supposed to knock you down and redirect it so that you keep standing, even if you're staggering, and can maybe even redirect that energy into a knockout blow of your very own.

No, it's not about getting up after you're knocked down. It's about how you can absorb all that pain, redirect it in a positive direction, and never hit the floor in the first place.

But how do we do this? Not surprisingly, I have a system for that, like everything else.

Before I get into it, I want to point out that this kind of thing is way easier when you are not in crisis. I was in crisis for about 25 years, in a constant state of suicidal ideation, panic attacks, and doom spiraling. I thought this was normal, and how everyone dealt with the world until I got on meds.

Even when I got out of it and started thriving, I assumed that what I went through was normal. I did not understand that most people are in crisis for weeks or months, or maybe a year, not since they were 15 until they were 40.

To succeed, I built structures that allowed me to create as a compulsive way to expel my overwhelming anxiety and created pathways to become successful even though I was in crisis. My structures did not make sense to any other human but me, but it was the only way I could make it happen.

How could I be in crisis if I was successful? Because I found ways to succeed despite my mental health crisis. I was constantly exhausted, panicked, and frightened, but I did it anyway. This is not normal.

You might think that you can't be in crisis if you are doing well, to which I say that you might be succeeding, but you are not thriving. Being in crisis does not always mean being unable to perform. Sometimes it means performing despite massive headwinds.

Doom spiraling is not normal. Suicidal ideation is not normal. Panic attacks are not normal. You do not have to feel like this all the time.

That doesn't mean you can't make these strategies work if you're in crisis. After all, I built my whole business while in crisis. I spent decades in crisis, and somehow made it work, but these things are way easier to handle if you aren't in crisis. I remember I felt like a superhero the first time the fog cleared because I'd been living with this huge weight my whole career.

Maybe you are not in crisis, but if you're wondering how people can do this when it's so hard, a big part of it might be that they are not in crisis.

Okay, let's get to it. How do we avoid getting knocked out by a knockout punch?

STEP 1: ANTICIPATE AND RESEARCH

- **Prepare before the setback:** Before diving into any venture, take the time to research potential challenges and their outcomes. Understand the risks involved and familiarize yourself with scenarios where similar setbacks have occurred to others in your field. Most people research the "good outcomes" but make sure you're looking at the "bad outcomes," too. What is the worst outcome?
- **Gather insights:** Investigate strategies others used to handle or avoid these setbacks, noting what worked and what didn't. This foresight will give you a mental map of possible situations, so if a setback does happen, you already know your options. How have people recovered from the worst outcomes and what has happened in

your life that you can use as a guide to do something similar?

- **Plan preemptive measures:** With knowledge of potential outcomes, consider implementing early safeguards. This might include contingency planning, creating a support network, or building specific skills that will help you pivot more effectively if needed. Most people don't want to look at the bad, but good risk assessment involves being prepared in any eventuality, even the worst ones. Just because you know the bad outcomes doesn't mean they will happen. It just means you will be ***prepared if*** it happens.

STEP 2: RECOGNIZE THE SETBACK EARLY

- **Identify warning signs promptly:** In the face of a challenge, pause and analyze the situation objectively. Recognize the signs that indicate a setback is unfolding, whether they're financial losses, a stalled project, or strained relationships. Early recognition is key to preventing the problem from escalating. This is usually only possible if you've done the research beforehand, and you are brave enough to look at the data objectively, even if you don't like it.
- **Assess the root cause:** Use the knowledge from your initial research to evaluate why the setback occurred. Is it due to an overlooked detail, an external factor, or an unexpected outcome? Pinpointing the cause helps ensure your response targets the real issue rather than just the symptoms. The quicker you can look at the data the better you will be at assessing the root cause of the problem, even if that root cause has many potential solutions.
- **Stay calm and grounded:** Resist the urge to react emotionally. A clear mind allows you to make better

decisions. Take a moment to reflect on the setback as part of the process, grounding yourself before you move to address it. You'll almost always have to sit with the data for a moment in order to react calmly and rationally. This is why developing a general plan before you even get started is so important. It prevents you from acting emotionally.

Notice that the first two steps, arguably the most important steps, are all about preparation, not action. If you aren't preparing for disaster, you are welcoming it to knock you down.

STEP 3: MAKE AN INFORMED CHOICE

- **Review your options with context:** Now that you understand the setback's root cause, review your possible responses. Your earlier research will guide you in selecting actions aligned with your goals and values. Consider options like pausing for further reflection, seeking advice, or implementing a pivot strategy.
- **Evaluate short-term and long-term impacts:** Consider the potential consequences of each option. Ask yourself questions like, "Will this choice support my goals, or is it a short-term fix that could cause more problems later?" Look for paths that balance immediate relief with long-term success.
- **Commit to a direction:** Once you've weighed the options, choose the approach that best serves your overall vision and commit fully. Acting decisively is essential—doubt and hesitation can magnify the setback rather than resolve it.

STEP 4: REFRAME FAILURE AS ENERGY

- **Embrace the Setback as Fuel for Growth:** Rather than viewing the setback as a defeat, treat it as an opportunity to generate momentum. Remind yourself that every obstacle has the potential to be redirected toward growth, creativity, or resilience.
- **Shift your perspective:** Focus on what you're learning rather than what you've lost. By embracing a mindset that sees adversity as part of progress, you transform a negative experience into a positive one, harnessing it as a catalyst for growth.
- **Apply insights actively:** Use the lessons from the setback to guide your next steps. If the experience revealed a skill gap, take time to develop it. If it highlighted a misalignment in your approach, adjust accordingly. These steps ensure that your setbacks lead to meaningful improvement.

STEP 5: TAKE SMALL, CONSISTENT ACTIONS

- **Avoid the pressure for instant fixes:** Rather than aiming to fix everything at once, commit to small, manageable steps that move you forward consistently. Each small action builds momentum and provides a sense of progress, even if the path feels slow.
- **Focus on building resilience, not just results:** Measure your progress by your ability to adapt and stay on course, not by the immediate outcome. This approach allows you to fortify your foundation, making it more resilient to future setbacks.
- **Keep a record of progress:** Document each small step and the insights you gain along the way. Over time, this record will serve as a testament to your resilience and provide encouragement during challenging moments.

STEP 6: CHANNEL ENERGY INTO A COMEBACK

- **Redirect the setback's momentum into new initiatives:** Once you've stabilized, consider how the setback can fuel a fresh start or an improved version of your original plan. Whether it's a new project, refining existing work, or launching an entirely different venture, use the energy you've built through resilience.
- **Share what you've learned with others:** The comeback phase can be empowering for others as well. Share your experience openly, using it to inspire those around you or to strengthen relationships with others in your field. People love an underdog and will often rally to your cause. Be forewarned, though, that people hate a hot mess, so this strategy can backfire if you don't have a plan to fix it.
- **Reinforce your self-belief:** Celebrate the steps you've taken to overcome the setback. Acknowledge that the resilience you've cultivated through this process is a permanent asset, ready to support you in future challenges.

STEP 7: REFLECT AND ADJUST

- **Conduct a post-setback review:** Once you've fully overcome the setback, take time to reflect on the entire experience. What prepared you well, and where were there gaps? This review turns the setback into a resource for your personal and professional development.
- **Document key takeaways:** Write down what worked, what didn't, and any insights gained. These notes will serve as a personal playbook, making you more prepared for similar challenges in the future.

- **Integrate adjustments into your plan:** Use this experience to refine your strategies and approaches. Each setback you've successfully navigated becomes part of your growth story, reinforcing your ability to face future obstacles with strength and foresight.

By following these steps, setbacks become less about loss and more about transformation, building resilience and strength with each experience. The goal is not just to survive the hits but to emerge stronger, armed with the energy they brought, ready to face whatever comes next.

I feel like my whole career is constantly learning how to hold a ticking bomb and finding ways to use the explosion to lift me up instead of blowing up in my face. After two decades of this kind of work, I've built up dozens of systems that help me evaluate potentially dangerous situations and react when they do.

One of the reasons I'm so obsessed with looking at data is because it can reveal insights I can use to fix mistakes moving forward and repair them in the moment.

I'm constantly reading and listening to strategies that I can apply in different situations because I know I'll be in a bad place again and need as many tricks in my toolbox to get out of the next jam. I keep standing because I'm informed and squirrelly. When the walls close in, I find ways to wriggle out without getting mortally wounded.

I'm also constantly learning new skills, even if they fizzle in the moment. Courses never worked for me in the 2010s, but all of that knowledge came in handy when we created The Kickstarter Accelerator. My podcast never really took off, even after 200 episodes, but all of that knowledge was super helpful in designing the Six Figure Author Experiment with my co-host Lee Savino. My first books didn't burn up the charts, but they still sell in bundles on my website and taught me what not to do when building The Godsverse Chronicles and <u>The Obsidian Spindle Saga</u>, which taught me so much about how to do it better next time.

Because I've learned how to do so much in my life, and have such a massive back catalog, I have tons of strategies to help me recover when something goes disastrously wrong. More than helping me succeed, which they do, I'm mainly trying to build the biggest buffer possible so I can eat in the lean times.

Make no mistake, though, the more successful you get, the more likely you'll run into these situations that can bankrupt you and need better and better strategies to get through them. Lee calls these "millionaire problems." If you do this right, the "smaller problems" won't phase you, but your ambition will slam you into new problems on every new rung of the success ladder with even more potential to knock you out.

As you learn and grow, you'll face bigger and bigger challenges, but you'll also know how to get through the ones you're dealing with now without batting an eye.

WHEN TIME HAS TO HAPPEN

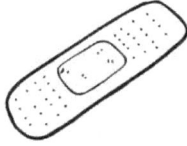

Too often in life, the answer to "why am I not having success?" is that time has to happen. It is not satisfying so most teachers and coaches will never say that part out loud, which leaves writers thinking that something must be broken in their own process.

So, I'll say the quiet part out loud. Even if you have a perfect strategy, it doesn't matter until you execute it.

- **If you want to make $100k in a year, guess what?** *The whole year still has to happen.*
- **If you want 10,000 new subscribers in the next six months, guess what?** *You have to set metrics and plod through a lot of muck to get there.*
- **If you want to write 12 books this year, guess what?** *You actually have to write those books, and it takes time.*

We often operate with the belief that if we have the right plan, success will follow quickly. But time is an inevitable factor that no one can circumvent.

This became a mantra for me during my Writer MBA days, because a conference is the ultimate "time has to happen product." Even though people do buy throughout the year, upwards of 25% buy within the last six weeks, and hardly anyone buys until three months before.

That said, vendors still want their money early, which makes for a fun cash crunch challenge. It's impossible to announce speakers until you, like, have speakers to announce.

You can run ads, craft highly persuasive email campaigns, or engage potential buyers in person, but for most people, it simply doesn't matter until a particular window opens. Most won't buy until three months before an event or product launch. Sure, there are tactics to create urgency and move things along, but if your portfolio consists of a few articles, a single book release, or if you've only been building your audience for a short while, success won't appear overnight.

This brings us to a crucial point: planning for time to happen. The reality is that time needs to pass for success to materialize, but the way you approach that time can make the waiting less stressful and more productive. Instead of focusing solely on speeding up the process, it's about getting comfortable with the time it takes and understanding how to plan for it wisely.

A lot of my consultations revolve around a key question: Is it reasonable to expect the success you want, based on everything you've done so far? It's a question that forces us to evaluate our progress realistically. Here are some indicators that can help you assess whether your success expectations are reasonable:

1. **Do you have a sufficient track record?**
   If you've been working at something for a few months but expect the results of someone who's been in the game for years, you may need to adjust your expectations. Success often builds over time, and a consistent body of work or long-term engagement with

your audience is usually necessary before you see big results.

2. **Are you measuring the right metrics?**
   Often, success doesn't show up immediately in the most obvious ways, like sales numbers or subscriber counts. Instead, it may appear as growing engagement, positive feedback, or increased visibility. Focus on the smaller, incremental wins that signal you're on the right path, even if they're not the ultimate goal.

3. **Have you put in the necessary effort?**
   Have you done everything in your power to set yourself up for success? This includes not just the creation of your product (whether that's writing, marketing, etc.) but also how effectively you've communicated with your audience, built relationships, and leveraged opportunities. If the effort isn't there, the results won't be either.

4. **Are external factors in your favor?**
   Sometimes, success hinges on things beyond your control, like market conditions or timing. If you're in a competitive industry or trying to launch during a time when the market is saturated, your success might take longer than expected. It's important to be mindful of factors that could affect your trajectory.

5. **Have you given it enough time?**
   Finally, and most importantly, have you allowed enough time for success to materialize? This is where the concept of letting time happen really becomes important. Many people give up just before they would have seen the fruits of their labor. Assess how long others in your field took to reach similar levels of success and give yourself that same grace.

Rather than obsessing over the final outcome, focus on the process. Every big goal, whether it's making $100k or publishing twelve books, can be broken down into smaller milestones. Those incremental steps not only help you feel a sense of accomplishment along the way but also make the passing of time feel more manageable. It's the routine that matters most: writing a certain number of words each day, engaging with your audience regularly, or refining your craft bit by bit.

Gary Keller and Jay Papasan wrote an amazing book called *The One Thing*. In it, they talk about the benefits of finding the single thing which could change your life forever, The Big Domino, and putting an inordinate about of time and effort into tipping it over. In order for the domino to tip, there are all sorts of smaller dominos that need to fall, too, but all in service of toppling the big domino.

Unfortunately, it takes time to set up these dominos to fall, but we humans want everything Veruca Salt fast.

Patience isn't a natural skill for most of us. It's something we have to practice. Every time you resist the urge to push too hard, every time you let things unfold at their natural pace, you're strengthening your patience muscle. Over time, you'll find the waiting period less overwhelming because you've trained yourself to endure it.

If you've just started writing or publishing, it's not fair to expect the same level of success as someone who's been at it for years. Success usually builds gradually, and part of getting comfortable with letting time happen is acknowledging that this growth takes time. Be patient but also be strategic.

I believe you only get 1-2 shots to level up a year, and 90% of your time is moving the pieces around in the background to make that lurch happen. You rise to the level of the structures you have in place, and most of life is building those structures so that when you make your leap, they catch and support you.

Yes, you might be able to make a gigantic leap quickly, but if your structure is shaky, or if you haven't constructed it at all, you'll likely fall back down to Earth and hurt yourself, possibly irreparably, in the process. Most of the successful people you see have either been building their support structure for years or are about to flame out because they grew too fast.

Now, this brings us to the question I ask many of my clients: *Is the success you expect reasonable given the efforts you've put forth and the support structures you've put in place?* Often, the answer is no. That's not a negative. We just have to realign your expectations with reality. Do you have a big enough track record to expect success at the level you're aiming for? Have you been consistent enough in your efforts? Do you have the network in place to support you? These are the questions we need to ask ourselves, honestly, when assessing our path.

I ask myself these same questions constantly. I'm incredibly ambitious, and with that comes impatience. I want to achieve my goals yesterday, and I sometimes forget I'm only human. I remind myself, and now I remind you, that it's not just you who feels this way. We all have to balance ambition with the understanding that time is a fundamental component of success.

THE ART OF HARNESSING CHAOS MAGIC

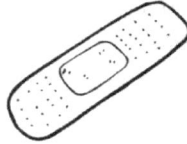

Most successful people I know are masters of chaos magic. I don't mean they are chaos; I mean they understand how to live in chaos, harness chaos, and use chaos in a restful way.

When I started on my path to success, I thought I'd eventually become like President Business from *The LEGO Movie*: structured, orderly, in control of everything. I pictured a well-oiled machine humming under my watchful eye, every piece in its place. But the reality turned out to be wildly different. The more successful I became, the more I channeled big Princess Unikitty energy.

People laugh when I say this but hear me out: Princess Unikitty is an absolute unit. Her kingdom thrives not because it's orderly, but because she knows how to ride the waves of chaos, harness its energy, and create something magical out of it.

Unlike President Business, who exhausts himself trying to force order on a chaotic world, Princess Unikitty understands that the world is inherently unpredictable. Chaos isn't a bug in the system; it's the main feature of it. Her genius lies in not fighting it but channeling it productively.

This was a game-changing realization for me.

Many of the people I coach think that achieving success means finally being able to impose order on their lives. But that's a trap. The true gift of success isn't eliminating chaos—it's having enough chaos working in your favor that good things start happening more often than not. It's learning to harness the unpredictable and thrive in its flow.

Imagine a life where chaos no longer feels threatening. You wake up each day grounded in your purpose, open to the unexpected, and ready to turn unpredictability into progress. You trust your systems, your community, and your ability to adapt.

This is the essence of chaos magic: not controlling the storm, but dancing with it.

WHAT IS CHAOS MAGIC?

Let's get one thing straight: chaos magic isn't about casting spells or invoking mystical forces. It's about cultivating a growth mindset to approach the swirling, unpredictable mess of life with curiosity, confidence, and creativity. Chaos magic is the art of thriving in uncertainty, of turning the unexpected into an ally instead of an enemy.

Chaos is inevitable, especially for those who are building something ambitious. The more you grow, the more connections you make, the more decisions you face, and the more opportunities you create. Each of these adds complexity, and with complexity comes chaos. The magic lies in recognizing that this isn't a problem to solve but a power to harness.

There was a time when I could have named every one of my readers and told you exactly when and where I met them. Now, with a much larger fanbase, and with so many potential touchpoints, it's impossible for me to tell someone where I met them.

This is one of the many paradoxes of success: the more you achieve, the more chaos you attract…and that's a good thing.

Imagine an author who writes their first breakout hit. With the success of that book comes a flood of new opportunities: foreign rights deals, movie adaptation offers, speaking invitations, collaborations with other creators. At the same time, the demands on their time and attention skyrocket. They must now juggle deadlines, navigate public appearances, and keep their creative energy alive, all while managing a growing fan base. The sheer volume of moving parts creates chaos.

Growing a bigger audience helps your business in a myriad of ways, but the most important thing might be that it allows for more chaos to swirl under and around you. More people talking about your work allows for more moments of serendipity to collide and more good things to happen for you. Opportunities amplify when you allow more chaos to swirl around you.

This isn't unique to authors. Entrepreneurs launching a startup, artists scaling their craft, parents navigating a growing family—success in any area of life adds layers of complexity. The trick isn't to fight this complexity but to work with it.

Chaos is the natural byproduct of growth. Learning to thrive in it is the hallmark of lasting success. Instead of fighting against it, we must learn to harness that chaos to our benefit.

Despite its inevitability, most of us instinctively resist chaos. From a young age, we're taught to value order, predictability, and control. Society celebrates the neatly planned, the perfectly executed, the tightly managed. Chaos, by contrast, is often framed as a sign of failure.

This mindset runs deep. Chaos triggers our fear of the unknown, our anxiety about making mistakes, and our discomfort with losing control. But chaos is also where breakthroughs happen. It's the fertile ground of innovation, creativity, and growth. In order to access its gifts, you have to let go of the illusion of control and embrace the unpredictability.

It's normal to feel overwhelmed, but the key is learning to reframe these emotions. Ask yourself, What can this chaos teach me? or How can I grow from this?

HARNESSING CHAOS: THE C.H.A.O.S. FRAMEWORK

In working with so many successful creators, and learning from their process, I developed a simple framework that can hopefully help you harness the power of chaos, learn to live with it, and use its magic to propel you forward.

This C.H.A.O.S. framework has five stages: **Center, Harness, Adapt, Observe, Simplify.**

Remember, harnessing chaos magic isn't about **being** chaos. It's about flowing with the chaos, aware and awake for opportunities when they present themselves, and being able to redirect its energy into productive outlets when you find them.

1. (C)ENTER YOURSELF

The first step to mastering chaos is grounding yourself. When everything feels like it's spinning out of control, your inner stability becomes your anchor. This might mean developing a daily ritual like meditation, journaling, or even a walk in nature to calm your mind and clarify your priorities.

Centering yourself isn't about eliminating chaos. It's about maintaining your equilibrium within it. Think of it like standing in the eye of a storm. The winds rage around you, but in the center, you remain calm.

2. (H)ARNESS PRODUCTIVE CHAOS

Not all chaos is destructive. Creative bursts, unexpected connections, and sudden opportunities can be incredibly productive. The key is learning to recognize the difference. Productive chaos adds energy to your life, while destructive chaos drains it.

When you encounter chaos, pause and ask: *Is this moving me closer to my goals, or is it pulling me away?* If it's the former, lean in. If it's the latter, let it go.

It's very possible that you won't know which bit of the chaos will be productive. In that case, try to isolate one bit of chaos, and start playing with it.

Which bit of the chaos seems fun to you? Which bit sparks your intuition? There are opportunities everywhere, so following the fun is a pretty good starting place, even if eventually it doesn't lead anywhere. At least then you did something that was fun, right?

3. (A)DAPT WITH FLEXIBLE SYSTEMS

Rigid systems break under pressure. Flexible systems bend and thrive. This means creating processes that allow for experimentation, iteration, and change. For example, instead of micromanaging every step of a project, set broad goals and empower your team to find their own solutions. Flexibility isn't a lack of structure. It's a structure that evolves over time, like one of those inflatable tube men waving their arms all over the place.

There is money everywhere if you look for it with intention. However, if we build our systems in a way that breaks instead of bends, we won't be able to flow in ways that capture it. I spent many years pursuing paths that didn't lead to money, mainly because I couldn't even see the opportunities all around me. Then, when I did start to see them, my business was so structured that pivoting toward them would have broken my foundation.

When I started holding my ideas more loosely and allowing myself to evolve with time in easeful ways, I started making much more money and having more success.

4. (O)BSERVE AND LEARN

Chaos is a powerful teacher, but only if you're willing to listen. Instead of rushing to control the situation, take time to observe. What patterns are emerging? What opportunities are hidden within the mess? Chaos often reveals insights you'd miss in a more orderly environment.

This is why I'm so big on analyzing data. It's not because I'm rigidly pursuing my goals. It's because I'm throwing a lot of chaos at the universe and observing results.

When you run a science experiment, the only one who doesn't know what's going to happen is you. The universe already knows what's going to happen when you combine certain things together.

Data is how I impose some amount of structure on experiments so I can repeat them. The universe is chaos, but it is often consistent chaos that can be harnessed in predictable ways.

I find something as simple as taking a few deep breaths helps center me on the deeper meaning behind a situation. Yes, things may be blowing up all around me, but there are ways to use those explosions to lift me up instead of letting them blow up in my face.

5. (S)IMPLIFY TO REBALANCE

When chaos becomes overwhelming, the solution isn't to fight it harder—it's to simplify. Cut back to what matters most. Eliminate distractions. Focus your energy on the essentials. Simplification isn't about giving up; it's about creating space for clarity and action.

Going back to the beginning and retracing your steps usually reveals the flaw in your process, and being fluid in your systems should allow you to backtrack to the problem and pick another path or abandon it completely. If something isn't serving you, feel free to stop working on it. You can always pick it up later. Your intuition is probably telling you that you missed something, and you need to reenter the chaos to find out how to move forward.

We might think we know what's going to happen, but even if we have run the same experiment a hundred times before there's a small chance that you'll get a wildly different result, which is fabulous and frustrating in equal measure.

THE LONG-TERM BENEFITS OF CHAOS MAGIC

Mastering chaos isn't just a short-term survival skill—it's a long-term strategy for success. Over time, chaos magic builds resilience, adaptability, and confidence. It makes you antifragile: instead of breaking under pressure, you grow stronger.

In practical terms, this means:

- **Resilience:** You bounce back faster from setbacks.
- **Adaptability:** You pivot gracefully when plans change.
- **Innovation:** You find unexpected solutions and opportunities.

These aren't just professional skills. They're life skills, too. Chaos magic makes you better equipped to handle the inevitable unpredictability of life, whether in your career, relationships, or personal growth.

Remember that you're the magician. Sometimes, magicians need to be chaos agents, but usually they stand in the center of a chaotic universe and wield that chaos to their benefit.

How do you know you're mastering chaos magic? Here are some signs:

- **Emotional resilience:** You feel less overwhelmed by unpredictability and more curious about what it can teach you.

- **Productive patterns:** You consistently turn chaotic moments into opportunities for growth or innovation.
- **Greater impact:** Your projects, teams, or creative endeavors thrive, even in uncertain conditions.
- **Increased confidence:** You approach challenges with a sense of calm and capability, knowing you can handle whatever comes.

Here are a couple of exercises that might help you harness your own brand of chaos.

1. **Chaos mapping:** Write down all the areas of chaos in your life. Separate them into two categories: "Productive chaos" (opportunities, creative sparks) and "Destructive chaos" (energy drains, unnecessary distractions). For each item, brainstorm one action to harness or reduce it.
2. **Controlled chaos challenge:** Pick a routine area of your life—like your morning schedule or a creative project. Intentionally disrupt it for a week (e.g., work in a new location, experiment with a wild idea). Reflect on how the change sparks new insights or opportunities.
3. **Post-chaos reflection:** After a chaotic event, write down what you learned. What went well? What didn't? What patterns or opportunities emerged? Use these reflections to improve your approach next time.

Chaos magic isn't about controlling the uncontrollable. It's about learning to dance with it. The most successful people I know aren't those who avoid chaos; they're the ones who embrace it, channel it, and turn it into fuel for their ambitions.

The next time life feels chaotic, remember, chaos isn't a problem to solve. It's an opportunity to grow. ***Be like Princess Unikitty.*** Channel the madness. Build your kingdom not in spite of the chaos, but because of it.

And when you do, you'll discover the real magic: thriving in the unpredictable and creating something extraordinary along the way.

HOW TO AMPLIFY YOUR MESSAGE

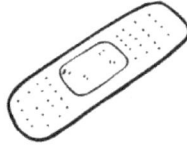

At the beginning of my career, when nobody paid attention to what I said, it was helpful to talk a lot to get people used to the cadence of my work, to know I had something to say, and frankly to make them pay attention.

Eventually, something switched, though, since I started working with Monica, and Lee, and Melissa, and Laurie, and Travis, and Andy, and Mel, and Tawdra, and all the wonderful humans who I've partnered with over the years

At this stage of my career, people very much do read my work, yet I'm using the same tactics I used when nobody was paying attention. Now, they don't work and even have a negative effect sometimes.

In fairness, it is considerably more overwhelming now when I send 10 emails a day because people don't want to ignore them. I've been working really hard to pull back on my sends (imagine what I would be like if I didn't, amirite?), but it's a really tough transition.

On top of that, if I send the right thing, it gets amplified without me doing anything, which is something I never had. Previously, I would have to create an echo myself by multiplying my own efforts.

I don't know if this is going to resonate with many of you, but I've built out a bit of a framework for amplification with expanded objectives for each stage of your career, ensuring a comprehensive and detailed guide for authors on their amplification journey.

WHAT IS AMPLIFICATION?

Amplification is the process of magnifying your message and reach to build and sustain audience engagement. It involves understanding when and how to communicate to ensure your voice resonates with the right people at the right time.

Amplification strategies evolve as your career progresses. as you grow your *owned, earned,* and *borrowed* media channels. We talked about that before in the amplification chapter, but here's a little summary of all four channels.

OWNED MEDIA CHANNELS

Owned media refers to the platforms and content that you have complete control over. These are the channels that you directly manage and where you can consistently communicate your message without relying on external parties. Owned media is essential for establishing your brand, building a loyal audience, and creating a hub where people can regularly engage with your work.

EXAMPLES OF OWNED MEDIA CHANNELS:

- **Website/blog:** Your personal website or blog is a central hub for your content, including articles, updates, resources, and other information about your work. It's a primary space where you control the user experience and the messaging.

- **Email newsletter:** Newsletters allow you to communicate directly with your audience, providing regular updates, exclusive content, and personal insights. Since you own your email list, it's a reliable way to reach your audience without depending on external algorithms.
- **Social media profiles:** While social media platforms themselves are not owned, the profiles and pages you maintain on platforms like Instagram, LinkedIn, and Facebook are spaces where you control the content and how often you post.
- **Podcasts and YouTube channels:** If you create and manage your own podcast or YouTube channel, these serve as owned media where you have complete control over the topics, format, and audience interaction.
- **Books and ebooks:** Your published works, whether traditional or self-published, are forms of owned media that reflect your voice, brand, and expertise.
- **Online courses or membership sites:** Platforms where you host your own content, such as online courses or member communities, provide a controlled environment to deliver value and engage deeply with your audience.

EARNED MEDIA CHANNELS

Earned media refers to the exposure you gain through organic, unpaid methods—essentially, it's the recognition you "earn" rather than pay for. This includes any media coverage, word-of-mouth, social media mentions, shares, reviews, and any other form of promotion that comes from outside your direct control. It's often seen as one of the most credible forms of media because it's driven by others talking about your work rather than by your own marketing efforts.

EXAMPLES OF EARNED MEDIA CHANNELS:

- **Press coverage:** Articles, interviews, or mentions in news outlets, blogs, or industry publications.
- **Social media mentions:** Shares, likes, comments, or posts by others on platforms like Tiktok, Facebook, LinkedIn, or Instagram.
- **Reviews and testimonials:** Reviews on platforms like Goodreads, Amazon, or endorsements from readers and other authors.
- **Word-of-mouth:** Personal recommendations from readers, peers, or influencers.
- **User-generated content:** Content created by your audience, such as fan art, videos, or blogs related to your work.

BORROWED MEDIA CHANNELS

Borrowed media, sometimes referred to as "shared media," involves leveraging someone else's platform to reach their audience. This type of media includes guest appearances, collaborations, or content that is published on platforms or channels not owned by you but where you have permission to share your message. The key here is that you're using someone else's established audience to amplify your voice, often through partnerships or mutual agreements.

EXAMPLES OF BORROWED MEDIA CHANNELS:

- **Guest blog posts:** Writing for other websites, blogs, or newsletters that have a built-in audience interested in your niche.

- **Podcast appearances:** Being a guest on podcasts to share your insights, which can reach new fans.
- **Social media takeovers:** Temporarily taking over someone else's social media account to interact with their followers.
- **Collaborative content:** Joint webinars, articles, or videos where you work with other creators to reach both of your audiences.
- **Influencer collaborations:** Working with influencers who share your content or discuss your work on their platforms.

While you can also amplify your message even at the beginning with *paid media*, especially as your budget expands, I generally think about amplification across these three media channels.

As you grow your audience, you'll gain access to more and more powerful media channels as you build the structure of your network.

You could, if you wanted, spend a millions dollars in advertising and overcome a lot of these effects, but otherwise most of your amplification over time will fall over your growth in these three channels.

It's important to note here that you should focus on one of these, and your success with them will naturally buoy your success with the others. Personally, my business is built upon *owned media,* with a significant amount of *borrowed media*, a little *earned media,* and *paid media* sprinkled in to keep growth steady.

Because I have a mailing list with over 44,000 people on it (*owned*), it's a lot easier to book partnerships (*borrowed*) and get press coverage (*earned*). My message naturally gets amplified now in a way it didn't 10 years ago. So, what does this look like?

THE EARLY STAGE: FILLING THE VOID

- **Objective:** Establish your voice and get people to notice you.
- **Key tactic:** Frequency over Refinement.
- **Media channel focus:** Owned media

In the early stages of your career, the primary goal is to create visibility and establish your presence in a crowded space. This is about making noise to ensure that your voice cuts through the clutter and begins to register with your intended audience. At this point, you don't have the luxury of a built-in audience or widespread recognition, so your focus is on showing up consistently and frequently enough that people start to associate your name with value.

You're essentially building a foundation, laying the groundwork for recognition, and signaling to the world that you have something to say. This stage is crucial for building initial momentum and getting your audience accustomed to your presence.

While you can focus on any of the four media channels at the beginning, it's probably going to be a lot easier if you have your own audience with your own projects that already have a little success.

STEPS TO IMPLEMENT:

- **Show Up consistently:** Consistency builds recognition and trust. Create a content calendar that outlines what you'll post and when—whether it's a weekly blog, daily social media updates, or frequent newsletters.

Stick to this schedule to build a rhythm that your audience can rely on. Even if engagement is low at first, regularity will help establish your presence. Don't be afraid to repurpose content across platforms; the goal is to be seen repeatedly in various places.

- **Don't overthink perfection:** Early on, the most important thing is to be seen and heard. Don't get bogged down by trying to make every piece of content perfect. Set a reasonable standard for quality but prioritize speed and frequency. Use templates, batching, and simple formats to keep content flowing without overextending yourself. Focus on delivering value and insights rather than polish; authenticity often resonates more than perfection.

- **Engage actively:** Be an active participant in your community. Respond promptly to comments, questions, or feedback on your posts. Go beyond your own platforms—comment on other creators' content, join relevant discussions, and make your presence felt. This not only boosts visibility but also shows that you're accessible and engaged. Set aside time each day to interact with your audience, fostering a sense of community and loyalty.

- **Experiment broadly:** This is your time to try everything. Test different content formats—blogs, videos, podcasts, infographics, and social media platforms. Track what gets the best response and refine your approach over time. Use analytics tools to monitor engagement and identify which types of content resonate most with your audience. Don't shy away from bold or unconventional ideas; early stages are perfect for discovering what truly sets you apart.

INDICATORS YOU'VE MOVED TO THE NEXT STAGE:

- **Organic engagement increases:** You notice that comments, shares, and likes on your content are happening more frequently and without prompting. This suggests that your audience is starting to engage with your content because they genuinely find value in it, not just because you're pushing them to.
- **Audience growth from external sources:** People start discovering your work through mentions, shares, or features on platforms you didn't directly engage with. This shows that your reach is extending beyond your immediate efforts.
- **Inbound opportunities:** Instead of you always reaching out, opportunities start coming to you—whether it's collaboration offers, speaking engagements, or media features. This shift indicates that others see value in associating with your voice and brand.

THE GROWTH PHASE

- **Objective:** Expand your audience by leveraging networks and collaborations.
- **Key tactic:** Leverage Networks.
- **Media channel focus:** Borrowed media

In the growth phase, your goal shifts from merely being noticed to actively expanding your reach through strategic partnerships and collaborations. At this stage, your voice has begun to resonate, and it's time to tap into larger networks to amplify your message further. By aligning with others who share similar audiences or values, you can accelerate your growth, reach new followers, and build credibility through association.

This phase is about moving from solo efforts to a more collaborative approach, using the power of community and connections to multiply your impact. It's not just about reaching more people but reaching the right people through trusted channels.

Once you get some traction, it's a lot easier to build your partnerships. This is a lifelong pursuit, as your partnerships will level up as you level up.

The bigger you can build your own network and the better you can hone your own skills, the more attractive you will be to more and more successful people.

STEPS TO IMPLEMENT:

- **Identify potential partners:** Start by mapping out potential partners who align with your audience's interests. This could include other authors, bloggers, influencers, or brands in your niche. Approach these partnerships with a clear value proposition—what can you offer them, and what do you hope to gain? Begin with small, low-commitment collaborations like guest blog posts or social media takeovers to build rapport. Keep track of your partnerships and their outcomes to refine your approach over time.
- **Contribute to communities:** Look for forums, social media groups, or online communities where your target audience spends time. Consistently add value by sharing insights, answering questions, and participating in discussions. Avoid hard sells; instead, aim to establish yourself as a helpful, knowledgeable presence. Track which communities drive the most engagement and focus your efforts there.
- **Cross-promote content:** Partner with others to share each other's content. This not only amplifies your reach

but also lends credibility to your voice through association with respected peers. Create joint projects, like webinars or collaborative articles, which allow both you and your partners to benefit from each other's audiences. Make sure to follow up and evaluate the success of these initiatives to identify the most fruitful collaborations.

- **Attend and speak at events:** Whether virtual or in-person, events are a great way to connect with others in your field. Use these opportunities to network, share your expertise, and learn from others. Prepare a brief pitch about who you are and what you offer and be ready to share it when the moment arises. After events, follow up with new contacts to keep the connection warm and explore potential collaboration opportunities.

INDICATORS YOU'VE MOVED TO THE NEXT STAGE:

- **Consistent external features:** Your work is being highlighted by others regularly, such as through guest posts, interviews, or mentions in newsletters and blogs. This indicates that your voice is resonating within your industry, and you're recognized as someone worth following.
- **Engagement depth over breadth:** Instead of just increasing the number of followers, you're seeing deeper engagement—people are asking specific questions, requesting more of certain content, or showing loyalty by following you across different platforms.
- **Greater influence in collaborations:** When you collaborate, your input is sought after and valued. You're not just a participant but a key contributor, showing that your partners see you as an equal or a leader in the space.

THE ESTABLISHED STAGE

- **Objective:** Refine your approach to ensure that your communication is impactful and well-received.
- **Key tactic:** Selective Amplification.
- **Media channel focus:** Paid media.

As you move into the established stage, the challenge becomes one of refinement rather than expansion. Your audience is engaged, but now it's about ensuring that every interaction and communication counts.

Over-communicating can lead to diminishing returns, as your audience may feel overwhelmed or begin to tune out.

This stage is about focusing on quality over quantity— sending fewer but more impactful messages that resonate deeply with your audience. It's about leveraging the trust and recognition you've built to make every message count, ensuring that each piece of communication drives action and reinforces your brand's value.

By now you know your products sell and your message works. At this point, you can start running ads to amplify your message to people who might not know who you are. You've probably capped out at the people you can reach individually, and this allows you to keep bringing in new people as they age into your work.

You'll also likely have enough work to break even on your costs, and enough word of mouth that a lot of people have heard of your work and are ready to try you out.

STEPS TO IMPLEMENT:

- **Audit your communication channels:** Regularly review all the platforms you're using to communicate with your audience. Identify which channels are driving the most engagement and which are not performing as expected. Consider scaling back or eliminating efforts on less effective platforms. Focus on where your audience is most active and responsive to streamline your efforts and maximize impact.
- **Prioritize high-impact messages:** Create fewer, more purposeful communications. Each piece should have a clear goal, whether it's driving engagement, boosting sales, or building brand awareness. Use data to refine your content strategy, focusing on topics and formats that historically drive the best results. Develop a hierarchy for your communications—reserve frequent updates for high-engagement channels and use broader announcements sparingly.
- **Segment your audience:** Use data to segment your audience based on behavior, preferences, or engagement levels. Tailor your messages to these segments to increase relevance and impact. For example, you might send more frequent updates to your most engaged followers while offering broader, less frequent communications to those less engaged. Experiment with A/B testing to see which approaches resonate best with each segment.
- **Measure and adjust:** Continuously track key metrics like open rates, click-through rates, and engagement to gauge the effectiveness of your communications. Use this data to refine your approach. Regularly survey your audience for feedback on your communication frequency and content preferences. Make data-driven adjustments and don't hesitate to pivot your strategy if something isn't working.

INDICATORS YOU'VE MOVED TO THE NEXT STAGE:

- **Noticeable drop in engagement with high volume:** When you send too many messages, you observe a decline in open rates, click-through rates, or general engagement, signaling that your audience feels overwhelmed. This drop is your cue that more isn't better anymore.
- **Action from minimal effort:** You begin to see that even small actions, like a single email or post, can drive significant outcomes—whether that's sales, sign-ups, or shares. This shows your audience is highly attuned and ready to respond to your cues.
- **Direct feedback:** You receive feedback from your audience or network indicating they feel overwhelmed or prefer more focused communication. This might come in the form of unsubscribes, replies asking for less frequent updates, or feedback from partners about your approach.

THE EVOLVING STAGE

- **Objective:** Leverage your established network and influence to amplify your message organically.
- **Key tactic:** Trust in Organic Reach.
- **Media channel focus:** Earned media

In the evolving stage, your strategy shifts to fully leveraging the ecosystem of influence and connections you've built over time. At this point, your content and brand have a life of their own, and your focus should be on letting your audience and network do some of the amplification for you. Trust in the strength of your previous work, your established relationships, and the content you've put out to continue spreading your message organically.

This stage is about embracing a more hands-off approach, knowing that your influence now extends beyond direct actions you take. It's about maximizing the power of organic reach, where your network amplifies your message naturally without needing a heavy-handed push from you.

You should be reaching out to the press throughout your journey, but this stage is when it will start paying dividends. Press coverage only really works if people know who you are and like your work. Yes, it's great to get backlinks, but the more people know you, the better the press is going to work.

On top of that, the press will likely reach out to you over time to cover your work and subscribe to your work to get announcements. They might even start as fans and grow into great press contacts.

STEPS TO IMPLEMENT:

- **Create shareable content:** Focus on producing content that your audience will want to share—whether because it's insightful, useful, or entertaining. Infographics, quotes, and actionable tips can often travel farther than lengthy articles. Regularly refresh your content based on trending topics and feedback from your audience to maintain relevance and shareability. Ensure your content is easy to share by including share buttons or prompts.
- **Empower your advocates:** Identify your most engaged followers or superfans. Create a system to reward or recognize them for their support, such as exclusive content, shout-outs, or early access to new work. Encourage them to share your content by making it easy—provide pre-written tweets, shareable graphics, or insider tips they can pass along. Cultivate a sense of

community among your advocates to foster organic growth.

- **Lean on your network:** When you have something important to share, don't hesitate to ask your network to help amplify it. A personal ask can be much more powerful than a generic broadcast. Leverage your relationships with peers, collaborators, and industry contacts to spread the word. Offer to reciprocate their support in the future, creating a mutually beneficial dynamic that strengthens your overall ecosystem.
- **Trust the process:** Recognize that your influence allows your content to have a life of its own. Give it space to breathe and grow within the ecosystem you've nurtured, rather than trying to push every piece manually. Monitor the natural flow of your content and step in only when necessary to nudge things in the right direction. Trust that your audience and network will amplify the right messages at the right times.

INDICATORS YOU'VE REACHED THIS STAGE:

- **Widespread organic amplification:** Your content frequently spreads beyond your immediate reach without direct intervention—through shares, mentions in articles, or even discussions in spaces you didn't target directly.
- **Recognition beyond your network:** You start getting noticed or approached by people, publications, or organizations outside of your immediate network who have been indirectly influenced by your work. This shows your reach is broadening beyond your direct influence.
- **Minimal effort, maximum impact:** You notice that major actions—like book launches or important announcements—require significantly less promotional effort from you. Your established ecosystem and

audience now play a significant role in spreading your message.

EVOLVING WITH YOUR AUDIENCE

This is not a perfect outline, especially when it comes to your area of focus. I know plenty of people that started with paid advertising before they had much owned media and killed it. They are more successful than I am at this point by a factor of ten.

I've built out this structure to give you the best odds for success and lowest chance of falling on your face. That said, you are gonna fail at this sometimes, and feel like a failure a lot of the time, as you work to amplify your message.

Even highly skilled experts working with world-renowned authorities have problems placing stories and breaking even on ads. Recognizing when to shift your amplification strategy is critical to maintaining and growing your influence.

By paying attention to these detailed indicators and implementing the expanded steps, you can confidently transition through each stage, ensuring your message continues to resonate and have the desired impact. Remember, it's not just about making noise; it's about making meaningful connections at the right moments.

BREACHING THE TRUST THERMOCLINE

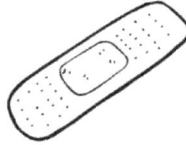

I think about trust a lot; probably too much. I think about the trust with my wife, my business partners, my collaborators, and readers all the time.

Maintaining trust with readers is a critical part of building a sustainable writing career. Readers don't just invest their money in a writer. They also invest their time, energy, and emotional engagement in the worlds and books they create.

Often, readers stick with writers for years, or even decades, building up a ton of trust with them. We often take that trust for granted, but it's not given. We are constantly gaining and losing trust with our readers.

In general, authors are good about building and retaining a positive relationship with readers, but as we move further and further into direct sales, more and more vectors of trust fall on us.

Now, we aren't just responsible for uploading our books to retailers, we're also responsible for shipping and handling books from our direct store, fulfilling Kickstarters, delivering for subscribers, and more.

In the past, we've been able to rely a lot on the trust our readers had with retailers, but over time we've taken a lot of that responsibility onto ourselves. I'm worried we're not worried enough about maintaining that trust over time.

If that trust erodes too much, readers may walk away from our brand, leading to a collapse in book sales, newsletter engagement, or even word-of-mouth recommendations.

This can happen suddenly, often without warning, but it doesn't occur after one bad incident or overnight. In fact, it's a gradual process, and understanding how to avoid breaching the trust thermocline can help authors build and maintain long-term, loyal audiences.

WHAT IS THE TRUST THERMOCLINE?

A thermocline is an ocean (or other body of water) layer where the temperature changes rapidly. In this layer, the water temperature decreases much more quickly than in the warmer layer above or the colder layer below.

In the same way, trust in an author can seem solid until one small, seemingly minor event triggers a rapid decline.

However, if we look closer it becomes clear that this sudden decline didn't *actually* happen suddenly. Instead, it resulted from the slow buildup of small issues over time.

Customer trust doesn't erode in a predictable, linear way but rather builds up until it reaches a tipping point, at which trust suddenly collapses. Businesses often fail to notice this tipping point forming because it happens over time through small, seemingly inconsequential actions.

The same applies to authors: readers won't abandon you after one missed deadline or a controversial book, but over time, these small frustrations can add up to them breaching the thermocline layer and abandoning your brand.

As an author, you might delay a book release, miss a newsletter, or put out a book that doesn't quite hit the mark, and your readers may forgive you. But each of these instances adds a little bit of weight to the relationship, and over time, if these things continue, trust begins to wear thin.

Additionally, it might take you additional time to fulfill a Kickstarter, or the book you deliver could not live up to expectations, or you suddenly stop updating your Patreon, or your direct store crashes, or you snipe at people who contact your customer service line, or any number of things, each of which move you closer and closer to the thermocline layer.

I am petrified of this layer, though I didn't have the language to describe it until now. I'm obsessed with making sure people have a great experience with every interaction, so they don't ever come close to that thermocline level.

Every time we have to delay a launch or do something we know will irritate our audience, I fear we get closer to that layer and I work extra hard to make it right with people.

AVOIDING THE TRUST THERMOCLINE

I don't want to get alarmist about this, because frankly it takes a pattern of breaches to break through this layer, but it's also why we need to be cognizant of it now. Buoying yourself and preventing this erosion is easier than the almost impossible task of pulling people back from the breach later.

Here are some easy ways to make sure you stay far away from the thermocline layer.

1. CONSISTENCY OVER TIME

Readers are forgiving of the occasional misstep. What they dislike is inconsistency over the long term. One (or more) missed release isn't going to hurt you, but if people can't trust you will deliver your book, they will eventually turn away from you. Just look at how fans talk about George RR Martin or Patrick Rothfuss now compared to how they first blew their deadlines or ask a reader how they feel about not getting a Kickstarter book they ordered months ago without any word from the author.

2. COMMUNICATE EARLY AND OFTEN

Most readers are patient when authors are upfront with them. If you have to delay a release or make a major change to your content, give your customers a clear explanation. Proactive communication allows people to stay invested in the journey and makes it less likely that they'll reach a breaking point. Remember, readers don't expect you to be perfect. They just want to feel included and valued. And if you've built up goodwill over time, readers will overlook small issues.

3. RESPECT READER EXPECTATIONS

Your readers trust you to deliver a certain kind of experience. If you write cozy mysteries and suddenly release a horror novel without any notice, you risk confusing and frustrating your readers. I call this "*The Last Jedi* syndrome." I love *The Last Jedi*, but it's not a *Star Wars* movie and breaks the brand promise people had built up with the series over decades. This doesn't mean you can't evolve as an author, but it's important to manage transitions thoughtfully. Explain why you're making a shift and maybe offer your core readers a sneak peek to bring them along for the ride. Additionally, if you're going to break your brand promise, start another series, or pen name, to explore it.

4. ENGAGE WITH READER FEEDBACK

Readers reach the trust thermocline slowly, so pay attention to early warning signs from your audience. If readers are expressing dissatisfaction with certain elements, whether in reviews, comments, or emails, don't brush them off. Addressing concerns early can help prevent those small grievances from building into larger ones. Think of it as fixing a leak before the dam bursts. That said, happy readers won't make their opinions known very often. I can count on one hand how many readers reach out and tell me when they like something, and yet they always buy the next thing. When they are unhappy, though, they will make their dissatisfaction heard.

5. BOND WITH YOUR READERS

Preventing a breach requires understanding your audience on a deep level. Share insights into your process, your struggles, or your future plans. Bring them into the fold, so they feel emotionally invested again. Readers want to support authors they feel connected to, and if you show that you're listening and engaging with them, they'll likely give you another chance.

For authors, the trust thermocline represents a real risk, but it's important not to let the fear of crossing it paralyze you. One mistake won't lead to a loss of readers, nor will it cause them to abandon you tomorrow. Trust is built over time, and so is its erosion.

It's the accumulation of unresolved issues that leads to a breach. But as long as you engage with your readers consistently, communicate openly, and respect their expectations, you'll avoid crossing that critical point.

Additionally, what you measure you manage. So, if you're aware of how your customers feel and make real efforts to maintain their trust and work in their best interest, you'll have a lot of leeway.

Trust is not a fragile thing, but it needs care and attention. By understanding that the process is gradual and focusing on long-term relationship building, you can protect your reader base and ensure that trust remains intact.

BUILDING AN INTEGRATED PUBLISHING ECOSYSTEM

The publishing landscape has become increasingly complex. Authors today face a constant barrage of "next big things" and "silver bullet" solutions. It's exhausting trying to keep up with every new platform, marketing strategy, and publishing trend.

But you *probably* don't have an information problem. You have a sequencing problem.

All the information you need already exists. The real challenge lies in putting it together in a way that works for your specific situation without burning yourself out in the process. What's even better? It's actually simpler to integrate these pieces than most people realize.

Why do so many authors struggle? Because the industry often overcomplicates things. Sometimes this happens because "experts" make money by doing it for you. Other times it's because authors try to do everything at once instead of building systematically.

This methodology comes from over fifteen years of research, testing, and real-world experience. I've experienced both spectacular failures and incredible successes. More importantly, I've learned what works sustainably versus what leads to burnout.

The key is building an integrated publishing ecosystem that:

- Makes the most of every piece of content you create
- Uses your resources efficiently
- Grows steadily without requiring constant attention
- Creates predictable, sustainable income
- Lets you focus on writing rather than constant marketing

We'll explore the five core components of a successful publishing ecosystem and how to implement them in a way that builds on your strengths while protecting your creative energy.

THE FOUNDATION OF YOUR ECOSYSTEM

Before diving into specific tactics, let's talk about the two core principles that make a publishing ecosystem work: leverage and sustainability.

Leverage means doing things once and getting multiple uses from them. Think of it like planting a tree. You do the work once, but that tree keeps producing fruit year after year. In publishing terms, we want our content and marketing efforts to keep working for us long after we create them. This might mean writing content that works across multiple platforms or creating marketing materials that can support multiple books.

Many authors burn out because they try to do everything at once. They launch a podcast, start a newsletter, run ads, and attempt to be active on every social media platform simultaneously. This approach almost always leads to failure. The smart approach is to start with one thing and make it work well. Only after you've mastered that should you consider adding new elements to your system.

Smart authors think about how to reuse their work before they even start creating. Your blog posts can become book content. Your book content can fuel social media posts. Your marketing copy can work across multiple platforms. Your launch systems can be reused for future books. This isn't about cutting corners. It's about being strategic with your time and energy.

The key to sustainability is understanding that everything you do should be repeatable without burning you out. It needs to be scalable as your audience grows, manageable within your available time, and compatible with your creative process.

Many authors try to copy what works for others without considering if it's sustainable for their situation. What works for a full-time author with a team might not work for someone writing on the side.

Remember, the goal is to build a system that can grow with you over time, not one that requires constant heroic effort to maintain. By focusing on leverage and sustainability from the start, you create a foundation that supports your long-term success as an author.

THE FIVE-STEP PUBLISHING SYSTEM

Many authors jump straight into publishing without a clear plan. They release a book, try some marketing, and hope for the best. But publishing success isn't about luck. It's about building a systematic approach that works reliably over time. Let's explore the five key steps that create a solid publishing ecosystem.

1. **Continuity through subscriptions** - The foundation of any strong publishing business is predictable, recurring revenue. Think of subscriptions like the undercurrent of your author business. While they take time to build, they provide stability that helps you weather the ups and downs of publishing. You shouldn't obsess over subscriptions when first setting them up, but everything you do should funnel readers toward becoming subscribers.
2. **Building your casual reader funnel** - Retail sales aren't the end goal. They're a means of customer acquisition. Think of retailer sales as a funnel to convert casual fans into devoted readers. The point is to cast a wide net to find readers and bring them into your ecosystem where you control the customer relationship. You don't need retail sales to turn a huge profit. They just need to work well enough to keep bringing new readers to your door.
3. **Using Kickstarter strategically** - Kickstarter serves as the first step in your publishing journey. It's how you can make the most money from your most ardent backers while creating all your marketing materials for direct sales. Kickstarter comes first because it's a testing ground. You can validate your marketing messages, test different price points, and build excitement before a wider launch.
4. **Creating a series landing page** - Once you've proven your marketing through Kickstarter, you can create series landing pages that use that tested copy. This

gives new subscribers a clear path to buying your work. You can create automated sequences offering special deals to new subscribers using the exact email messages that converted best during your campaign. The key is making these landing pages evergreen assets that keep working for you.

5. **Building your web store** - Your web store becomes the final piece, allowing you to sell directly to readers ongoing. While you'll offer all your books, focus on exclusive bundles readers can't get elsewhere. This gives people a reason to buy directly from you rather than retailers. Remember that once someone buys from you directly, they're much more likely to do so again.

The beauty of this system is that each piece builds on the others. Your Kickstarter creates marketing materials for your landing pages. Your landing pages feed subscribers to your web store. Your web store offers exclusive products to reward your most loyal readers. Everything works together to create a sustainable ecosystem that grows stronger over time

SUBSCRIPTIONS

Many authors launch their subscription program with grand ambitions. They promise daily content, personal attention, and exclusive access to everything they create. While this enthusiasm is admirable, it often leads to burnout and disappointment when reality sets in.

Instead, subscriptions should grow naturally as part of your overall ecosystem. They aren't meant to be your primary income source when you start. Instead, they're a steady stream that builds over months and years, eventually becoming a reliable foundation for your business. They are the undercurrent of your business, but they don't matter much until they matter a lot.

The key is starting small and sustainable. When you first launch a subscription, focus on delivering what you can easily maintain. This might mean sharing "burn off" content from your existing work - early drafts, character designs, behind-the-scenes glimpses. Don't create entirely new content streams until you have enough subscribers to justify the extra effort.

Even with 1,100 paying members almost everything I generate is being used multiple times in multiple ways, without spending a ton of time servicing my membership. Now that we are making $20k/yr on subscriptions, it is now worth it to spend more time working on more community activities.

You don't need to spend tons of time worrying about subscriptions when you first set them up. The goal isn't to create an overnight subscription success. Instead, everything you do should naturally funnel readers toward becoming subscribers over time. This brings more recurring revenue into your business steadily and sustainably.

We use periodic pledge drives to increase subscriptions in bunches, usually 2-4 times per year, and augment them with special discounts that last 24-72 hours. These focused efforts let us boost our numbers and gain attention without constantly pushing subscriptions.

Here is how our membership looked after each big launch in 2024:

- **January 1, 2024** – 324

- **March 1** – 470 (+*146*)
- **August 1** – 789 (+*319*)
- **September 15** – 888 (+*99*)
- **October 31** – 952 (+*64*)
- **December 10** – 1,052 (+*100*)
- **January 1, 2025** – 1,150 (+*98*)

As you can see, the biggest pledge drive was still only 319 members (and it lasted 6 weeks, way too long). Each launch built on the previous one, and we welcomed more people into our membership. It takes 1-2 years to build a sustainable membership like this, which is why it's the undercurrent of your publishing ecosystem, not the focus of it.

When starting out, stick to one simple price plan until people are literally begging to pay you more. Don't add features or tiers that people aren't actively requesting inside your community. Only introduce higher price plans once your base plan is sustainable. When done right, you should see 10-20% of people upgrading over time.

Remember, subscriptions are not the focus of your business, but they are the undercurrent of it. Everything should lead back to the membership, but you shouldn't spend a ton of time executing on it until it is sustainable to do so for you.

THE CASUAL READER FUNNEL

Most authors see retail sales as the end goal. They obsess over Amazon rankings and BookBub features, thinking these metrics define success, but this approach misses the bigger picture. Retail sales aren't the destination. They're the start of a journey to convert casual readers into devoted fans.

Think of retailer sales as your wide net. Amazon, Barnes & Noble, and other platforms give you access to millions of potential readers. These casual browsers might stumble across your book through algorithms, ads, or recommendations. That first sale is just your foot in the door.

The real magic happens when you turn these casual readers into direct customers. Every retail book should include clear pathways back to your ecosystem. Your back matter needs strong calls to action that guide readers to join your mailing list or visit your website. Once they're in your world, you control the relationship.

This is where most authors get it backward. They worry about making huge profits from retail sales when those platforms should really be customer acquisition channels. Your retail books don't need to generate massive profits. They just need to avoid losing money while bringing new readers into your ecosystem.

The beauty of this approach is that it's infinitely scalable. As long as your retail presence stays profitable (or at least breaks even), you can keep expanding your reach. Every new reader who discovers you through retailers becomes a potential direct customer.

Anything that increases exposure is good until it sacrifices customer acquisition costs below profitability. You can experiment with pricing, promotions, and marketing as long as you're not losing money to gain readers. The goal is sustainable growth, not quick spikes that drain your resources.

This funnel approach also protects you from platform changes. When you build your business entirely on retail sales, you're vulnerable to algorithm updates, commission changes, or platform shifts, but when retailers are just one part of your ecosystem, feeding readers into your direct sales funnel, you maintain control of your business destiny.

Remember, the most valuable asset isn't your retail rankings or reviews. It's your direct connection to readers. Every retail sale should be viewed as an opportunity to build that connection, moving casual readers closer to becoming loyal, direct customers.

KICKSTARTER

Once you have the base and funnel set up, Kickstarter should be your first step in your publishing journey for most projects.

When used correctly, Kickstarter serves three crucial purposes. First, it lets you make the most money possible from your most ardent supporters. Second, it creates all your marketing materials for future direct sales. Third, and most importantly, it acts as your testing ground for everything that comes after your launch.

Kickstarter is not just about raising money. Every campaign is a marketing laboratory. We test the copy on our page to make sure it converts before spending money to drive traffic to it. We experiment with email messaging to see what drives the most sales. We track which products and reward tiers resonate most with our audience.

This testing is invaluable. Instead of guessing what will work in your marketing, you get real data from real buyers.

Every successful element from your campaign becomes a proven asset you can use in your broader publishing strategy.

We also use Kickstarter to fund production of extra inventory. This lets us take advantage of economies of scale, getting better rates on printing and production. We can then sell this inventory through our direct sales website and in future campaigns. While the campaign should still be profitable on its own, this extra inventory becomes rocket fuel for future sales.

A successful Kickstarter campaign should end with three things:

- *All* your production costs paid off,
- A *seed budget* for marketing and advertising, and
- Enough profit for *at least* one reward for yourself.

More than that, you should end with proven marketing materials and a clear understanding of what resonates with your audience. Everything you build after - your landing pages, your web store, your email marketing - all grow from what you learn during your campaign. It's not just about the money raised. It's about creating the bedrock for your entire publishing ecosystem.

This is why timing matters so much. Running a Kickstarter too late in your publishing journey means missing out on all this valuable testing and foundation building. Start with Kickstarter, learn from your campaign, then use those insights to build everything else.

LANDING PAGES

Once your Kickstarter wraps and you've proven your marketing copy works, it's time to turn that success into something permanent. This is where series landing pages come into play. They're not just web pages. They're conversion machines built on proven messaging.

We create a series landing page using the exact copy we just tested in our Kickstarter. No guessing, no reinventing the wheel. We know this messaging works because we've already seen it convert real buyers, but now, instead of a time-limited campaign, we're building an evergreen asset that keeps working for us.

We're using a landing page instead of a web store because we know our Kickstarter page works, and we want to replicate that success as easily as possible.

Once the page is set up, we create a sequence to present new subscribers with a "special offer" for our series at a healthy discount. This sequence uses the exact email messages that converted best during our Kickstarter campaign. Again, we're not guessing. We're using proven winners.

This becomes your reader's first introduction to your direct sales environment. You're training them to buy directly from you instead of retailers. Our offers use evergreen countdown timers, so everyone who hits the site starts at the same place, no matter when they join, and considers that initial discount an investment in our relationship with them.

It's really important to note here that we never offer this discount again. This first discount should be the absolute best deal anyone can ever get on your series. When you stick to this rule, it creates real urgency and rewards people for taking quick action. If readers know they can always get the same deal later, they have no reason to act now.

We use heat mapping and session recording to test these pages with new readers. This lets us make small improvements over time that increase conversion rates. Once we have a template that works well, we can create additional special offers periodically with limited-time deals.

The beauty of this approach is that until this point, we haven't spent a dollar on advertising. We're building our foundation on organic reach and proven messaging. Only after we know our funnel works do we consider adding paid traffic to accelerate growth.

WEB STORE

Your web store isn't just another sales channel. It's the final piece of your integrated publishing ecosystem. It's the place where all your previous efforts converge to create direct relationships with readers.

After creating landing pages and testing your marketing through Kickstarter, your web store becomes the mechanism for ongoing direct sales. The goal isn't to compete with retailers, especially since they are funneling casual readers to you, but to create an exclusive experience that gives readers a compelling reason to buy directly from you.

While you'll offer all your books, the focus should be on creating exclusive bundles readers can't find elsewhere. This approach gives people a unique reason to visit your site and purchase directly from you.

The most important metric? Repeat purchases. Once somebody buys from you, they become open to buying from you again. This is the entire game of direct sales.

Create a strategic approach to discounts that make each purchase feel like a special opportunity. Make sure to segment customers who purchase through your web store, so they don't get your even better offer.

Your web store isn't an isolated channel. It's the final step in a carefully constructed publishing ecosystem. Your Kickstarter creates marketing materials. Your landing pages feed subscribers. Your web store offers exclusive products that reward your most loyal readers. Everything works together to create a sustainable ecosystem that grows stronger with each sale.

The beauty of this approach is its simplicity. You're not just selling books. You're building a direct relationship with readers, one exclusive bundle at a time. And in a world of increasingly complex publishing strategies, sometimes the simplest approach is the most powerful.

THE ADVANCED SET

Advanced optimization isn't about doing more. It's about doing the right things strategically and efficiently. Most authors chase every marketing tactic, burning themselves out in the process, but true optimization is about understanding where your energy creates the most impact.

Advertising enters the ecosystem only after you've tested and proven your foundational elements. Running ads before your funnel is optimized is like pouring water into a leaky bucket. You'll waste resources without seeing meaningful returns.

When you're ready to add advertising, focus on your best bundle offer or series landing page. The goal isn't immediate massive sales but creating a sustainable pathway for reader acquisition.

The key is testing. Not endless, exhausting testing, but strategic experiments that provide clear insights. Track your metrics carefully. Understand which elements of your funnel convert most effectively. A small, targeted ad spend can generate spillover sales across multiple platforms, potentially reaching six-figure results when done correctly.

Optimization isn't about maximizing every single metric. It's about creating a system that generates predictable, sustainable income while protecting your creative energy.

The Joy of Missing Out (JOMO) isn't just a cute phrase. It's a strategic approach to building your author business. Many authors leave money on the table by trying to optimize everything. Instead, focus on the 20% of activities that generate 80% of your results. Your time and creative energy are your most valuable resources. Protect them fiercely.

This doesn't mean being lazy. It means being intentional. Choose the platforms and strategies that align naturally with your strengths. Build systems that work even when you're not actively pushing them. Create an ecosystem that grows with minimal constant intervention.

The most successful authors aren't those who work the hardest. They're those who work the smartest. They build repeatable processes. They create content that serves multiple purposes. They understand that true optimization is about working in harmony with your natural strengths, not fighting against them.

Remember, your goal isn't to become a marketing machine. Your goal is to create a sustainable publishing business that supports your writing, not consumes it. Advanced optimization is about finding that delicate balance— generating enough income to support your creative work while maintaining the freedom and autonomy that drew you to writing in the first place.

BRINGING IT ALL TOGETHER

The publishing world loves to overcomplicate things. Authors are bombarded with endless strategies, platforms, and "revolutionary" marketing techniques. But direct sales isn't about chasing every shiny new opportunity. It's about creating a systematic approach that works reliably and grows with you.

Direct sales isn't just selling books outside traditional retail channels. It's about building a direct relationship with your readers. Every sale is an opportunity to transform a casual reader into a loyal fan. This means thinking beyond individual transactions and focusing on creating an entire ecosystem around your work.

Your direct sales strategy should integrate multiple channels—Kickstarter, landing pages, web stores, subscriptions—each working together to create a seamless reader experience. The goal isn't to replace retailers but to create additional pathways for readers to discover and engage with your work.

Platforms like Kickstarter become more than just funding mechanisms. They're testing grounds for marketing messages, ways to validate audience interest, and opportunities to build excitement before a wider launch. Your landing pages transform from static web pages into conversion machines, using proven messaging from your most successful campaigns.

Most authors approach their writing as a creative pursuit, separating it completely from business strategy, but the most successful authors understand that creativity and business are deeply interconnected. Your publishing ecosystem isn't just about selling books. It's about creating a sustainable business that supports your creative vision.

This means thinking strategically about every piece of content you create. How can one piece of work serve multiple purposes? A blog post might become a book chapter. A character sketch could become newsletter content. A Kickstarter campaign becomes a marketing laboratory for future projects.

The key is leverage. Do the work once but create multiple pathways for that work to generate value. This isn't about working harder. It's about working smarter. It's about building systems that continue generating value long after the initial creative effort.

Sustainability isn't just a buzzword. It's a strategic approach to protecting your creative energy. Many authors burn out trying to be everywhere, do everything, chase every trend. But the most successful authors are selective. They understand their strengths and build systems that amplify those strengths.

Your author business should feel like an ecosystem; interconnected, adaptable, and capable of growth with minimal constant intervention. It should support your writing, not consume it. Each element should work together, creating a whole that's greater than the sum of its parts.

This approach requires a mindset shift. Stop thinking like a struggling artist hoping for a big break. Start thinking like a creative entrepreneur building a sustainable business. Your writing is your product. Your ecosystem is your business strategy.

The most powerful publishing strategy isn't about finding the perfect marketing hack. It's about creating a system that works for you, protects your creative energy, and grows steadily over time. It's about building an author business that feels less like constant hustle and more like a natural extension of your creative work.

THE AUTHOR STACK FRAMEWORK

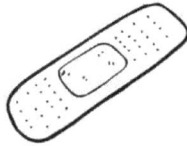

I've written a lot about author growth in my career. So much that it often paralyzes people from taking action. While we have loads of books and frameworks, I've been trying to collect my most powerful concepts together into one place to help you stack processes on top of each other to generate outmoded success.

I believe that most authors, at the end of the day, have a sequencing problem. They are trying to do step six before step two and after step twelve. If we could just get writers to take these challenges in the right order, then each would build on the last to amplify each other. Instead, what happens is that their process often negates their previous effort, forcing them to start over and they lose all the momentum they built up.

If instead we can sequence our author careers correctly, then we would keep gaining momentum over time, and be able to get to success faster.

This is my best attempt at showing you the correct sequence of events to think about to get you to success faster and to stop spinning your wheels. Much of it is compiled from other articles I've put out recently, but there's a lot of new and bulked out content as well.

1. PRODUCTIVITY VS MONETIZATION

If you've been in authorship for any length of time, you've probably heard people talk about "sustainability" in order to prevent burnout. The conversation around sustainable productivity and slow growth often emphasizes the personal benefits of aligning work with natural rhythms and patterns, such as reducing burnout, enhancing creativity, and fostering a healthier work-life balance.

Writers and content creators are encouraged to cut back, focusing on quality over quantity, and to create in ways that are more attuned to their personal energy levels and creative flow. This approach can lead to a more fulfilling and sustainable creative process, where the pressure to constantly produce is replaced by a more mindful and intentional pace.

However, what often gets overlooked in this discussion is the impact that sustainable productivity can have on income. When you slow down and produce less, especially in industries where output is directly tied to earnings, there can be a significant reduction in revenue.

If you drop your output from 12 books a year to 2 books a year because that's what you can sustain, then you have to figure out how to make up for that drastic reduction in revenue or you're just going to replace burnout of one type with burnout of another type.

You can't sustainably create content if you can't sustainably monetize that content.

We usually talk about sustainable productivity as a function of our own work, but sustainable monetization requires a broader thought process. It should take all the stakeholders into account, including the ecosystem of authors, and readers, and publishers, who collectively work together toward creating an environment that is mutually beneficial for all parties.

Unfortunately, the publishing industry is not set up to work that way, and neither is capitalism on a broader scale. It's set up so that every person is incentivized to maximize their own needs while giving the least to the collective as possible.

This is incredibly short sighted and why America's infrastructure is crumbling. Collectively, we can build enough leverage into society to land on the moon. However, if we don't all contribute a little bit, we don't have enough to fill the potholes on main street.

In today's society, we celebrate those who amass the most wealth and resources for themselves, viewing it as a mark of success and intelligence. Individuals and businesses are praised for their shrewdness in maximizing profits, cutting costs, and leveraging every possible advantage to come out on top.

This "winner takes all" mentality glorifies self-interest and often incentivizes actions that prioritize personal or corporate gain over the broader societal good. For instance, executives who drive up stock prices by slashing jobs or outsourcing labor to cheaper markets are often rewarded with bonuses and praise, while the broader impacts on employees, communities, and economic stability are overlooked.

On the flip side, those who choose to invest in the collective good—whether through paying fair wages, contributing to social programs, or supporting environmental initiatives—are often criticized for not maximizing their profit potential. Companies that prioritize ethical practices or sustainability over short-term financial gain can be seen as naive or inefficient, and individuals who advocate for higher taxes on the wealthy or more robust social safety nets are sometimes scorned as unrealistic or anti-business.

This scorn stems from a deeply ingrained belief that the primary goal of any financial endeavor should be to extract as much value as possible for oneself, even if it means skirting ethical lines or neglecting the welfare of others.

This dynamic creates a cultural environment where contributing to the collective good is not just undervalued but actively discouraged. Maybe, on a small scale, we can build a community that looks out for each other, but once you get beyond 150 or so players, all of that collapses. I am deeply sympathetic to socialism, but I can also admit it doesn't work on a societal level. Neither does libertarianism, though, which is what's left when we over-index for the needs of each individual actor.

As an individual actor, being self-motivated by making the optimal decision to maximize your own needs is almost always the correct choice, especially in the short term. If you know everyone else will make the selfish choice, then game theory says the only logical move is to also do the same thing.

But to what end?

Each individual actor might not do much damage to the ecosystem by themselves, but collectively they become like a horde of economic locusts picking everything clean as they carve a path of destruction through an industry. When you think that way, you create and perpetuate an industry that offers an asymmetrical upside for people who act in their own self-interest at the expense of anyone else.

You might say "but I'm not talking about systemic issues. I just want to monetize my own work in a sustainable way" and that's great, but what happens when a customer exits your perfectly balanced ecosystem and runs headlong into a creator who's only interested in making the most money, even at the expense of the customer. Worse, what happens when they run into that person first? Then, they probably won't even give your work a shot.

This is a rampant problem in the coaching space, where we are constantly trying to find people before they get jaded and indoctrinated by bad actors propped up by endless capital.

You can't build sustainability in an environment where everyone is singularly focused on leveraging their own best interest.

Whether it's overusing resources, cutting corners, or exploiting loopholes, these actions collectively contribute to a system that is fragile and prone to breakdown. When everyone is making decisions toward optimizing their own self-interest, cooperation breaks down, and the collective good suffers—resources are depleted faster, markets become volatile, and inequality widens, leading to a cycle of instability that harms everyone in the long run.

The longer this goes on, the worse the problem gets, as more and more actors have no choice but to act in their own self-interest simply to survive. True sustainability thrives on cooperation, shared responsibility, and a long-term view that balances individual and collective needs. It requires an understanding that personal success is intricately linked to the health and stability of the broader community.

When individuals recognize that their actions impact more than just themselves, they are more likely to engage in practices that support the greater good, such as conserving resources, supporting fair policies, and investing in community well-being.

By shifting the focus from short-term personal gains to sustainable practices that consider the collective impact, we create environments where stability, equity, and resilience can flourish. Without this shift, any efforts toward sustainability are undermined by the constant friction of competing self-interests pulling in different directions.

Unfortunately, thinking beyond the individual to the platform needs, or the genre, or anything is only possible if you expect everyone else to make the same decision and that would be lunacy, right? If you decide to help the group at the expense of yourself and everyone else goes the other way, then you are left holding the bag.

That would be irresponsible to yourself and your loved ones.

When you make the best decision for you to maximize your own needs, then who cares if they are bad, or boring, or turn people off listening to them, because that's somebody else's problem.

That's the next guy's problem.

And that is intrinsically not how a society works. Or how an ecosystem works. Or how sustainability works.

Sustainability only truly works when you take the entire supply chain and all the stakeholders into consideration and realizing every part of the process, from raw material sourcing to production, distribution, and consumption, is interconnected.

A company might boast about using eco-friendly packaging, but if the materials are sourced from suppliers who exploit labor or degrade the environment, the overall impact is still harmful. Involving all stakeholders—suppliers, workers, consumers, and communities—ensures that sustainability efforts are comprehensive and not just surface-level fixes.

So, how do you build sustainable monetization when at least half the industry is working actively to burn it all down at any one time and human nature amplified by capitalism pushes people toward the most selfish and thus least sustainable choice?

I don't know the answer, but it's not to keep making the same choices we've been making and hoping for different results.

That's how we got into this stupid mess in the first place.

What I do know is the two things we need to think about first are:

- What does sustainable production look like to me?
- What does sustainable monetization look like to me?

We don't have to have those answers yet. We'll get to them, but as you go forward, it will be helpful to keep that in the back of your mind.

2. MONEY AS MEANS OR MONEY AS ENDS?

Most advice about "growth" comes from people who see money as the ultimate goal. They are usually agnostic about what they sell or how they sell it. To them, the process, whether it is crafting a book, building a platform, or designing a marketing plan, is just a means to an end. Their focus is on the outcome: the accumulation of wealth.

For many creators, this mindset grates against their souls. Writers tend to care deeply about the process and the work itself. Writing is not just a job; it is a craft, a calling, and often a form of self-expression. For most authors, money is not the ultimate goal. Instead, it is a tool, a necessary means to create more books, connect with readers, and sustain a writing career. Once the basics are covered—keeping the lights on, buying time to write—money often fades into the background.

This difference in priorities creates a disconnect. Advice aimed at maximizing revenue can feel out of sync with what authors truly value. When money is the end goal, the strategies you use are very different than when writing and creating are the end goals. This misalignment leads to authors and growth experts talking past each other, unable to connect because they are speaking entirely different languages.

MONEY AS MEANS

For authors, money serves as a way to sustain their writing lives and foster creativity. It enables them to invest in their craft, expand their audience, and build a sustainable career without constant financial stress. Writers who see money as a means prioritize creative integrity and long-term growth over short-term gains.

This approach often involves reinvesting earnings into areas like editing, cover design, marketing, or learning opportunities. For example, an author might use royalties to pay for a professional editor or a marketing campaign that helps their book reach a wider audience. The goal is not to accumulate wealth for its own sake but to create a virtuous cycle where financial stability supports better work and better work leads to greater impact.

Seeing money as a means allows authors to focus on their craft and their readers. It aligns their financial decisions with their creative values, ensuring that their work remains authentic while still reaching those it is meant to serve. This perspective often leads to careers that are deeply fulfilling, even if they do not yield massive financial rewards.

Most importantly, when money is the means, you aren't spending a lot of time focusing on how to make more, unless it aligns with the work you are already doing.

- **Focus on growth through craft**: Authors reinvest earnings to improve their skills and their books, prioritizing quality over quick wins.
- **Create stability for creativity**: Money is used to remove financial stress, allowing authors to focus on what matters most—their writing.

MONEY AS ENDS

For most entrepreneurs, money is not a tool but the ultimate goal. This mindset shifts the focus from the process of writing to the financial outcomes it can deliver. Authors who take this approach often prioritize market trends, scalability, and profitability over personal or artistic considerations.

This perspective can lead to strategies that emphasize quantity over quality. An author might focus on publishing quickly in high-demand genres, even if the work feels formulaic or disconnected from their true interests. While this approach can result in financial success, it often leaves little room for creative satisfaction or personal fulfillment.

When money is treated as the end goal, decisions are driven by external metrics like sales rankings or revenue targets. The creative process becomes secondary, valued primarily for its ability to generate income. This can create a disconnect between the author and their work, as well as between the author and their audience.

These types of entrepreneurs don't care about what they are selling (with some exceptions) just that they are making money doing it.

- **Prioritize market trends**: Decisions are driven by what is profitable rather than what is personally meaningful.
- **Measure success by financial metrics**: The focus shifts to sales and revenue, often at the expense of creative satisfaction.

TWO WORLDVIEWS COLLIDING

The tension between these two perspectives is why authors often feel disconnected from conventional growth advice. For those who see money as the end goal, the strategies are straightforward: focus on the numbers, optimize for profitability, and treat the process as a means to a financial end.

For authors who see writing as the end goal, these strategies can feel alien or even harmful. Writing is deeply personal and treating it as just another "product" in the marketplace can feel like a betrayal of what brought them to the craft in the first place. This misalignment leads to frustration. Growth experts may feel that authors are resistant to proven strategies, while authors feel misunderstood and pressured to compromise their values. The real issue is not resistance to growth; it is resistance to treating their art as someone else's financial means.

When growth advisors offer advice, they often assume that all creators share the same goal: making more money. For authors, though, money is only part of the equation. Their goals often include writing books that matter, building meaningful connections with readers, and leaving a legacy. When advice ignores these deeper motivations, it fails to resonate. For example, a growth advisor might suggest aggressive pricing strategies or upselling tactics that feel exploitative to an author. What the advisor sees as a way to increase revenue, the author sees as a threat to their authenticity and their relationship with readers.

The tension between money as means and money as ends will always exist, but it does not have to divide us, and we don't have to stay consistent. Maybe one project is focused on money as the means (like your passion project) while another is about money as ends (where you are very focused on hitting market trends).

The tension between money as means and money as ends will always exist, but it does not have to divide us. Authors and advisors can find common ground by respecting each other's goals and values. Growth does not have to mean chasing money at all costs; it can mean building a sustainable career that allows you to keep doing the work you love. When approached with mutual respect and understanding, growth becomes not just a financial outcome but a way to amplify your voice and reach as an author.

3. MONEY TO GROWTH PARALLEL

On top of sustainability, we have to decide whether we're in a period of growth, monetization, or a balance of both. To help with that, I'd like to introduce you to the growth-to-monetization parallel.

On one end of this parallel, you have growth. In order to grow your audience, you need to invest in marketing to get in front of them and reduce friction to hook them. Basically, you have to give stuff away to lots of people for free by spending lots of money.

At the other end of this spectrum, you are trying to maximize your money in the bank to keep your business running and pay your bills, which means paywalling content, raising prices, and severely *increasing* friction.

These two actions consume most business actions, and it's nearly impossible for a small business to do both at the same time. Each of us lies somewhere on the growth to monetization parallel, but it's a bit nebulous where for most of us, most of the time.

Once you understand this parallel and give context to it, though, hopefully you can make better decisions in your business moving forward.

GROWTH PHASE

For most writers, their initial focus is on building an audience, or even just growing as a writer who can create content consistently, sharing your work widely, and engaging with readers to build a loyal following. These types of writers are heavily indexing for growth, knowing that in order to be read they have to be found.

However, this growth-focused approach comes with financial sacrifices.

You are almost always undercutting your money situation in a growth phase because you're almost always giving at least some portion of your work for free.

Maybe it's just a story or maybe it's whole books, but growth is about removing friction, and the biggest friction point to somebody reading your work is spending money on it.

Many self-published authors on platforms like Wattpad or A03 start by sharing their work for free. These platforms allow them to reach a broad audience, but monetization opportunities may be limited initially. As their stories gain traction and readership grows, these authors often transition to monetization strategies like offering paid versions of their books, setting up Patreon accounts, or selling exclusive content.

However, this problem exists even with writers who build a big, engaged audience. Sometimes, successful people are actually struggling financially even harder than newbie authors under the weight of all their expenses. Many leverage all their time and resources to maintain audience growth, leaving little room for income-generating activities.

The illusion of success, driven by high follower counts or large subscriber lists, can mask brutal (and unstable) financial instability.

Bloggers and social media influencers who amass large followings often face this challenge. While they may have millions of subscribers or followers, the income generated from ads, affiliate marketing, or donations may not be enough to sustain them. The pressure to continually produce free content to maintain and grow their audience can lead to burnout, especially when the financial returns are minimal.

Meanwhile, if they stop hustling, so does the growth of their channel, which puts them in a very dangerous doom loop, especially as they try to change their content to appeal to a broader audience.

MONETIZATION PHASE

After writers build their audience, their focus eventually shifts from growth to monetization—finding ways to generate income from the readership they've cultivated. This might involve introducing paid content, offering services like editing or coaching, launching a Patreon, or selling books directly to their audience.

Money is great. I enjoy the act of exchanging it for things we need and want, but most authors have trouble simply asking people to financially support their work. Even if a writer grows comfortable with selling their work, it's a tricky balance to maintain, especially when many people are only in your audience for the free stuff.

Nothing kills growth like monetization.

I run a lot of launch events, and I always lose the most subscribers when I'm promoting one, which means I have to make a concerted effort to grow my audience and nurture them once the event is done.

On the other side, if you're giving away too much for free, you are undercutting your own revenue. So, you end up with a volatile and precarious balancing act that you're trying to walk at all times, but especially during a monetization event.

THE BALANCING ACT

Successfully navigating the growth-to-monetization parallel as a writer involves finding the right balance between expanding your audience and generating revenue.

The growth-to-monetization parallel is not just a one-time challenge but a continuous, fluid process that ebbs and flows throughout a writer's career.

Sustainability is key in this journey. Writers need to recognize that growth and monetization are not distinct phases but intertwined elements of their ongoing career. The balance between expanding an audience and monetizing that growth is something that evolves over time, requiring constant adjustment and adaptation.

The question to ask here is:

- Where on this axis am I now, and what actions can best support my growth toward that end?

4. HOW MUCH DO YOU WANT TO MAKE?

I'm not saying everything comes down to money, but I ***am*** saying that it is good to have enough that you can sustainably exchange it for goods and services without struggling. In this section, we are gonna help you find that number for you.

What you measure you manage, so we're gonna figure out how much money you need and the best way to get it.

This is the first true exercise we'll run during this framework, and it should take about an hour to get right, as long as you have easy access to financials. If not, it's going to take as long as it takes for you to get comfortable with the whole money situation.

We talked a lot about sustainable monetization in the first section, and this is how we come to put a number onto that concept. By the end of this, you should know your sustainable monetization number, or at least what you're shooting for in the next year.

STEP 1

 This is the longest and hardest part because it requires you to go back to last year and figure out how much revenue you generated across all projects, including your job (if applicable). ***This is your baseline.***

STEP 2

Once you have looked back, it's time to project forward until the end of this year and ask yourself how much money you want to make. Not necessarily how much you think you'll make, but how much you want to make.

Don't worry, we'll bring you back to reality later, but for now, just pick a number and, as they say, dream big, honey.

STEP 3

Get out a sheet of paper (but a different sheet of paper you used for the last exercise) and separate it into four columns. Label the columns **Q1, Q2, Q3,** and **Q4**.

If you don't do a lot of financial stuff, then those labels mean quarters 1, 2, 3, and 4.

Quarter 1 runs from January 1-March 31st. Quarter 2 runs from April 1-June 30. Quarter 3 runs from July 1-September 30. Quarter 4 runs from October 1-December 31.

Now, under your quarter heading, take the number you want to make this year and divide it by four, then put the final number at the top of each column.

So, if you've made a goal of $100,000 (which is what most people use if you want a guidepost for what number to choose), then you would put $25,000 at the top of each column.

STEP 4

Next, take any recurring revenue you make and put it under what you just wrote. This could include your average Amazon revenue, your salary, your membership income, etc.

The thing is, though, you have to add this up by quarter, not by month. So, if you make $3,000 a month, then you're going to put $9,000 down on the sheet.

Why do we do this by quarters?

Because things change month to month throughout the year, and it's not a very good predictor of year-over-year growth. Quarters are easier to analyze and better to budget around.

Additionally, often a marketing action starting in January won't pay off until February or even March, so judging a campaign by any one month is folly. Judging it by the complete three-month cycle is more accurate to chart success.

STEP 5

Now that you've got your recurring revenue down, write out any planned launches you have for the year, and how much you estimate making on them.

If you've never launched anything before, I'll be frank with you...this is probably not the time to do this exercise. You need baseline data before you can grow.

However, if you insist, then a single launch on Amazon for a new author will probably make between $250-$500, and a first-time Kickstarter will make about $1000-$2500 if you use our system. If you're trying to launch a membership without a fanbase, I would have a hard time believing you would make more than $25/mo. in the beginning, but your mileage may vary.

It's much better to use baseline metrics and then chart growth from there, but if you really want to do this early in your career, bully on you for getting ahead of the game. There will just be more variance than an established author doing this same exercise.

Back to our exercise, if you have three launches in Q1, then you need to add them all up. So, if you plan a book launch in January, February, and March, and you estimate to make $1,000 at each launch, then you'll put $3,000 in that column.

Make sense?

If you're wondering how to come up with your estimates, I recommend taking your baseline number and measuring it against your mailing list and social media reach at the time of your launch.

Then, find out how much growth you've had since that launch and use that growth to project your number out.

If you had 300 people on your mailing list and made $1,000 back in March of last year, and you currently have 600 people on your list, your reach doubled, and you can expect to make $2,000 on that same launch this year.

Please note that even the best models are guesses and while you can get very good at guessing, there is variance at even the best estimations.

The biggest culprit of bad estimation is inorganic email list growth strategies.

I have no problem with inorganic email list strategies like viral builders and have run them for authors for years, but authors tend to believe that when I ethically deliver a list to them that all their problems are over, which is simply not the case.

If you use a service to help you grow your email list, they might deliver 1,000 or even 5,000 emails to you at the end of a campaign, but that does not mean your potential income grew by that much.

You have to do the painstaking work of whittling those subscribers down to find the people who will love and buy your work. It could take a year or more of nurturing those subscribers before you see any tangible value from them.

I recommend that if you've participated in these high-growth strategies, use your previous baseline number as a predictor until you see how the new subscribers perform.

In general, the best way to estimate well is to be ultra-conservative until events tell you otherwise. I often use my previous baseline when I estimate how something will perform without accounting for any growth.

STEP 6

Let's take stock of where you are by subtracting everything you've done so far from your topline number. If you're tracking our example, we put $25,000 as the topline number and then put $9000 in recurring revenue and $3,000 in launch revenue for Q1.

If we subtract all that out that would leave us with $13,000 remaining in Q1 to "make up" in order to hit our targets.

How do we do that? Let's continue. We're almost done.

STEP 7

- Here is where we brainstorm what other actions we can take in order to make up that deficit.

- Can you run a Kickstarter for a special edition hardcover? I've seen people make $10,000+ on something like that, though only 25% of campaigns ever pass that threshold.
- Could you put together a direct sales offer? I've made thousands on just one offer, and I know people who run 2-3 a month.
- Are you able to do a membership drive to get new subscribers? Maybe you could add $100+ a month using that.
- Could you add more advertising possibilities to help your series make even more money?
- Do you need a new pen name, or to jump to another subgenre in order to make the kind of money you want?
- Are there conventions you could attend that might put some fast cash in your pocket, or book signings you could set up?
- Could you write a signature series that will up your baseline number with every release so that by the end of the year you're making thousands more a month?
- Is there a new project you can spin up like an anthology that would put additional money into your pocket without adding a backbreaking amount of work?

As you come up with these options, write their potential income on your list *with a different color pen.* I like to use black for income I'm confident I'll receive, and red for income that is theoretical.

This is another reason you should break things up into quarters instead of months. Making up a big deficit in any one month is next to impossible, but making it up in three months is considerably more attainable.

Multiple times in my career, I have, for example, added additional launches and extra conventions into my schedule when I've seen budget shortfalls that accounted for $10,000+ in additional income to my bottom line and literally saved my business.

Being able to make money out of nothing is the kind of magic every successful business knows how to do and is essential for long-term sustainability.

Don't stop adding options until you have either made up that deficit or run out of ideas.

STEP 8

Now it's time for an "oops here comes gravity" moment. Is your number achievable this year? Were you able to easily make up that deficit or did it seem impossible?

If it seems impossible this year, that's okay. Now you know the scaffolding you have to build next year in order to make it work. This is why we call it long-term planning.

Or, did you easily make up that deficit? Maybe you undershot and can look at even bigger and better things this year.

Maybe you can't make it up this quarter or even next, but could you start seeing a bigger impact later in the year, or early next year?

The whole point of this exercise is to show you what is possible and how to expand your mind to different ways of making money.

It's all one bucket of money at the end of the day, and there are hundreds of ways to expand it.

The question to ask during this is:

- What is your sustainable monetization number?
- Does your schedule allow you to reach that number without stretching?

5. USING A MODIFIED EISENHOWER MATRIX

One of the best tools I use is a modification of an Eisenhower Matrix, one of the single best prioritization tools I've ever found.

The Eisenhower Matrix is a powerful time management tool that helps you prioritize tasks by dividing them into four distinct quadrants: urgent and important, important but not urgent, urgent but not important, and neither urgent nor important.

Building one for yourself allows you to focus your energy on what truly matters, ensuring that essential tasks are addressed promptly while avoiding the trap of busywork that often feels pressing but yields little value.

My process isn't exactly an Eisenhower Matrix, but it's very, very close. If you've never done one before, then I highly recommend taking some time to audit your business.

Here's the exercise I do every year.

1. Write down all your responsibilities and tasks, no matter how small, either on a notepad, a spreadsheet, or a whiteboard. Really it doesn't matter where you write it down but try to make it comprehensive.
2. Create two new columns with headers NECESSITY and ENJOYMENT. The necessity column deals with how important a task is to the day-to-day functionality of your business. The enjoyment column deals with how much you like doing that task.

3. Now, rank each of your tasks on a scale from 1-10. Something with high necessity can be monetary or functional, but not always. Some admin tasks are critical for a business, even if they don't add any revenue to your business. Meanwhile, some monetary tasks might not be very necessary at all. The enjoyment level should be self-explanatory. *Here's the rub.* You can't use the number seven as an answer. Seven is the default when you don't want to make a hard choice, so you can't use it here. You must choose either a six or an eight, for reasons that will be clear very soon.

4. Once you have your list, it's time to make a hard break between 1-6 and 8-10. *This is why you can't use seven.* Everything on the 1-6 side falls on the DON'T LOVE/DON'T NEED side of the barrier. Everything 8-10 falls on the LOVE/NEED side of the barrier depending on the column.

5. Draw a grid with four quadrants. Mark the X-AXIS as ENJOYMENT and the Y-AXIS as NECESSITY. Everything you LOVE and NEED should end up on the TOP RIGHT QUADRANT. Everything you NEED but don't LOVE should end up in the TOP LEFT QUADRANT. Everything you DON'T NEED and DON'T LOVE should be in the BOTTOM LEFT. Everything you LOVE but DON'T NEED should end up in the BOTTOM RIGHT. It should end up looking something like this when you are done.

6. Now, you assess. *What is in the top right quadrant?* Those should be your core products and offerings. You might even find some new services you could offer that more align with your passions. *What is in the bottom right quadrant?* How can you make those more important to your business? *What is in the top left quadrant?* How can you outsource those, or change them so you love them? *What ended up in the bottom left quadrant?* Cut those things ASAP.

The more time you can spend doing those, the more your company will grow.

,What you should find are the things in your business that bring the highest return and provide a high level of satisfaction. You should immediately find ways to double down on those parts of your business.

The question to ask during this is:

- What are you keeping in order to have your best quarter ever?

6. YOUR TRANSITION POINT

As an author, understanding the psychological and emotional triggers that drive people to buy books is crucial. People are most likely to make purchases when they are in flux—times of transition when their lives are changing, and they're seeking clarity, support, or an escape.

This is true whether you're writing fiction or non-fiction. By recognizing these pivotal moments, you can craft books that resonate deeply with readers who are in search of solutions, inspiration, or stories that reflect their inner world.

Readers in transition are often dealing with uncertainty, and as they navigate major life changes, they look for things to bring them clarity, comfort, or perspective.

During these times, people seek books that either provide practical guidance (in the case of non-fiction) or offer emotional resonance and escapism (in the case of fiction). Understanding this need gives authors an opportunity to position their work as timely and relevant, creating an emotional connection with potential readers when they are most vulnerable and receptive.

NON-FICTION: PROVIDING CLARITY AND SOLUTIONS

In non-fiction, the connection to life transitions is clear. Readers who are in a state of flux often want answers, strategies, and a roadmap to help them navigate their new circumstances. Whether it's a guide on starting a new job, a self-help book on personal growth, or a memoir about becoming a parent, non-fiction books provide readers with the information and insights they need to make sense of their evolving lives.

For example:

- **Graduating from school or college:** Non-fiction books about career planning, financial literacy, and life skills become essential as young adults step into an unfamiliar world, looking for practical advice.
- **Starting a new job or career:** Readers in this phase want reassurance or tips to succeed, and books on career advancement or leadership fill that gap.
- **Becoming a parent:** Parenting guides or memoirs about the challenges of family life provide new parents with valuable advice and comfort during an overwhelming transition.

The more your book aligns with these transition points, the easier it will be to reach readers who are actively searching for content that speaks to their current situation.

FICTION: OFFERING EMOTIONAL RESONANCE AND ESCAPE

When I talk to fiction authors about this, they usually say "Well, that's great for non-fiction, but that doesn't apply to me," and yes it does, absolutely apply to fiction. Fiction is just a different way to incept knowledge into people by letting them empathize and learn from a parable instead of a real event.

For fiction authors, these same transition points offer rich opportunities to connect with readers on a deeper, emotional level. Fiction allows readers to see themselves in characters facing similar challenges or provides an escape from the stress and uncertainty of their real lives. Here's how fiction can play a vital role during transitions:

- **Starting a new job or career:** Novels about characters striving for success, navigating office politics, or starting over in a new field provide relatable stories that resonate with readers in similar circumstances.
- **Moving to a new place:** Fiction that explores themes of belonging, identity, and the search for home can offer solace to readers uprooting their lives.
- **Getting married or entering a long-term relationship:** Romance novels, or literary fiction exploring the complexities of relationships, resonate deeply with readers experiencing love and commitment, offering both an escape and a mirror to their own lives.
- **Divorce or breakup:** Fiction about heartbreak, rediscovery, and the strength to move on provides emotional catharsis for those recovering from a breakup. Readers in this phase often seek out stories that help them feel understood or inspired by characters who overcome similar challenges.
- **Loss of a loved one:** Novels dealing with grief and loss can serve as a source of comfort for those navigating the emotional turmoil of losing someone close to them.
- **Health changes:** Stories about resilience, healing, or characters overcoming physical challenges can offer

hope and emotional support to readers facing their own health battles.

Escapism also plays a key role here. For readers overwhelmed by transitions, fiction provides an escape into another world—a necessary break from the stress of real life. Whether it's diving into a fantasy realm, a thriller, or a romance, readers in flux often use fiction to recharge emotionally, and authors who provide that escape will find a loyal audience.

FICTION THAT REFLECTS SELF-DISCOVERY

Another major transition point that fiction can speak to is personal growth or self-discovery. Readers at these stages are often drawn to novels where characters embark on similar journeys—whether it's a coming-of-age story, a novel of self-transformation, or a plot centered around identity and belonging. As fiction writers, weaving these universal themes into your narratives makes your stories more relatable to readers experiencing their own personal evolution.

For example:

- **Young adults** facing identity issues might gravitate toward stories that explore self-discovery, offering them the emotional resonance they need to feel seen.
- **Midlife transitions** often trigger a desire for stories about second chances, reinvention, and rediscovery of purpose—fiction that mirrors this process resonates with readers seeking to redefine their lives.

WHY TARGETING TRANSITIONS WORKS FOR BOTH

Readers buy during life transitions because these are moments of vulnerability, uncertainty, and emotional intensity. For **non-fiction authors**, this means offering content that directly addresses readers' immediate needs—whether it's how-to guides, memoirs that inspire, or advice that offers clarity.

For **fiction authors**, targeting these transition points means crafting stories that emotionally resonate with readers who are grappling with similar themes in their own lives. Whether they're seeking escape or reflection, readers in flux are looking for books that provide an emotional anchor.

By tailoring your marketing and messaging to readers going through these transitional moments, you can position your books as essential resources for readers seeking connection, understanding, or a break from their current reality.

Whether through practical advice or an immersive story, your book becomes part of their journey through change.

No matter what genre you write in, understanding the psychology of transitions allows you to connect with readers when they are most likely to seek out content. By addressing their emotional needs, offering clarity, or providing an escape, your books can become a pivotal part of their process of navigating life's many transitions.

The question to ask during this section is:

- What is your transition point where your customers are most likely to buy?

- Are you focused on it or scattered around working with less effective transitions?

7. PLATFORM, AUDIENCE, AND ASSETS

Building a sustainable author career requires aligning three things in a strategic way: *Platform, Audience,* and *Assets*. If you can make these three things work for you, then you'll be on your way to reach your priorities.

- **Platform** refers to the online or offline space where you promote, sell, and engage with your work. It's the foundation for how you share your writing with the world and includes the tools, websites, or systems that allow you to connect with readers and manage your author business.

- **Audience** consists of the people who consume your content, whether that's reading your books, following your blog, engaging with your social media, or subscribing to your newsletter. Understanding your audience is essential because their needs, preferences, and engagement directly impact your success.

- **Assets** are the tools, resources, and intellectual property you already have that can help you grow your author career. These include everything from your backlist of books, your email list, your social media following, and your unique skills or experiences.

Each of these elements plays a distinct role in how you grow, engage, and monetize your work. When aligned, they create a cohesive system that supports both your creative output and business goals.

PLATFORM: MEETING THE DEMANDS OF THE MARKET

Your platform, whether it's Amazon, Patreon, your website, or social media, has its own unique demands and dynamics. Each one requires a tailored approach to content, engagement, and sales. The key to success is understanding what the platform prioritizes and how you can meet those demands while staying true to your voice and goals.

The main thing I want to get through here is that if a platform isn't helping you grow, then there's no reason to give them your money, time, or attention. So many people are on every platform, even when their incentives are not aligned with, or even in direct opposition with, their goals.

You should only be working on platforms that actively help you grow.

TYPES OF PLATFORMS

- **Online Platforms**: Amazon, Patreon, Substack, your own author website, social media (e.g., Instagram, Bluesky, TikTok).
- **Offline Platforms**: Bookstore events, speaking engagements, writer conferences, and book signings.

WHAT MAKES A PLATFORM IMPORTANT FOR AUTHORS?

- **Visibility**: Platforms like Amazon or social media provide access to a wide audience, allowing your books or content to be discovered.
- **Sales channels**: Platforms such as your website or eBook stores like Kobo or Amazon are where readers can buy your books directly.

- **Audience engagement**: Platforms like Patreon or a newsletter are where you can build direct, ongoing relationships with your audience, nurturing superfans who support your work long-term.

EXAMPLES:

- **Amazon**: A powerful platform for discoverability, leveraging its algorithm for ranking books and reaching a large, diverse audience.
- **Patreon**: Focuses on community building and deeper, more personal engagement with fans through memberships and exclusive content.

WHAT DOES THE PLATFORM WANT?

Platforms like Amazon are driven by algorithms that favor popular categories, frequent releases, and reader engagement. To thrive here, you need to write to market and optimize your work for the genres or keywords that are currently trending. In contrast, platforms like Patreon may prioritize deeper connections with your audience and regular, smaller updates that foster a sense of community. On social media, platforms reward engagement and shareable content—creating bite-sized insights or visuals can help your work go viral.

- **What kind of content does well on the platform:** On Amazon, writing consistent, genre-specific books helps you show up in search results and recommendation algorithms. For Patreon, exclusive behind-the-scenes content, serialized fiction, or fan engagement polls often work best. On social media platforms like Instagram or Tiktok, eye-catching visuals or quick, meaningful interactions are vital for expanding your reach.

- **How to align with platform expectations:** To give the platform what it wants, optimize your content. On Amazon, use targeted keywords, book covers that match the expectations of your genre, and release schedules that keep your name in front of readers. On Patreon, offer tiered rewards that reflect your creative process, giving fans a reason to engage at different levels of commitment. On social media, post regularly, engage with your audience, and create content that encourages shares and comments, driving the platform to boost your visibility.

DIFFERENTIATING BETWEEN PLATFORMS

Each platform has different requirements for success. For example:

- **Amazon** requires a focus on keywords, genre conventions, and release frequency.
- **Patreon** is about nurturing your community with regular, exclusive content.
- **Social media** is driven by engagement metrics—frequent posts, interactive content, and shareability.

Tailoring your approach to fit the specific platform you're using can maximize your success. Authors often make the mistake of trying to apply the same strategy across platforms, but recognizing and adapting to each platform's demands can dramatically improve your results. I recommend 1-3 platforms, expanding beyond that only when you are established on your previous platforms.

AUDIENCE: ALIGNING YOUR CONTENT WITH READER NEEDS

Types of audience:

- **Super fans:** These are the types of people who will fly to meet you or spend $100 on a special edition of their favorite book.

- **Core audience**: Your most loyal readers or superfans who engage with your content regularly, buy your new releases, and advocate for your work.
- **Casual readers**: Readers who may have enjoyed one or two of your books but aren't deeply invested in everything you create.
- **Potential Readers**: People who fall within your target demographic but haven't yet discovered your work. These are readers you aim to convert into fans.

WHY UNDERSTANDING YOUR AUDIENCE MATTERS:

- **Targeted content**: Knowing what your audience loves allows you to tailor your work to meet their preferences, increasing the likelihood that they will buy and recommend your books.
- **Engagement**: A clear understanding of your audience helps you build strong relationships through direct engagement, offering them content they're eager to support.
- **Marketing efficiency**: When you know your audience, your marketing becomes more focused and effective. Instead of casting a wide net, you can reach people who are most likely to become loyal readers.

EXAMPLES:

- **Romance readers**: If your audience is primarily romance fans, they may expect certain tropes, like happily-ever-afters, and knowing this helps you write and market accordingly.
- **Newsletter subscribers**: These are readers who have given you their contact information and have expressed a deeper interest in your work, making them a valuable group to nurture for long-term success.

Your audience has specific needs, preferences, and pain points. As an author, your success hinges on how well you can align your content with those desires while considering the platform's demands.

WHAT DOES MY AUDIENCE WANT?

Your audience could want different things depending on where they engage with you. For instance, readers on Amazon are often looking for the next book in a series, consistent quality in their favorite genre, or books that fit popular tropes. On social media, your audience may be looking for updates on your writing process, personal engagement, or sneak peeks of upcoming projects.

- **How does this align with the platform's needs?** Your challenge as an author is to align what your audience wants with the platform's mechanisms. If your readers want updates on your writing journey, Patreon is a great platform to offer behind-the-scenes content. If your readers are looking for consistent new releases, Amazon's algorithm will reward you for frequent publishing. On social media, timely posts and interactions keep your readers engaged and can help build buzz for new releases.

- **Creating a feedback loop:**
Consistently engaging your audience allows you to understand their changing needs. Use surveys, beta readers, or email list engagement techniques to see what they want and how it aligns with your platform. For instance, if you notice that readers are highly engaged with certain types of updates or book previews, you can double down on those types of content to enhance both audience satisfaction and platform performance.
- **Tailoring for different audience stages:**
Newer authors may focus more on building their audience by offering free content or engaging on platforms like Wattpad or social media where discovery is easier. Established authors, on the other hand, might focus on monetization by launching higher-priced products, exclusive content, or more personalized interactions.

ASSETS: LEVERAGING YOUR UNIQUE STRENGTHS

As an author, you have assets beyond just the words you write—these include your mailing list, social media following, your backlist, or even your personal story. Your assets are the tools that help spur your success and grow your reach beyond your core audience.

WHAT ASSETS DO I HAVE?

Your assets could include:

- **A robust email list**: A direct line to your readers that you own, which allows you to promote new releases, offers, or collaborations without relying on platforms.

- **A backlist of books**: Multiple titles that allow you to leverage different parts of your catalog, bundling books, running sales, or promoting lesser-known works.
- **A strong social media presence**: This is where you can engage fans, run promotions, and drive traffic back to your website or Amazon page.
- **Personal experience or expertise**: If you have unique insights or a niche area of expertise, this can be a powerful asset, especially when building a thought leadership platform or writing non-fiction.

WHY ASSETS ARE CRUCIAL

- **Monetization**: Assets like your backlist or email list can be leveraged to generate income, whether through book sales, memberships, or exclusive content.
- **Growth**: By leveraging your assets strategically, you can expand your reach and increase your visibility across platforms.
- **Audience engagement**: Assets like exclusive content, book bundles, or direct access through email make readers feel more connected to you, which encourages loyalty and repeat purchases.

LEVERAGING ASSETS

To grow beyond your current audience, consider how you can leverage what you already have:

- **Collaborations and partnerships**: Use your network to team up with other authors or influencers in your genre. This can introduce you to new readers while also enhancing your credibility.
- **Cross-promotion**: Utilize your backlist by cross-promoting new releases with older works. For instance, you can offer discounts on previous books when

promoting a new release or offer exclusive bundles to your email list.

- **Scaling your brand**: If you have a strong email list or a loyal social media following, consider launching exclusive products, like limited edition signed books, merchandise, or even offering workshops or coaching.

GROWING YOUR ASSETS OVER TIME

Continue nurturing your assets by:

- **Building your email list**: Use lead magnets like free chapters or exclusive short stories.
- **Strengthening your social media**: Be consistent and interactive, offering unique insights that make people want to follow you.
- **Refreshing your backlist**: Update book covers, run promotions, or reformat for new platforms to keep older works generating revenue.

COMMON PITFALLS TO AVOID

Authors often make a few key mistakes when aligning platform, audience, and assets. These include:

- **Neglecting platform demands**: Not optimizing your work for the specific platform, such as failing to use relevant keywords on Amazon or not engaging regularly on social media.
- **Ignoring audience needs**: Focusing too much on what the platform wants without keeping an eye on what your readers are asking for.
- **Underusing assets**: Failing to leverage existing assets like your backlist, email list, or social proof (e.g., reviews and testimonials) to grow your reach.

MEASURABLE ACTION STEPS

To align these three elements, here are some concrete steps you can take:

1. **Platform optimization**: Choose two key platforms and optimize your content (e.g., update keywords on Amazon, increase social media engagement). Track your progress monthly.
2. **Audience feedback loop**: Send out a survey to your email list or social media followers and adjust your content strategy based on the feedback.
3. **Asset leveraging**: Run a promotion using your backlist or cross-promote your new release with older works to boost sales across your catalog.
4. **Growth goals**: Set specific growth targets for each asset, such as increasing your email list by 20% over the next six months or doubling social media engagement through regular posts.

To thrive as an author, you need to think of your platform, audience, and assets as interconnected parts of your overall strategy. Understanding the demands of the platform helps you tailor your content to what will succeed, while knowing your audience ensures that you meet their needs in a way that aligns with the platform's strengths. By leveraging your assets strategically, you can amplify your reach beyond your core audience and build a sustainable author career.

When you align these elements, you create a system where each part supports the others, allowing for growth, engagement, and monetization to happen in a balanced, sustainable way.

There are a lot of questions for this part, but they boil down to:

- What platforms do I want to focus on?
- How can I gather my audience?
- What assets do I need to make best use of my platform and audience?

8. AUTHOR SUCCESS PATHS

We've identified five author success paths to help authors build sustainable, thriving careers by focusing on different aspects of their writing and marketing strategies. Each path is a proven way to grow your audience, increase visibility, and drive revenue. Let's explore each of these paths in detail.

VIRALITY / WRITING TO MARKET

Virality refers to content that spreads quickly and organically among readers, often driven by word-of-mouth or social media. Writing to market, on the other hand, means aligning your content with popular trends, tropes, and reader expectations in a specific genre. Both of these strategies focus on maximizing visibility by producing work that resonates widely with readers.

KEY COMPONENTS:

Understand reader expectations: Identify the current trends in your genre by researching bestsellers, reading reviews, and following discussions on forums or social media. For instance, if enemies-to-lovers romance is trending, crafting a novel that fits this trope can increase its appeal.

Target high-demand genres: Writing in popular genres such as romance, thrillers, or sci-fi increases your chances of virality because readers in these markets are actively searching for content that fits their tastes.

Optimize for discoverability: Use relevant keywords, engaging covers, and compelling descriptions to ensure your books stand out on platforms like Amazon or BookBub, where visibility can lead to a viral effect.

ACTIONABLE STEPS FOR AUTHORS:

Market research: Research trends in your genre and choose a high-demand category to write in.

Align content: Write to market by using familiar tropes and delivering the story beats that readers expect, but with your own unique spin to stand out.

Encourage sharing: Include features in your book or marketing strategy that make it easy to share, like social media-ready quotes or special editions that encourage fans to spread the word.

In our Author Ecosystem framework, we call these Deserts.

Deserts are pliable creators who are good at writing to market and audience. They can make unemotional business decisions and can also ride a trend by delivering a solid experience. When they find a trend they want to ride, they are usually very good at hitting the market at the right time and place. They also do a good job of doubling down on things that seem to be working and tend to put all their chips on one square.

Because Deserts are good at riding trends, they need to have a few different skill sets, including strong research skills, ability to produce quickly, and willingness to detach—both to double down on what's working well, and to cut activity on anything that's not working. Deserts tend to put all their sustenance in one cactus and build a highly profitable pathway of readers to sales. This brings more money in the short-term, though it can put their business at risk if any aspect of their system—audience, money, or market forces—dries up. Many Deserts balance this risk by having multiple pen names or by maintaining a freelance career on the side that they can always fall back on.

Healthy Deserts maintain a camel hump (or several) where they can store away their "riches in the niches" to get them between oases where water is plentiful. They watch the warning signs that the market is changing, and they pivot when necessary—to another genre, to another source of readers, or to another platform. Unhealthy Deserts stray too far from a water source and end up thirsty when one or several of their money makers dries up. Because this type is focused more in the short-term, it's extremely important that they feel confident in their ability to figure it out, though in their unhealthy versions, they fly too close to the sun.

CONTENT MARKETING / THOUGHT LEADERSHIP

Content marketing involves consistently producing valuable content that attracts and engages your target audience. Thought leadership takes this a step further by establishing you as an authority in your niche, building trust with your audience, and positioning you as a go-to resource.

KEY COMPONENTS:

Write for your readers: Focus on delivering content that solves a problem or provides valuable insights. This could be in the form of blog posts, newsletters, or videos. For non-fiction authors, this is especially critical, but even fiction authors can build thought leadership by discussing writing craft, industry trends, or the themes in their books.
Engage consistently: Whether through your blog, social media, or newsletter, build a steady stream of content that keeps you top of mind for your audience.
Establish authority: Use guest posts, podcast interviews, or articles to share your insights and experiences with a wider audience. By consistently delivering valuable content, you establish yourself as a thought leader in your niche.

ACTIONABLE STEPS FOR AUTHORS:

Content strategy: Develop a plan for producing blog posts, podcasts, or newsletters that speak directly to your audience's needs.
Authority building: Contribute guest content to other platforms to expand your reach and establish yourself as a credible expert in your field.
Community engagement: Respond to comments, ask for feedback, and create content that sparks discussion and engagement, helping you build stronger relationships with your audience.

In our Author Ecosystem framework, we call these Grasslands.

Grasslands are focused, deep delvers that seek out popular topics that align to their interests. They plant grass to feel out a plain, but when they find something that takes root with a large potential audience, they quickly go extremely deep with it—deeper than anyone else has the energy to do! They tend to consider every angle of their genre, niche, or topic, so when they put something out, it tends to blow people's minds and rise to the top. In nonfiction, they tend to be correct about whatever their thesis is. Grasslands are capable of becoming the absolute best-in-class at whatever they do, which is why they need to choose new potential projects carefully!

Because Grasslands are intense and obsessive about their chosen topic, they must stay focused to see the fruits of it. It does not serve them well to have multiple projects going at once because they don't have the energy to devote to each one. It also doesn't typically work for them to cross over audiences between two different interests, unlike some of the other types.

Healthy Grasslands find fertile soil to take root in and grow the tallest, most epic tree in the garden. They also dedicate so much of their energy to one area that they become above reproach. Unhealthy Grasslands plant a lot of seeds but never gain momentum in any one area, and struggle to deliver on deadlines they've set for themselves.

LAUNCH CYCLES

A well-executed launch cycle can make or break the success of a new book. This path involves planning your book launches strategically to maximize sales and visibility during the critical launch period and sustain momentum afterward.

KEY COMPONENTS:

Pre-launch planning: Build anticipation for your book well before its release. This can involve cover reveals, sneak peeks, ARC (Advance Reader Copy) distribution, and pre-order campaigns.

Release strategy: Launch events, special promotions, and partnerships with bloggers or influencers can help generate excitement and ensure that your book gets noticed.

Post-launch momentum: After the initial release, continue to promote the book through advertising, guest appearances, and continued engagement with readers.

ACTIONABLE STEPS FOR AUTHORS:

Pre-launch timeline: Create a timeline for each launch phase (3–6 months before the release) and assign specific tasks like cover reveals, pre-orders, and reader engagement.

Leverage influencers: Build relationships with bloggers, podcasters, and reviewers to get your book in front of new audiences.

Sustaining sales: After the launch, maintain momentum through promotional campaigns, cross-promotions with other authors, and ongoing audience engagement.

These people utilize the build, launch, recover cycle. In our Author Ecosystem framework, we call these Tundras.

Tundras love to build cool things and launch them, and they are extremely well-versed in turning a ton of attention to themselves and their project for a short period of time. They are the type to study the platform and see what trends they can tap into to make their next launch bigger, and they are most likely to know how they are going to market and sell something before creating it. Once done with a project, they wipe their hands free of it and rarely think much of it again—the launch is over!

Because Tundras survive on a feast and famine cycle, they need to be able to peel as much meat from the bone as possible. Tundras become stackers—stackers of trend, stackers of value, stackers of audience. They are comfortable with having a lot of one-off projects and comfortable with building a diverse audience that only likes a portion of their catalog—though they welcome superfans who enjoy everything, too!

Healthy Tundras have a firm understanding of their seasons and build safeguards to make sure there's never a point of starvation. They also learn to connect their body of work—usually somewhat disparate projects—under one banner so that every launch offers a bigger feast on their backlist. Unhealthy Tundras struggle to create enough feast to get through the famine periods, leaving them burnt out and under-resourced before the next launch.

AMBASSADOR MARKETING / COMMUNITY BUILDING

Ambassador marketing involves turning your most loyal readers into advocates who help spread the word about your books. Community building focuses on cultivating a dedicated fanbase that actively supports your work and feels personally connected to your journey as an author.

KEY COMPONENTS:

Identify ambassadors: Your superfans can be your biggest asset in marketing your books. These readers will often volunteer to share your work, leave reviews, or even promote your books on social media.

Foster community: Build spaces (Facebook groups, Patreon communities, Discord channels) where your readers can engage with each other and with you. By creating these spaces, you build a sense of belonging, turning casual readers into lifelong fans.

Reward loyalty: Give ambassadors exclusive content, early access to new releases, or special shout-outs. This strengthens their connection to you and motivates them to continue spreading the word.

ACTIONABLE STEPS FOR AUTHORS:

Superfan engagement: Create a group or community where your most engaged readers can connect with you directly. Offer special perks like early access or exclusive content to incentivize deeper engagement.

Incentivize ambassadors: Encourage your readers to share your work by creating referral programs or offering rewards for their advocacy.

Nurture relationships: Regularly check in with your ambassadors, involve them in your creative process, and make them feel like a valued part of your author journey.

In our Author Ecosystems framework, we call these Forests.

Forests are often marching to the beat of their interests and putting their own unique spin on everything they do for their readers. They have a close relationship with their fans largely because they inject so much of their own personality into all their books. They could write a murder mystery, a sweet romance, and cozy comedy, and readers will gobble it up because it's [insert name here]'s take on the genre!

Because Forests are multi-passionate, they tend to have multiple pen names going at once. Whereas this might overwhelm other types, Forests are good at watering each of their trees every year on a consistent schedule so everything grows steadily. They are extremely competent and tend to stack an impressive number of skills to deliver high-quality work across everything they do. Forests are good at being top of the class and being part of the conversation. To do this, Forests must be consistent, hardworking, and patient, as it takes time, energy, and money to stand up each of their trees. (And they still need to do so one at a time to get a bit of momentum in one area before moving on to another!)

Healthy Forests survive by cross-pollinating their work across all their interests. The key connection is their personality, and their fans gravitate toward them for *who they are* rather than what they do or write. Unhealthy Forests chase trends, explore too many interests at once, and don't pay close enough attention to the marketplace to ensure enough others will share their interests.

STRATEGIC PARTNERSHIPS

Partnerships with other authors, influencers, or organizations can amplify your reach and create opportunities for mutual growth. This strategy is about leveraging the networks of others to extend your visibility and credibility.

KEY COMPONENTS:

Collaborate with authors: Whether through co-writing projects, shared marketing initiatives, or group anthologies, teaming up with other authors in your genre can open you up to their readers and expand your reach.

Cross-promotions: Partner with other creators, such as podcasters, bloggers, or YouTubers to cross-promote your work. This helps you tap into new audiences that may not have discovered you yet.

Joint events: Hosting webinars, live chats, or virtual book tours with other authors or experts can increase engagement and attract attention from a larger audience.

ACTIONABLE STEPS FOR AUTHORS:

Identify potential partners: Look for authors or influencers in your genre or niche who share your values or target audience.

Plan collaborative projects: Work together on anthologies, book bundles, or cross-promotions to reach new readers.

Leverage shared networks: Use your partner's platform (and vice versa) to promote your joint venture, ensuring that both parties gain new followers and increased visibility.

In our Author Ecosystems framework, we call these Aquatics.

Aquatics are excited about everything and want to create an immersive experience for their readers. They know exactly what their fans want and this dictates both what they create and how they sell it. If their fans won't follow them to this or that platform, they don't go there! If their fans want to see their bestselling novel as a comic book, they create it for them—even if they have no idea how to make a comic book. (They'll learn!)

Because Aquatics build their business horizontally and have their hands in many different formats as well as merchandise, they must be competent at many skill sets, like building large stories and worlds, delegating, building a functional team that understands the bigger vision, maintaining a strong connection to fans, and expanding slowly and as time, energy, money, and other resources allow.

Healthy Aquatics survive by creating cool new things that both service their current audience and help them grow a larger audience. Unhealthy Aquatics create too many things with disparate audiences, spreading themselves too thin and losing momentum across everything.

Each of these paths offers a different route to success, and most authors will benefit from a combination of these strategies. Whether you're focusing on writing to market for virality, building thought leadership through content marketing, or cultivating a loyal community through ambassador marketing, the key is to align your approach with your goals, audience, and assets. Understanding these paths helps you structure your career for sustainable growth and long-term success.

The questions you should ask here are:

What ecosystem/strategy feels the best to me right now? Where do my natural strengths lie?

9. MEDIA CHANNELS

Amplification strategies evolve as your career progresses. as you grow your *owned, earned,* and *borrowed* media channels. Here's a little summary of all four channels.

OWNED MEDIA

Owned media refers to the platforms and content that you have complete control over. These are the channels that you directly manage and where you can consistently communicate your message without relying on external parties. Owned media is essential for establishing your brand, building a loyal audience, and creating a hub where people can regularly engage with your work.

EARNED MEDIA

Earned media refers to the exposure you gain through organic, unpaid methods—essentially, it's the recognition you "earn" rather than pay for. This includes any media coverage, word-of-mouth, social media mentions, shares, reviews, and any other form of promotion that comes from outside your direct control. It's often seen as one of the most credible forms of media because it's driven by others talking about your work rather than by your own marketing efforts.

BORROWED MEDIA

Borrowed media, sometimes referred to as "shared media," involves leveraging someone else's platform to reach their audience. This type of media includes guest appearances, collaborations, or content that is published on platforms or channels not owned by you but where you have permission to share your message. The key here is that you're using someone else's established audience to amplify your voice, often through partnerships or mutual agreements.

PAID MEDIA

Paid media involves any form of advertising or promotional content that you pay for to reach a broader audience. This includes ads on social media, search engines, display ads, paid influencers, sponsored posts, and more. Paid media is an effective way to quickly increase visibility, drive traffic, and boost engagement, especially when you're looking to reach specific demographics or expand beyond your existing audience.

10. CATALOG/RETAILER SALES VS. DIRECT SALES

For authors, understanding the distinction between catalog/retailer sales and direct sales is crucial, especially when considering how to write to market. Writing to market means aligning your work with popular trends, genre expectations, and what readers are currently buying. This strategy plays directly into the strengths of catalog sales, where fitting into what's popular can lead to greater visibility and success. However, balancing this with direct sales can give you the freedom to explore more niche or personal projects.

CATALOG/RETAILER SALES: WRITING TO MARKET FOR BROAD APPEAL

In the world of catalog or retailer sales, such as selling through Amazon, Barnes & Noble, or other major platforms, writing to market is key. Much like the classic JC Penney catalog, which was designed to offer products that were trending and widely appealing, these platforms thrive on mass-market demand. To succeed in catalog sales, authors must be aware of what genres, tropes, and themes are popular and align their books with those trends.

HOW WRITING TO MARKET WORKS WITH CATALOG SALES

- **Fitting into popular categories:** Retail platforms rely heavily on genre categorization and search algorithms. Writing to market ensures that your book fits neatly into one or more high-demand categories (e.g., romance, thrillers, or self-help), increasing its chances of being discovered by readers searching for specific types of books.
- **Tapping into reader expectations:** Readers browsing large retailer platforms are often looking for books that meet certain genre conventions. For example, romance readers expect happily-ever-afters, while mystery readers look for suspense and plot twists. Writing to market means you're delivering exactly what these readers are searching for, which increases your chances of making a sale.
- **Leveraging trends:** Much like JC Penney would stock up on the season's hottest clothing styles, successful catalog sales often depend on your ability to recognize and write within trending genres or themes. If thrillers with unreliable narrators or cozy mysteries are in demand, writing a book that fits that trend can help you stand out in crowded categories.

CHALLENGES OF WRITING TO MARKET FOR CATALOG SALES

- **Competition:** Writing to market means your book will likely compete with a large number of similarly themed books. To stand out, you need to offer something that's not only aligned with current trends but also distinct enough to grab attention.

- **Conformity:** While writing to market can increase sales, it may also limit your creative expression. To succeed in retailer channels, your book often needs to fit into a predefined mold, which can stifle innovation or exploration of unique ideas.

DIRECT SALES: FREEDOM TO WRITE OUTSIDE THE MARKET

In contrast to catalog sales, direct sales allow authors more freedom to explore niche markets or pursue more creative or unconventional projects. When you sell directly to readers—whether through your website, a subscription model, or another direct platform—you have more control over your marketing and messaging. This freedom lets you connect deeply with a specific audience that may not be interested in what's popular but is passionate about your unique perspective.

ADVANTAGES OF DIRECT SALES FOR NICHE OR PERSONAL PROJECTS

- **Freedom to experiment:** Direct sales platforms allow you to write and market books that may not fit into mainstream trends. If you have a unique voice or want to explore cross-genre works, this is the space to do it. You're not bound by the strict genre conventions that drive catalog sales.
- **Building a loyal audience:** Direct sales enable you to cultivate a dedicated following of readers who appreciate your work, regardless of whether it fits current trends. These readers often value the personal connection they get through newsletters, exclusive content, and a direct line to the author.

- **Higher profit margins for unique projects:** Since direct sales don't involve third-party platforms taking a percentage, you can price your books in a way that reflects their true value. This is particularly useful for limited editions, special releases, or books that don't conform to mass-market pricing expectations.

WRITING TO MARKET VS. WRITING FOR YOUR AUDIENCE

When planning your author strategy, it's important to understand when to write to market and when to follow your own creative instincts. Catalog sales heavily favor authors who can write to market, aligning their books with popular trends to capture the broadest possible audience. Direct sales, on the other hand, allow authors to focus on personal projects or niche genres, building a smaller but highly engaged readership.

HYBRID STRATEGY: COMBINING BOTH APPROACHES

- **Use catalog sales to gain broad exposure:** Writing to market for retailer platforms can help you build an initial audience, gain visibility, and generate sales volume. This is where you align your writing with what's currently popular in the market, positioning your work to fit reader expectations.
- **Utilize direct sales to nurture long-term relationships:** Once you've built a fan base, use direct sales to nurture deeper connections with your readers. Here, you have the freedom to write outside market trends, explore passion projects, or offer exclusive content. Your loyal readers will follow you for your voice, not just your ability to fit into genre trends.
- **Adapt to market shifts:** Trends in catalog sales change rapidly, much like seasonal clothing lines in the JC

Penney catalog. As an author, staying flexible and aware of these shifts allows you to adapt and write books that continue to align with market demand, while still using direct sales to showcase your broader creativity.

Writing to market is a powerful strategy for authors focused on catalog/retailer sales. Like the JC Penney catalog, which stocked what was trending, retailer platforms favor books that fit into popular categories and trends. However, direct sales offer an opportunity to write for niche audiences and experiment with ideas that may not conform to mass-market expectations. By balancing these two approaches, authors can expand their reach while maintaining creative control, maximizing both their visibility and their long-term connection with readers.

The questions to ask here are:

- Which channel do you feel the strongest at right now?
- Which do you want to pursue?

11. SET YOUR WIN CONDITION

A win condition is the ultimate goal that makes all your hard work worth it. It's not necessarily about hitting specific revenue targets or achieving fame.

It's about what makes you feel fulfilled in your work.

This is such a powerful exercise because it cuts through all the noise and settles on how winning feels to you. It probably has nothing to do with having a million followers, either. It's probably about having the security to live your best life.

Nobody's best life is livestreaming their every thought to their followers, not even the Kardashians. Sometimes, you just wanna have a think and a poo in peace and quiet.

One major key to finding happiness in your business is to pick a win condition that's aligned with what *you* truly want, not what the industry or society says success should look like. *Many people make the mistake of setting a win condition based on external validation*, like money or fame, when their *real* desire might be more personal, like more time with family or space to pursue their creativity.

Once you have your win condition, you can work backwards to the platform, audience, and assets that help you get there. Then, you can work forward to find the actions that can best help you get to your win condition without betraying your values.

If you haven't ever thought about this before now, trust me you're not alone. I talk to writers all the time who've planned and prioritized their whole adult life who have never set a win condition for their career.

My personal win condition looks a lot like my life now. I want to be able to take any weird idea in my head and find enough people excited to make it happen that it will make me money. I want to do very few things and have my whole day free to dicker around with people that inspire me, without having to worry about the money piece of it all because there is always more than enough and it's growing all the time.

I've slowly been able to expand doing that kind of thing 10% of the time a decade ago to 60% of the time these days, but it wouldn't have been possible if I couldn't visualize my win condition.

When your win condition doesn't match your actions, you're setting yourself up for burnout and frustration. You might feel like you're constantly hustling but never getting closer to what you really want. Worse, if you don't know your win condition, you could create a plan at odds with what you really want out of life, which is my nightmare situation.

At NINC this year, I met several authors who were successful by traditional standards, but were miserable because their win condition was different from their actual plans and they had no idea.

One author felt guilty for not writing as much this year because she'd spent most of her time getting three kids off to college. She was measuring her success by books written when, in reality, her personal win condition was more about her family life.

She had achieved something remarkable, but because her KPIs (Key Performance Indicators) didn't align with that win condition, she felt like she'd failed.

Another author spent an hour each day gardening and felt guilty for not writing, but gardening was what got her in the right mindset to write. Her win condition was having the mental space to create, but she was tracking the wrong metric.

Realigning your actions with your win condition isn't easy by any stretch. You may find that old habits die hard or that you're tempted to revert back to traditional measures of success. The key is to stay focused on your true goal. Don't be discouraged if it doesn't happen overnight.

It's kind of like meditation. We all know that it's impossible to clear your mind for long, but the process is the point. It's okay to take small steps toward realignment, and it's normal for the process to take time.

Some authors may fear that shifting their KPIs could hurt their business in the short term. For example, if you stop obsessing over sales and start focusing on conversations with readers, you may initially see a dip in revenue. But over time, this realignment can create a more sustainable business model that's rooted in the things you actually care about.

If you're feeling burnt out or like your work isn't moving you toward success, it's time to reflect on your win condition. Here are some steps to help realign your actions with your true goals:

1. **Reflect on your most rewarding experiences.**
   Think back to moments in your life where you felt a deep sense of accomplishment or fulfillment. What were you doing? Why did it matter to you? These moments often reveal your real win condition. For example, if you felt most alive while traveling or mentoring others, your win condition might be more about freedom or impact than financial success.

2. **List what you truly enjoy doing.**
   Write down the activities that bring you joy, even during challenging times. These are the things that energize you, rather than drain you. If you consistently find joy in brainstorming with others, or spending time outdoors, those activities are likely more aligned with your win condition than, say, endless hours of marketing.

It's easy to get caught up in what the industry says your KPIs should be, whether that's book sales, social media followers, or revenue. ON top of that, it's very easy for external pressure to push you further away from your win condition, especially if you don't have one. The challenge is to resist these external markers of success and focus on the internal metrics that matter most to you. Your journey may not look like anyone else's, and that's okay. In fact, it *should* be different.

BRINGING IT ALL TOGETHER WITH KPIS

Now that you've done all of this stuff, we can tie it all up by focusing on your most important metrics, or KPIs. Most people aren't stagnating. They are just focusing on the wrong metrics. I talked to somebody today who didn't write much in the past year…but they got triplets off to college.

That's an epic year, but their KPIs are misaligned.

KPIs, or Key Performance Indicators, are measurable values that help authors assess the success of their activities in relation to specific goals, such as productivity, audience growth, and monetization.

While there are hundreds of performance indicator metrics, your KPIs are the 3-5 that you're looking to improve at any one time, which should be reanalyzed every quarter.

By regularly monitoring these indicators, authors can make data-driven decisions to ensure consistent growth, adapt to changing market trends, and create a sustainable, thriving career.

To align your KPIs (Key Performance Indicators), follow these steps. The KPIs at the end of this chapter will be tied to the key themes discussed in each section to help you measure progress in both creative and business aspects of your author career.

1. PRODUCTIVITY VS MONETIZATION KPI

KPI focus: Balance sustainable productivity with sustainable monetization.

KPIs to track:

- **Number of books written vs. revenue generated**: Compare the number of books you produce to the revenue from those books. This helps determine if fewer high-quality books generate more income.
- **Burnout vs. revenue impact**: Measure the impact of slowing down production on your revenue and burnout. Track mental health or energy levels with productivity rates.
- **Revenue per book**: Track how much each book generates in revenue to gauge the effectiveness of fewer, more impactful releases.

2. MONEY AS MEANS VS. ENDS KPI

KPI Focus: Understand how effectively you are using money as a means to sustain your creative work and career longevity.

KPIs to Track:

- **Revenue Reinvestment Percentage:** Track the percentage of income reinvested into your writing career, such as for editing, marketing, or professional development. This shows how much of your earnings are fueling sustainable growth.

- **Revenue-to-Impact Ratio:** Measure how effectively each dollar spent translates into meaningful outcomes, like audience growth, reader engagement, or book quality improvements.
- **Creative Output vs. Financial Input:** Compare the creative projects completed (e.g., books, articles) against the money spent to support them. This ensures your financial investments align with your productivity.
- **Sustainability Score:** Develop a metric that factors in income stability, burnout levels, and work-life balance to evaluate whether your current financial strategy is sustainable long-term.
- **Audience Expansion Efficiency:** Track how financial investments (e.g., in ads or outreach) result in tangible growth in your audience base, such as increased email subscribers or loyal readers.

3. GROWTH-TO-MONETIZATION PARALLEL KPI

KPI focus: Understand your position on the growth-to-monetization spectrum and manage expectations.

KPIs to track:

- **Audience growth (Subscribers/Followers)**: Track your social media, newsletter, and platform follower growth to measure audience expansion during the growth phase.
- **Revenue growth from monetization**: Track income from book sales, services (coaching, Patreon), and product launches to see how monetization efforts contribute to the bottom line.
- **Content giveaway vs. sales conversion rate**: Measure how giving away free content (e.g., chapters, books) converts into sales and long-term audience growth.

4. MONETARY GOALS KPI

KPI focus: Set financial goals and break them down quarterly.

KPIs to track:

- **Quarterly revenue goals**: Set a target revenue for each quarter and track progress.
- **Recurring revenue**: Track monthly or quarterly recurring income from sources like memberships or royalties.
- **Launch revenue**: Set goals for launches and compare actual income to the estimates.
- **Shortfall adjustments**: Track how new initiatives (Kickstarter, promotions, conventions) help cover any shortfall from your initial revenue goals.

5. PRIORITIZATION KPI (MODIFIED EISENHOWER MATRIX)

KPI focus: Identify high-impact, enjoyable tasks and eliminate low-priority ones.

KPIs to track:

- **Task efficiency**: Measure how much time is spent on tasks in the "NEED/LOVE" quadrant vs. the "DON'T NEED/DON'T LOVE" quadrant.
- **Outsourcing success**: Track the success and efficiency of tasks you outsource (from the "NEED but DON'T LOVE" quadrant).

- **Time spent on core business activities**: Measure time allocation on tasks that have the most impact (from the "NEED/LOVE" quadrant).

6. TRANSITION POINTS KPI

KPI focus: Identify life transitions when readers are most likely to buy.

KPIs to track:

- **Purchase timing**: Track the timing of book sales and correlate them with reader transitions (e.g., graduations, new jobs, breakups).
- **Reader engagement during key life moments**: Track interactions, such as email opens or social media engagement, during peak transition points.
- **Content resonance**: Monitor which content resonates with readers in different transition points by tracking feedback, reviews, and direct messages.

7. PLATFORM, AUDIENCE, AND ASSETS KPI

KPI focus: Align your platform, audience, and assets for long-term success.

KPIs to track:

- **Platform optimization**: Track platform-specific performance metrics, such as Amazon ranking, Patreon memberships, or social media engagement.
- **Audience growth and engagement**: Measure email list growth, open rates, and click-through rates.

- **Asset Utilization**: Track how effectively you are leveraging existing assets (books, backlists, email list) to generate consistent income.

8. AUTHOR SUCCESS PATH KPI

KPI focus: Determine which author success path aligns with your strengths.

KPIs to track:

- **Virality KPIs**: Track the reach of your content through social media shares, reviews, and recommendations.
- **Content marketing KPIs**: Measure the growth of blog readers, podcast listeners, or newsletter subscribers.
- **Launch cycle KPIs**: Track the success of book launches in terms of pre-orders, launch day sales, and post-launch momentum.
- **Community building KPIs**: Track the number of active members in your fan groups, participation rates in exclusive events, and superfan engagement.

9. MEDIA CHANNEL KPI

KPI Focus: Amplify your reach across different media channels.

KPIs to Track:

- **Owned media growth**: Track growth in your owned media, such as website traffic, email subscribers, or podcast downloads.
- **Earned media mentions**: Monitor the number of mentions, shares, and organic reviews you receive.

- **Paid media ROI**: Track the return on investment (ROI) from paid ads and sponsored posts.

10. CATALOG VS. DIRECT SALES KPI

KPI focus: Balance writing to market for catalog sales and pursuing niche audiences through direct sales.

KPIs to track:

- **Catalog sales revenue**: Measure sales performance on platforms like Amazon, Kobo, or Apple Books, and track how writing to market improves visibility and sales.
- **Direct sales growth**: Track the growth of direct sales through your website or platforms like Gumroad and measure how personalized content resonates with readers.
- **Catalog vs. direct sales ratio**: Monitor the ratio between catalog sales and direct sales to ensure a healthy balance.

Here's your section broken down into a KPI template format, following the structure you provided earlier:

11. WIN CONDITION KPI

KPI focus: Define and align your actions with your personal win condition to ensure fulfillment in your work.

KPIs to track:

- **Personal fulfillment vs. external success**: Measure how aligned your actions and goals are with your personal values (e.g., time with family, creative freedom) rather than traditional success markers like sales or followers.

- **Reflection on most rewarding experiences**: Regularly reflect on and track the moments in your career or personal life that bring the most fulfillment. This helps clarify whether your win condition is still relevant and provides insight into your true priorities.
- **Time spent on enjoyable activities**: Track how much time you dedicate to activities that energize you (e.g., brainstorming, creative projects) versus activities driven by external expectations (e.g., social media marketing).

HOW TO DETERMINE YOUR KPIS USING THIS FRAMEWORK:

- **Step 1**: Identify your current position within each section (productivity vs. monetization, platform optimization, etc.).
- **Step 2**: Set clear, measurable goals for each section, making sure they are aligned with your long-term vision.
- **Step 3**: Break down your yearly financial and creative goals into quarterly or monthly KPIs.
- **Step 4**: Regularly track your progress through simple, actionable KPIs.
- **Step 5**: Adjust your strategies based on performance, ensuring that you maintain balance across all areas of your author career.

This approach ensures that you're not only building toward short-term financial success but also establishing long-term creative and business sustainability.

Building a sustainable author career is a complex process that requires thoughtful sequencing, balancing productivity with monetization, and aligning your platform, audience, and assets.

As authors, we often get caught up in doing too much at once, losing momentum by skipping steps or focusing on the wrong areas. By following a clear, structured approach—whether that's prioritizing growth over monetization, tapping into life transitions to drive sales, or leveraging owned and borrowed media channels—you can create a career path that amplifies itself over time.

Success isn't achieved overnight, but through consistent effort, strategic decisions, and adaptability, you can position yourself for long-term growth. Remember, the key is to understand where you are, what your audience wants, and how to best utilize your assets to build a sustainable, thriving career in authorship.

365 SIMPLE WAYS TO TALK ABOUT YOUR WRITING

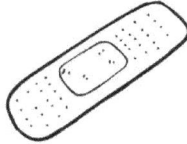

Marketing your book can feel overwhelming, especially if you're worried about sounding repetitive or running out of ideas. But successful book marketing is about consistent, creative engagement, not just pushing sales.

Whether you're running a preorder campaign, launching a Kickstarter, or selling direct, your success hinges on your ability to communicate why your book is worth a reader's time, money, and emotional investment.

A strong case for your book isn't built in a single moment. It's a layered, evolving narrative that unfolds over time.

When you first introduce your book, the case is simple. It's available, and readers can be among the first to get it. But as the days go on, your messaging needs to evolve.

One day, you might share the inspiration behind the story. Another, you might reveal an early review or a behind-the-scenes look at your writing process. Maybe you dive into a character's backstory or offer a sneak peek of the first chapter. Each piece adds depth, helping readers connect with your book on an emotional level.

This ultimate guide gives you 365 unique ways to talk about your book without sounding like a broken record. It covers social media, reader engagement, direct sales, email marketing, book launches, and long-term strategies to keep your book selling every single day of the year.

Whether you're an indie author, traditionally published, new, or experienced, this guide should work for everyone, just pick and choose the strategies that fit your style.

Ultimately, making the case for your book is about creating a conversation, not a hard sell. Every post, email, or update should give readers another reason to care. Over time, as you layer in different angles and deepen their emotional investment, you turn casual browsers into committed fans, and that's what builds a lasting career.

We're first going to spend some time laying the foundation for marketing before getting into the list.

LAYING THE FOUNDATION FOR EFFECTIVE BOOK MARKETING

Before you can market your book effectively, you must understand it so deeply that you can communicate its value in a way that resonates with your ideal readers. Before you create ads, post on social media, or run giveaways, you need to pinpoint what makes your book special and who will love it.

The strongest book marketing strategies start with clarity on your book's core message, audience, and positioning.

KNOW YOUR BOOK INSIDE AND OUT

As you start planning your marketing, ask yourself:

- **What is my book about in one sentence?** *(Your elevator pitch—the quick, compelling hook that grabs attention.)*
- **Who is my ideal reader?** *(Demographics, psychographics, interests, where they spend time online.)*
- **What emotions does my book evoke?** *(Adventure, nostalgia, heartbreak, humor? What does the reader feel while reading it?)*
- **How is my book different from others in the genre?** *(Your competitive edge—why should someone pick yours over similar books?)*
- **What themes and messages does my book explore?** *(Are there deeper ideas or social issues it touches on?)*

If you can't clearly articulate why someone should read your book, neither can your audience. Readers don't buy books because the author wants them to. They buy because something in your pitch, blurb, or marketing connects with them emotionally.

Your answers to the questions above will form the foundation for your book blurb, social media posts, ad copy, and pitch emails, so take the time to get them right.

DEFINE YOUR MARKETING STYLE

Marketing isn't one-size-fits-all. Some authors love engaging on social media, while others prefer a quieter, content-driven approach. Finding a marketing style that aligns with your strengths and personality will make promoting your book feel natural instead of forced.

The Educator – You love sharing **insights, tips, and knowledge.** Your marketing will likely involve:

- Blogging about writing, publishing, or research behind your book.
- Creating YouTube videos, podcasts, or Twitter threads breaking down industry insights.
- Teaching workshops, webinars, or courses based on your book's themes.

The Entertainer – You thrive on **humor, storytelling, and personality.** Your marketing will likely include:

- Posting funny or engaging TikToks and Reels about your book's world.
- Running interactive Q&As, live readings, or dramatic reenactments of scenes.
- Writing behind-the-scenes emails with hilarious stories from your writing process.

The Thought Leader – You love **deep discussions, industry trends, and meaningful conversations.** Your marketing will likely involve:

- Writing guest posts or essays on relevant topics tied to your book's themes.
- Speaking at events, conferences, or panels in your niche.
- Engaging in long-form, high-value content like newsletters and Substack articles.

The Community Builder – You excel at **engaging directly with readers and building fan loyalty.** Your marketing will likely include:

- Running an interactive Facebook group or Discord server for readers.
- Encouraging fan art, book clubs, and reader-led discussions.
- Offering personalized experiences like live events, exclusive behind-the-scenes content, and fan features.

The biggest mistake authors make? *Trying to do it all.* You don't need to be everywhere. Lean into what feels natural and sustainable for you. A successful marketing plan is one you can stick with consistently.

HOW YOUR MARKETING STYLE AND AUTHOR ECOSYSTEM WORK TOGETHER

Your marketing style and Author Ecosystem will likely complement each other. Let's match them up:

- **The Educator → Grassland / Forest** (Deep expertise and content marketing)
- **The Entertainer → Desert / Tundra / Aquatic** (High-energy, social media-driven)
- **The Thought Leader → Tundra / Forest / Grassland** (Industry engagement, personal branding)
- **The Community Builder → Forest / Aquatic** (Fan-driven, reader-focused engagement)

Understanding your Author Ecosystem allows you to lean into strengths, avoid pitfalls, and market in a way that feels natural.

HOW TO APPLY THIS TO YOUR MARKETING PLAN

- **Identify your Author Ecosystem.**

- **Match your ecosystem to your marketing strengths.** Don't fight against your natural style, leverage it!
- **Focus on the 2-3 marketing strategies at a time that fit your strengths.** Don't try to do everything. Do what works for you.
- **Refine over time.** Test strategies, adjust based on results, and keep evolving.

When your marketing aligns with your strengths, it feels natural, effective, and sustainable. Instead of forcing yourself into marketing tactics that don't feel right, build a system that works with your strengths, not against them.

365 WAYS TO MARKET YOUR BOOK

Now that we've got the foundation out of the way, let's dig into how to keep talking about your book all year without it sounding the same, being boring, or wearing people out.

A. BOOK CONTENT & WRITING PROCESS

Your book's content and your writing process are some of the most engaging and natural ways to market your book. Readers love behind-the-scenes insights, character deep dives, and creative storytelling.

1. **Share the inspiration behind your book.** Was it a dream, a real-life event, or a random idea?
2. **Talk about the first moment you knew you had to write this book.**
3. **Post a screenshot of your first draft vs. the final version of a paragraph.** Show how much your writing evolved.

4. **Reveal a deleted scene.** Explain why it was cut and how it would have changed the story.
5. **Discuss your book's themes.** What deeper messages are hidden in the story?
6. **Share a writing challenge you faced.** Was it structuring the plot? Developing a character? Staying motivated?
7. **Post an early synopsis or outline.** Compare it to the final version.
8. **Explain why you chose your book's setting.** Was it inspired by a real place?
9. **Talk about how long it took you to write your book.** Readers love hearing about the journey.
10. **Reveal the original title ideas for your book.** Did you change it? Why?
11. **Introduce your protagonist.** What makes them unique and compelling?
12. **Share a "character interview."** Answer questions from their point of view.
13. **Post a mood board for a character.** Include images that capture their personality.
14. **Describe your antagonist.** What motivates them? Are they misunderstood?
15. **Share a fun fact about a side character.** Do they have a secret backstory?
16. **Write a letter from your protagonist to the reader.** What would they say?
17. **Compare your main character to a well-known fictional character.**
18. **Ask your audience: If you could have lunch with one character from my book, who would it be?**
19. **Post a "Day in the Life" of your protagonist.** What do they do on a normal day?
20. **Describe your character's worst fear.** How does it shape their journey?
21. **Post a timelapse video of you writing or editing.**

22. **Share your biggest distraction while writing.** How do you overcome it?
23. **Talk about a major plot change that happened during edits.** What made you change it?
24. **Show a messy page of your notebook or Scrivener draft.** Give readers a peek into your process.
25. **Explain how you name your characters.** Are they based on real people or historical figures?
26. **Describe a moment when you struggled with writer's block.** How did you get past it?
27. **Share your daily writing routine.** Do you write in the morning, at night, or in bursts?
28. **Ask readers: What do you think is the hardest part of writing a book?**
29. **Post a picture of your favorite writing snacks.**
30. **Share a playlist that helped you focus while writing.**
31. **Share your book's first sentence.** Hook readers right away.
32. **Post a powerful quote from your book.**
33. **Reveal an excerpt from an intense or emotional scene.**
34. **Tease a line from a future book (if writing a series).**
35. **Post a funny or witty dialogue exchange.**
36. **Create a "Guess the Character" game.** Post a quote and ask readers who said it.
37. **Share an excerpt and ask readers to describe the mood in one word.**
38. **Post a short passage and ask, "What happens next?"**
39. **Describe your favorite scene to write and why.**
40. **Turn an excerpt into an aesthetic Instagram Story.**
41. **Describe a key location in your book.** What makes it special?
42. **Share a fun fact about your book's setting that didn't make it into the story.**
43. **Create a travel guide based on your book's world.**

44. **Post a map (if applicable) and highlight important locations.**
45. **Talk about real-life places that inspired your book's setting.**
46. **Ask readers: Would you want to visit the world of my book? Why or why not?**
47. **Describe the culture or traditions in your book's world.**
48. **Share a piece of "in-world" writing—a poem, a historical text, or a letter.**
49. **Create a weather report for your book's setting.** What's the climate like?
50. **Post a behind-the-scenes look at how you designed your book's world.**
51. **Describe your book in three emojis.** Ask readers to guess the plot.
52. **Run a "What's your fantasy name?" generator based on your book's world.**
53. **Share a fun fact about how a character's personality changed during editing.**
54. **Post a "character wardrobe" collage.** What do they wear?
55. **Create a book trailer or a short cinematic teaser.**
56. **Ask readers: What song would be the perfect theme for my book?**
57. **Host a live reading of a chapter.**
58. **Create a TikTok or Instagram Reel showcasing a pivotal scene.**
59. **Make a "Starter Pack" meme for your book.** Include items that represent the themes or characters.
60. **Run a giveaway where readers guess a secret from the book to enter.**

Your book's content is one of your biggest marketing assets. By consistently sharing insights into your writing process, world-building, and character development, you'll keep readers engaged and excited about your work.

B. READER ENGAGEMENT & COMMUNITY BUILDING

Marketing attracts the right readers that help you build a loyal community that supports and champions your work. Engaged readers are more likely to leave reviews, recommend your book, and stay excited for future releases.

1. **Host a live Q&A session.** Let readers ask you anything about your book and writing process.
2. **Start a poll: Which character would survive a zombie apocalypse?**
3. **Ask readers what actor they'd cast in a movie adaptation of your book.**
4. **Run a "What's your favorite quote?" challenge.** Let readers share their favorite lines.
5. **Encourage fan theories.** Ask: "What do you think happens after the final chapter?"
6. **Post a "What's your book's vibe?" mood board and ask readers to describe it in one word.**
7. **Start a caption contest.** Share an illustration, scene snippet, or book cover and let readers caption it.
8. **Ask: "If you could rewrite one scene, what would you change?"**
9. **Post a "Who said it?" quiz with quotes from your book.**
10. **Ask readers to describe your book in 5 words.**
11. **Host a fan art contest.** Encourage readers to submit illustrations of your characters.
12. **Run a short fan fiction contest based on your book.**
13. **Ask readers to create memes inspired by your book.**
14. **Encourage fans to take "shelfies" (selfies with your book) and tag you.**

15. Post a fun "bookish problem" (e.g., "Falling in love with a fictional character") and ask for reader experiences.
16. Ask readers to share a real-life moment where they felt like a character in your book.
17. Create a unique hashtag for your book and encourage readers to use it.
18. Encourage readers to record video reactions to key moments in your book.
19. Run a "Rewrite a Scene" challenge—have fans rewrite a chapter in a new genre or perspective.
20. Feature a "Fan of the Month" who actively engages with your book content.
21. Run a "Two Truths and a Lie" about your book's characters.
22. Create a TikTok or Instagram Reel reenacting a scene from your book.
23. Ask: "If my book had a theme song, what would it be?"
24. Create a book-inspired outfit challenge (e.g., dress like your main character).
25. Host a "Would You Rather?" poll based on events in your book.
26. Run a "This or That?" Instagram Story poll featuring choices from your book.
27. Create a book-themed Instagram filter or GIF.
28. Host a live Twitter/X thread reading through a fan-favorite chapter.
29. Ask: "If you could have dinner with any character from my book, who would it be?"
30. Challenge readers to "Spot the Easter Egg" in your book—hidden details or references they may have missed.
31. Start an online book club discussion about your book.

32. **Post book club discussion questions related to your story.**
33. **Offer to join a book club virtually if they're reading your book.**
34. **Create a downloadable book club guide.**
35. **Run a live-streamed "Author AMA" (Ask Me Anything) session.**
36. **Encourage book bloggers to review and discuss your book.**
37. **Partner with another author to do a joint book club crossover.**
38. **Host a book club giveaway where members can win a signed copy.**
39. **Ask: "What life lesson did you take away from my book?"**
40. **Create a discussion thread for controversial or thought-provoking themes in your book.**
41. **Share a reader review on your social media and thank them.**
42. **Run a giveaway for readers who leave an honest review.**
43. **Encourage readers to leave video testimonials of why they loved your book.**
44. **Ask your ARC (Advanced Reader Copy) team to post their favorite quotes.**
45. **Create an Instagram Story highlight featuring your best reviews.**
46. **Post a "Reacting to My Reviews" video.** Read and respond to positive (and funny) reviews.
47. **Ask: "What's one word that describes my book?" and compile the answers into a graphic.**
48. **Host a review challenge.** Encourage readers to leave reviews across multiple platforms.
49. **Share a heartfelt message about what good reviews mean to you as an author.**

50. **Use a testimonial in an Instagram Reel to create a dynamic, engaging review post.**
51. **Host a "Guess the Next Line" challenge.** Post an excerpt and let readers predict what happens next.
52. **Post a visual storyboard showing your book's timeline.**
53. **Turn your characters into zodiac signs and explain why.**
54. **Create a "Which Character Are You?" personality quiz.**
55. **Do a "Character Face-off" where two characters "compete," and readers vote for the winner.**
56. **Create a "Day in the Life" blog post.** What would your protagonist's daily routine look like?
57. **Write a scene in an alternate universe (e.g., your fantasy characters in modern-day NYC).**
58. **Ask readers: "If my book had a perfume/candle scent, what would it smell like?"**
59. **Post a fun "author confession" (e.g., "I almost killed off this character!").**
60. **Turn your book into a one-line joke or pun and see how readers react.**

A loyal reader base isn't just about selling one book. It's about creating lasting relationships with fans who will follow your career for years.

C. STORYTELLING & BRAND MARKETING

Telling a compelling story that makes readers care about you and your work is key to great marketing and in getting readers to love your world. This section focuses on leveraging storytelling, branding, and emotional engagement to create a lasting connection with your audience.

1. **Share a personal story that connects to your book's themes.** Did a real-life experience inspire a scene?
2. **Talk about how your life influenced your writing style.**
3. **Write a blog post on why you wrote this book.** What message did you hope to share?
4. **Explain a real-world event that inspired your book.**
5. **Create a "Lessons I Learned While Writing This Book" post.**
6. **Share the biggest challenge you overcame to publish your book.**
7. **Post a "How It Started vs. How It's Going" about your writing career.**
8. **Write about a moment of self-doubt you had as an author and how you pushed through it.**
9. **Talk about a rejection that made you stronger.**
10. **Share a list of books or movies that inspired your writing.**
11. **Tie your book to current events or trending topics.**
12. **Ask: "What conversations do you think my book will spark?"**
13. **Share a controversial or unexpected take related to your book's themes.**
14. **Write an op-ed or personal essay for a magazine or website related to your book.**
15. **Host a discussion about the social or political issues that your book explores.**
16. **Ask your readers how they would handle a moral dilemma from your book.**
17. **Relate your book's themes to real-life historical events.**
18. **Encourage teachers to use your book in their classrooms (if relevant).**
19. **Discuss how different cultures might interpret your book's message.**

20. **Invite guest authors to debate a topic related to your book.**
21. **Define your personal author brand in three words.** What makes you unique?
22. **Share a "Why I Write" post.** What motivates you to keep going?
23. **Tell the story of how you got your first book deal or self-published your first book.**
24. **Post about a time when you felt like giving up—but didn't.**
25. **Explain how your childhood influenced your storytelling voice.**
26. **Describe your ideal writing environment.**
27. **Talk about your creative process.** Do you plot meticulously or write freely?
28. **Ask readers to describe your writing style in three words.**
29. **Share a "favorite failure" that led to a breakthrough in your career.**
30. **Tell the story behind your pen name (if you use one).**
31. **Create a book trailer or cinematic teaser video.**
32. **Post a "behind-the-scenes" look at your book cover design process.**
33. **Showcase an alternative book cover that wasn't chosen.**
34. **Post a "Character Aesthetic" collage for your protagonist.**
35. **Create a "Book as a Movie" poster featuring your dream cast.**
36. **Turn a favorite book quote into a beautiful social media graphic.**
37. **Make a visual timeline of your book's events.**
38. **Design a fake "movie ticket" for your book adaptation.**
39. **Create an animated GIF featuring your book's tagline.**

40. Show an artist's interpretation of your book's world.
41. Write an Instagram caption that teases your book's biggest twist.
42. Share a "Book Hook" one-liner to grab attention.
43. Post an excerpt with a cliffhanger ending and say, "Want to know what happens next?"
44. Turn a pivotal book moment into a short video reenactment.
45. Ask: "If you were trapped in my book's world, what's the first thing you'd do?"
46. Write a micro-story related to your book that isn't in the novel.
47. Post a "Did You Know?" about your book's backstory or lore.
48. Describe your book's plot using only emojis and let readers guess.
49. Ask your audience to pitch your book in one sentence.
50. Share a piece of foreshadowing from early in the book that readers may have missed.
51. Write a "What to Read After My Book" list. Recommend books with similar vibes.
52. Create a "Book Starter Pack" with images that represent the themes.
53. Write a blog post about your research process and surprising facts you learned.
54. Turn your book into a listicle ("10 Life Lessons from My Novel").
55. Create a "Reading Guide" PDF for book clubs.
56. Post a "Where Are They Now?" update about your characters.
57. Write a short spin-off story featuring a minor character.
58. Compile your best book-related posts into a blog series.

59. **Create an audiobook teaser and post a sample clip.**
60. **Use your book's themes as the basis for an online course or coaching session.**

Marketing *is* storytelling. The more you integrate your book into compelling conversations, visual content, and your personal journey, the more readers will feel connected to you and your work.

D. LONG-TERM STRATEGY & AUTOMATION

Book marketing should help you sustain visibility and engagement long after release. The best authors set up systems that work for them over time so they don't have to market constantly. This section covers automated strategies, evergreen content, and audience-building techniques that will help you sell books consistently with less effort.

1. **Schedule social media posts in advance.** Use tools like Buffer, Hootsuite, or Later to stay consistent.
2. **Batch-create content to save time.** Spend one day a month writing all your posts.
3. **Use AI or templates to repurpose content across platforms.** Turn a blog post into tweets, Instagram captions, or TikTok scripts.
4. **Set up an evergreen email sequence for new subscribers.** Include a welcome message, book recommendations, and an exclusive excerpt.
5. **Create a FAQ page on your website to handle common reader questions.**
6. **Set up a chatbot on your website to answer reader queries instantly.**
7. **Use Pinterest to drive long-term traffic to your book.** Create pins linking to your book's sales page or blog.

8. **Upload Instagram Stories in bulk and schedule them for the week.**
9. **Automate welcome messages for new followers on social media.**
10. **Use analytics to determine your best-performing content and recycle it.**
11. **Write blog posts that link back to your book.** This helps with SEO and keeps your book discoverable.
12. **Record an audiobook to tap into a new market.**
13. **Optimize your book's metadata for better discoverability on Amazon.** Use keywords readers actually search for.
14. **Run Amazon ads on a low budget to keep your book visible.** Even $1/day can help.
15. **Create a free resource related to your book's topic and offer it as a lead magnet.** Great for nonfiction!
16. **Partner with another author for ongoing cross-promotion.** Feature each other's books in newsletters.
17. **Turn your book into a webinar or live workshop.**
18. **List your book in discount and deal sites.** BookBub, Bargain Booksy, and Freebooksy keep traffic coming.
19. **Post once a week in relevant Facebook groups to keep your book in conversations.**
20. **Create an evergreen sales funnel where readers get a free book in exchange for an email address.**
21. **Send a weekly or biweekly email to your readers.** Consistency builds loyalty.
22. **Create an autoresponder series to introduce new subscribers to your books.**
23. **Use "cliffhanger emails" to keep readers engaged.** End with a teaser for your next email.
24. **Offer exclusive bonus content to email subscribers.**
25. **Ask your audience for feedback on future book ideas.**
26. **Run a "secret sale" for email subscribers only.**

27. **Share your writing progress in a behind-the-scenes email series.**
28. **Send a "reader spotlight" email featuring fan reviews or reactions.**
29. **Use email segmentation to send targeted content.** Fiction readers get different emails than nonfiction readers.
30. **Include a call-to-action in every email.** Ask readers to review, share, or reply.
31. **Update your Amazon Author Central page regularly.**
32. **Make sure your Goodreads author profile is complete.**
33. **Optimize your website for book sales with clear buy buttons.**
34. **Create a dedicated "Start Here" page for new visitors to your site.**
35. **Add an excerpt of your book to your website for free sampling.**
36. **Include an easy way to sign up for your newsletter on every platform.**
37. **Use a tool like Linktree to direct followers to all your book links.**
38. **Write guest blog posts on websites your ideal readers visit.**
39. **Make sure your book is available in multiple formats (ebook, paperback, audiobook).**
40. **Regularly update your book's description to keep it fresh.**
41. **Post a mix of content: behind-the-scenes, quotes, personal updates, and promotions.**
42. **Pin a tweet with a direct buy link to your book.**
43. **Use Instagram Story Highlights to organize your book content.**
44. **Create an annual content plan so you're not scrambling for ideas.**

45. **Share content from readers (with permission).** Screenshots of reviews, fan art, and more.
46. **Create an Instagram Guide featuring all posts related to your book.**
47. **Use hashtags strategically—mix popular and niche ones.**
48. **Schedule Facebook group posts in advance so they go up regularly.**
49. **Keep an ongoing "content bank" of post ideas so you're never stuck.**
50. **Ask: "What's your biggest struggle with reading/writing?" to start conversations.**
51. **Bundle older books with new ones to refresh sales.**
52. **Run a limited-time sale on an older book to bring in new readers.**
53. **Repackage your book with a new cover or edition.**
54. **Write a blog post explaining why you wrote your older book.**
55. **Offer a "First in Series Free" promotion to hook new readers.**
56. **Record a "Behind the Scenes" video about your past books.**
57. **Create new ads featuring older books.**
58. **Run a giveaway where one of the prizes is an older book.**
59. **Revamp your book's categories and keywords to reflect current trends.**
60. **Ask: "Who here has read my first book?" and start a discussion about it.**

Marketing doesn't stop after launch. It evolves. By setting up automated systems, creating evergreen content, and keeping older books fresh, you can keep selling books without burning out.

E. RETAILER & PLATFORM-SPECIFIC MARKETING

Selling books becomes much easier when you're optimizing your book's presence on every major platform. This section covers Amazon, Goodreads, BookBub, libraries, indie bookstores, and direct sales, ensuring your book reaches the widest audience possible.

1. **Optimize your Amazon book page with A+ Content.** Add comparison charts, images, and an author bio.
2. **Make sure your book's keywords match what readers are searching for.** Use tools like Publisher Rocket.
3. **Test different categories to improve visibility.** You can be in 10 categories—choose strategically.
4. **Update your book's blurb using copywriting best practices.** The first line should hook readers instantly.
5. **Use Amazon's Look Inside feature to let readers sample your book.** Make sure the first few pages are compelling!
6. **Encourage readers to follow you on Amazon.** They'll get notified when you release a new book.
7. **Set up an Amazon Author Central page with a professional bio and photos.**
8. **Respond to reader questions on your Amazon book page.**
9. **Use the Editorial Reviews section to showcase blurbs from influencers or reviewers.**
10. **Run an Amazon ad campaign to keep your book visible in search results.** Even $1/day can boost exposure.
11. **Claim and update your Goodreads Author Profile.** Add a bio, photos, and a link to your website.
12. **Encourage readers to shelve your book on their Goodreads "Want to Read" list.**

13. **Run a Goodreads giveaway to attract new readers.** More people will see your book in their feed.
14. **Join Goodreads groups related to your genre and engage in discussions.** No spamming!
15. **Post updates on Goodreads about your writing progress or upcoming releases.**
16. **Ask readers to post their reviews on Goodreads after finishing your book.**
17. **Create a Goodreads list and add your book.** Encourage fans to vote for it!
18. **Host a Goodreads Q&A session to interact with readers.**
19. **Rate and review books in your genre to increase your visibility.**
20. **Encourage readers to recommend your book in Goodreads' recommendation threads.**
21. **Claim and update your BookBub Author Profile.** Readers can follow you for updates.
22. **Apply for a BookBub Featured Deal to reach thousands of potential readers.**
23. **Run a BookBub ad campaign to promote your book.**
24. **Encourage readers to review your book on BookBub.**
25. **Use BookBub's "New Releases for Less" to promote a discounted launch.**
26. **Ask fans to "recommend" your book on BookBub to boost visibility.**
27. **Announce a sale or discount via a BookBub Author Alert.**
28. **Collaborate with other authors for a joint BookBub promotion.**
29. **Engage with readers who comment on your BookBub posts.**
30. **Use BookBub to track which ads or promos bring in the most sales.**

31. Submit your book to library distributors like Overdrive, Hoopla, and Bibliotheca.
32. Encourage readers to request your book at their local library.
33. Reach out to indie bookstores and ask if they'll carry your book.
34. Offer to do a book signing or reading event at a local bookstore.
35. Join the American Booksellers Association to connect with indie booksellers.
36. Create a sell sheet for bookstores with key info about your book.
37. Offer a bookstore-friendly discount on IngramSpark or direct sales.
38. Partner with indie bookstores for signed book bundles.
39. Pitch your book to local library book clubs.
40. Send a personalized letter to bookstores explaining why your book fits their audience.
41. Sell books directly from your website using Shopify, Gumroad, or Payhip.
42. Offer signed copies as an exclusive perk for direct buyers.
43. Create limited edition hardcovers or special editions for direct sales.
44. Bundle your book with exclusive extras (stickers, bookmarks, art prints).
45. Run a discount for email subscribers who buy direct.
46. Create a pre-order campaign where early buyers get exclusive bonuses.
47. Use a landing page to drive traffic to your direct sales store.
48. Offer personalized dedications for direct sales copies.

49. **Create a book box subscription where fans get signed books & merch.**
50. **Use Patreon or Substack to offer books as part of a paid membership.**
51. **Make your book available on multiple platforms (Kobo, Apple Books, Google Play).**
52. **Run a Kobo promotion to reach international readers.**
53. **Use Draft2Digital to distribute wide without managing multiple accounts.**
54. **Apply for a Chirp audiobook promotion (run by BookBub).**
55. **List your book on specialty sites like Radish (serial fiction) or Ream (subscription fiction).**
56. **Use Smashwords to reach indie bookstores and libraries.**
57. **Run a B&N Press promotion to reach Nook readers.**
58. **Experiment with serializing your book on Wattpad.**
59. **Offer a direct-buy audiobook version on platforms like Findaway Voices.**
60. **Use direct email outreach to tell readers about your book's availability on all platforms.**

Your book's success largely depends on how easy it is for readers to find and buy it. By optimizing Amazon, Goodreads, BookBub, libraries, indie bookstores, and direct sales, you increase the chances of sustained, long-term sales.

F. ADVANCED, EVENT-BASED & EVERGREEN STRATEGIES

Once you've built your author platform and optimized your book's presence, the next step is leveraging long-term, high-impact marketing strategies to keep sales growing over time. This section focuses on live events, advanced marketing strategies, creative promotions, and evergreen tactics to help you consistently sell books without constantly promoting.

1. **Host a virtual book launch event on YouTube, Facebook Live, or Zoom.**
2. **Partner with an indie bookstore for an in-person signing event.**
3. **Run a live "Ask Me Anything" (AMA) on Reddit, Instagram, or Twitter/X.**
4. **Offer a "Meet the Author" event for book clubs reading your book.**
5. **Attend a local book festival or convention and sell signed copies.**
6. **Host a themed event based on your book's world or characters.** (e.g., a masquerade for a fantasy novel)
7. **Run a live "Writing Sprints" session where fans watch you write in real-time.**
8. **Create a scavenger hunt where readers find clues in your book.**
9. **Set up a pop-up bookshop event in a unique location.** (e.g., coffee shop, park, museum)
10. **Organize a multi-author panel or roundtable discussion about writing.**
11. **Run Amazon ads that target similar bestselling books in your genre.**
12. **Use Facebook ads to retarget visitors who viewed your book page but didn't buy.**
13. **Experiment with BookBub ads to test different ad copy and images.**
14. **Set up a Google Ads campaign targeting keyword searches for books like yours.**
15. **Use TikTok ads to reach readers who engage with #BookTok content.**
16. **Run a "re-engagement" ad campaign to bring back past readers for your next release.**

17. Test different price points to see what converts best for your book.
18. Use A/B testing on ad creatives to see which ones perform better.
19. Use Instagram Story ads with a direct swipe-up link to your book.
20. Run a short-term boosted post on Facebook to promote a book sale.
21. Create a limited-time "buy one, gift one" promo for holiday sales.
22. Turn your book into a serial podcast and release a chapter weekly.
23. Offer a collector's edition hardcover with exclusive bonus content.
24. Partner with a subscription box service to include your book.
25. Sell personalized, signed bookplates for fans who already bought the ebook.
26. Create a digital "Behind the Scenes" book with concept art, deleted scenes, and author notes.
27. Run a contest where readers submit cover design ideas for a future book.
28. Create a "Secret Chapter" and offer it exclusively to email subscribers.
29. Offer a special print edition with a unique cover design.
30. Host a charity event where a portion of book sales goes to a cause related to your book's themes.
31. Refresh your book's description every 6-12 months to test new angles.
32. Update your keywords and metadata to match current trends.
33. Schedule seasonal promotions for holidays and key shopping periods.
34. Bundle your book with other authors in a themed box set.

35. Create a long-term email marketing sequence that promotes your backlist.
36. Make a "How to Pronounce My Character's Name" post if your book has unique names.
37. Run a "Read My Book for Free" weekend for Kindle Unlimited users.
38. Offer your book as a freebie for a limited time to boost visibility.
39. Record a new audiobook version with updated narration.
40. Use new AI-generated translations to expand into international markets.
41. Launch a Patreon or Ream membership for superfans with exclusive perks.
42. Offer writing coaching services or masterclasses based on your expertise.
43. Turn your book into a video course if it's nonfiction.
44. Create a merchandise line inspired by your book (shirts, mugs, posters).
45. Write a spin-off novella featuring a fan-favorite side character.
46. Develop a board game or card game based on your book's world.
47. Turn your book into a screenplay and pitch it for adaptation.
48. Offer a writing retreat or workshop for aspiring authors.
49. Write a new book using reader feedback from your last one.
50. Launch a Substack where you share insights, book updates, and behind-the-scenes content.
51. Co-write a book with another author and cross-promote to both audiences.
52. Join a multi-author book bundle deal to boost sales.
53. Guest on 5+ podcasts to talk about your book and writing journey.

54. **Partner with book influencers for reviews and features.**
55. **Host a joint giveaway with other authors in your genre.**
56. **Write a guest blog post on a major book-related website.**
57. **Join a BookTok creator's reading challenge and submit your book.**
58. **Sponsor a bookstagrammer's giveaway in exchange for exposure.**
59. **Do a book signing event with multiple authors to attract more readers.**
60. **Collaborate with an artist to create book-inspired artwork.**
61. **Plan a five-year roadmap for your writing and marketing strategy.**
62. **Experiment with new social media platforms to stay ahead of trends.**
63. **Create a secondary revenue stream (book coaching, editing, etc.).**
64. **Ask readers what they want to see from you next, and build your next project around that.**
65. **Never stop talking about your book!** Marketing isn't a one-time event. It's an ongoing journey.

Marketing isn't just about launching. It's about staying visible. By implementing these live events, paid ads, creative promotions, and long-term engagement strategies, you can ensure your book continues selling for years to come.

YOUR NEXT STEPS

Instead of overwhelming yourself with endless marketing tactics, focus on picking 3-5 key strategies from each section to try this month. By narrowing your focus, you can implement new approaches effectively without burning out.

Once you've chosen your strategies, treat them as tests rather than definitive solutions. Some will work better than others, and that's okay. The key is to measure your results, see what resonates with your audience, and refine your approach over time.

Marketing is about constant learning, iteration, and adaptation.

Most importantly, keep your marketing efforts sustainable. It's easy to get caught up in the business side of writing, but your primary job is still to create. Build a system that allows you to engage with readers, sell books, and grow your audience without taking away from your ability to write your next book. A successful author career isn't just about short-term wins; it's about long-term consistency and balance.

Marketing a book isn't about shouting into the void or hoping for a one-time sales spike. It's about building a lasting connection with readers, keeping your book discoverable, and ensuring it sells long after launch.

If you've made it through all 365 strategies, you now have a powerful, year-long marketing plan that covers every angle from social media engagement to direct sales, platform optimization, and evergreen strategies. But knowing these strategies isn't enough. The real key is execution and consistency.

- **Many authors make the mistake of treating marketing like a sprint instead of a marathon.** They push hard for the first few weeks after launch, see some sales, then disappear expecting their book to sell itself. But here's the truth:

- **Readers won't remember your book if you don't remind them it exists.**
- **Most people need multiple touchpoints before they buy.** If you talk about your book once and never again, you're leaving sales on the table.
- **Your biggest fans are waiting for you to show up.** If you stop engaging, they'll move on to someone else who does.
- **Marketing doesn't have to feel like a chore. It should feel like storytelling.** You're not just selling a book; you're inviting readers into a world you created.

If you want consistent book sales, steady fan growth, and a career that lasts, you need a strategy that's sustainable, engaging, and built for the long term. It's impossible to do all 365 strategies at once. Instead, take a targeted, layered approach that builds momentum over time.

STEP 1: PICK YOUR MARKETING FOCUS FOR THE NEXT 30 DAYS

Whether you're just starting out, building momentum, or scaling to new heights, your focus should align with your current stage. By staying focused and adaptable, you'll make consistent progress without feeling overwhelmed.

- **New authors:** Focus on reader engagement (polls, excerpts, book clubs) and platform optimization (Amazon, Goodreads, BookBub).
- **Mid-career authors:** Prioritize long-term automation (email marketing, evergreen content) and scaling your audience through ads.

- **Established authors:** Double down on direct sales, strategic partnerships, and audience monetization (Patreon, Substack, high-ticket offers).

Regardless of your stage, Choose 5-10 strategies to test this month, then adjust based on results.

STEP 2: CREATE A SUSTAINABLE MARKETING HABIT

Long-term success is about creating a marketing habit that fits seamlessly into your writing life without overwhelming you. A sustainable system ensures you're consistently reaching readers while still having time to create. By following this structured approach, you'll keep growing your audience without sacrificing your writing time.

- **Daily (10-15 min):** Post a piece of content (quote, poll, behind-the-scenes) or engage with readers.
- **Weekly (1-2 hrs):** Schedule posts, email your list, update your ads, or pitch guest opportunities.
- **Monthly (2-4 hrs):** Check analytics, refresh content, plan next month's strategy, and try one new advanced tactic.
- **Quarterly (4-6 hrs):** Optimize your retailer and direct sales pages, test a price change, create a new marketing asset (webinar, bundle, new ad campaign).
- **Annually:** Revamp your brand, set big-picture goals, and plan how you'll keep your backlist fresh.

STEP 3: TRACK, TWEAK, AND REPEAT

Pay attention to engagement levels, reviews, and sales to determine which tactics are driving real results. If something isn't landing, don't be afraid to pivot. Most importantly, focus on what feels sustainable. Keep testing, keep tweaking, and most of all, keep showing up. The authors who thrive are the ones who refuse to fade into the background.

- **Which strategies are working?** (More engagement, more reviews, better sales)
- **Which ones fell flat?** (Low engagement? Maybe it's the wrong platform or audience.)
- **What feels sustainable?** (Lean into what energizes you, not what drains you.)

Marketing is about iteration and momentum. Keep testing, keep tweaking, and keep showing up. The authors who succeed are the ones who refuse to disappear.

Right now, pick 3-5 strategies from this list and implement them today. Commit to showing up every week, even when it feels slow, and most importantly, never stop talking about your book. Your next reader is always out there. You just have to reach them.

This is how authors build long-term success. This is how books stay relevant for years. This is how you turn a single book launch into a thriving writing career.

WHAT'S NEXT?

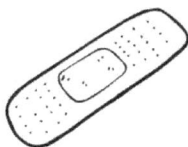

It's over!

If you've read this far, I want to thank you for your persistence and perseverance. I know that learning about business isn't any creator's favorite thing to do in the world; however, just by reading this book, you are so much further ahead than most creatives on this planet.

I would say to give yourself a round of applause, but I've worked very hard throughout this book not to be cheesy and don't want to ruin it now.

Well, maybe just a little applause would be okay. Not too long, though, because now the real work begins.

That's right…work.

As much knowledge as I crammed into this book, it's truly just a primer to gear you up for a lifelong pursuit of learning about the business of art. The goal of this book is to give you the necessary tools so you can go out there and build the foundation of a creative career.

It's not an endpoint. It's a beginning.

You made it to the end of this book. Now, you are prepared for the horrible and yet consistent world of late-stage capitalism. However, you still have to live in it.

If you loved this book, I hope you go check out *The Author Stack,* my weekly newsletter that goes into even more depth about how to build your creator career.

https://www.theauthorstack.com/

There's probably even more now since I update it every couple of months.

You can also find my work at: www.russellnohelty.com

Feel free to email me at russell@wannabepress.com and let me know what you think, and please leave a review. The only way I know I should keep writing these kinds of books is from your reviews and kind words.

Find more of my work at my blog:

www.theauthorstack.com

Find all my work at my website:

www.russellnohelty.com

Bookbub:

https://www.bookbub.com/profile/russell-nohelty